I0688349

Livingston Stone

Domesticated trout
How to breed and grow them

ISBN/EAN: 9783337145699

Printed in Europe, USA, Canada, Australia, Japan

Cover: Foto ©Andreas Hilbeck / pixelio.de

More available books at **www.hansebooks.com**

DOMESTICATED TROUT.

How to Breed and Grow Them.

BY

LIVINGSTON STONE, A. M.,

DEPUTY U. S. FISH COMMISSIONER, PROPRIETOR OF COLD SPRING TROUT PONDS,
SECRETARY OF AMERICAN FISH CULTURISTS' ASSOCIATION, AND
EDITOR OF FISH CULTURISTS' DEPARTMENT OF
"NEW YORK CITIZEN."

"Purpurisque Salare stellatus tergora guttis."
Ausonius, Idyl Tenth.

"Make assurance double sure."
Macbeth, Act iv. Scene 1.

BOSTON:
JAMES R. OSGOOD AND COMPANY,
LATE TICKNOR & FIELDS, AND FIELDS, OSGOOD, & CO.
1872.

TO

THEODORE LYMAN,

THE LEADING SPIRIT IN THE NEW FISH RESTORATION MOVEMENT
IN NEW ENGLAND,

THIS BOOK IS RESPECTFULLY DEDICATED

BY

THE AUTHOR.

CONTENTS.

----•----

PART I.

TROUT-BREEDING WORKS.

CHAPTER I.

INTRODUCTION.

CHAPTER II.

PONDS.

CHAPTER III.

BUILDINGS.

CHAPTER IV.

HATCHING APPARATUS.

CHAPTER V.

THE NURSERY.

PART II.

PROCESSES IN TROUT BREEDING.

CHAPTER I.

TAKING THE EGGS.

viii CONTENTS.

CHAPTER II.

HATCHING THE EGGS.

CHAPTER III.

CARE OF ALEVINS.

CHAPTER IV.

REARING THE YOUNG FRY.

CHAPTER V.

GROWING THE LARGE TROUT.

CHAPTER VI.

CONCLUDING CHAPTER.

APPENDIX.

DOMESTICATED TROUT.

PART I.

TROUT-BREEDING WORKS.

DOMESTICATED TROUT.[*]

CHAPTER I.

INTRODUCTION.

WHEN the writer of the following pages asked Seth Green, in 1866, " how many of those who engaged in trout breeding would succeed," he answered, with his well-known quickness of manner, " One in a million." There was so much wanting, at

---

[*] How fully the word " domesticated " will finally apply to trout that are bred and grown artificially, time alone can decide. It is still a very doubtful question whether they will ever become so accustomed and attached to the habitations of man that they will *prefer* to remain around his homes and under his protection, like dogs and fowls, and so become in the strictest sense domestic creatures.

Still, this result is not impossible, perhaps not improbable. Cattle and horses become as wild as buffaloes and deer when left to run wild long enough. Artificial influences have given these creatures their domestic habits. Why may not a sufficiently long course of similar influences create a similar change in the habits of trout?

Trout are not naturally averse to man in their primitive wildness, before they have learned to fear him. I have seen wild trout in the uninhabited forests of New Brunswick as little disposed to avoid man as sheep in a pasture. Why, then, may we not, by taking away their fear of man through domestication, restore that

that time, in the knowledge required to insure success, that Mr. Green's reply was hardly an exaggeration. Since that time, however, the whole aspect of the matter has been changed, and the care and study bestowed on the subject have evolved a set of rules and principles, the careful observance of which will render a degree of success almost certain. I think it may safely be said that the time has come when trout can be hatched, reared, and brought to maturity in great numbers and with comparatively little loss; and I think it is also safe to say that success in raising the fish will of necessity be accompanied by pecuniary success while the present relations exist between the prices of trout and the cost of the food on which they are reared.

primitive state of feeling towards him, which is free from aversion?

Again, I have at my ponds trout that were hatched from parents that were themselves hatched there artificially. Now, it may have been wholly a fancy, but there has seemed to me to be a difference between these fish and the offspring of wild parents in respect to shyness, and that the artificially hatched progeny of domesticated parents were less shy than the artificially hatched offspring of wild parents. If this is so, and the trout show an improvement in one generation, what may we not expect of fish in which domestication has been hereditary for many generations?

The time may come when continued domestication, together with the overcoming of their fear of man, will so modify the present action of their instincts, that, when pains are taken with the domesticated trout, they will *prefer* to seek the shelter and food which they find around the homes of men to the precarious chances of a wild and roaming life. This may not be probable, but I do not think it is impossible.

I do not wish to be understood, however, in saying that following certain rules will insure success, that a mechanical adherence to rules will make any one succeed. On the contrary, to raise trout successfully demands a vast deal more than that. It requires not only the ordinary force, foresight, and tenacity of purpose requisite to success in any business, but also, in an unusual degree, constant vigilance and caution, and that peculiar blending of insight, skill, and precision which makes a successful sportsman, and which seems to be a gift, rather than an acquirement.

I do not say that without these qualities a *degree* of success may not be obtained, but for the *best success* these traits are indispensable.

You can see at once why this is so. In the first place, the trout breeder has to deal with the most elusory, the most treacherous and capricious thing in the world, namely, running water. To make running water go *as* you would have it and *where* you would have it, from one year's end to another, through all the vicissitudes of weather of the four seasons, including the extremes of frost and heat, freshet and drought, is a task the difficulty of which only those know who have tried it. Then it must be remembered that your charge is a wild creature, which has never been domesticated or taught domestic habits, and every one knows the vast difference in the difficulty of the work between the rearing of wild and domesticated creatures.

Furthermore, the trout lives in an element not yours, but foreign to you, and one which you can never by any

possibility learn the nature of by living in it yourself;
and lastly, in the earlier stages of its growth the de-
velopments and functions of the trout and the progress
of its diseases are almost or wholly microscopic, —
all of which considerations call for a peculiar watchful-
ness and skill.

But though so much is required for great success, it
is also true that the knowledge which has now been
gained of the art will enable most persons to raise
trout with very gratifying results, and almost any one
in a favorable locality can raise trout enough to feel
rewarded for his pains.

The Principle of Security.

Before taking up the various branches and processes of trout raising, I beg to mention one principle, the most important, in the writer's opinion, of
any in the whole prosecution of the enterprise, and
one which, on account of its importance, will be im-
pressed upon the reader at every favorable opportunity throughout this little treatise.   This is the principle of insuring the *utmost degree of security* in every
department of your work.

The emphasis with which this principle of security
is urged upon the trout culturist will be understood
when the following points are considered.

1. All you have to do to be successful in trout
raising, or to make your fortune from it, if you have
a good place, is to *keep* your fish alive and growing.
The hundred thousand trout you hatch this spring,
if you keep them thirty months, will bring you thirty

thousand dollars, if you get only thirty cents apiece for them ; and they will be poor trout if they do not bring that.

This calculation is very simple, but sound. The fact is, that trout are produced in the first instance in such enormous quantities, and at so little cost, they can be raised with so little outlay of money, and they bring, when matured, such a high price in the market, that all you have to do is to keep the fish alive and growing, and your success will be all you can wish. The prize is already in your hand. All you are required to do is to hold it. Hence the importance of making what you have secure. It is important, because that *alone* will bring you almost incredible returns ; and if security alone will make you successful, it must be important.

2. The utmost degree of security is demanded, because, when losses do occur, it is generally on so large a scale. The peculiar nature of the things you deal with, namely, fish and running water, and the magnitude of the numbers you operate with, are such that there is hardly an occupation in the world where insecurity is followed by such wholesale loss. For instance, the stream that supplies fifty thousand fry is cut off a few hours, we will suppose, in a hot night in summer, by an accident. In the. morning fifty thousand trout are dead. It is not the loss of a few, as the farmers in the provinces lose their sheep by the attack of the black bear, or the spring lambs are killed by foxes, but it is the whole fifty thousand. As an illustration of this, a visitor, one July evening, about seven o'clock,

accidentally moved a small gate which regulated the supply of twelve thousand fine, healthy trout fry belonging to the writer, and at half past ten the same evening every fish was dead on its back. The gate was not moved over an inch ; the consequence was the death of twelve thousand beautiful young trout.

For instance, again, a freshet that you have not guarded against comes down unexpectedly, and sweeps over your ponds ; when the waters subside, you will not have lost one or two of your fish, but, it is very likely, three fourths of them. Or a screen insecurely placed may let them all go ; or an epidemic, bred by foul meat, may take off half your brood before you can check it.

A score of instances within the writer's knowledge might be mentioned, where actual losses of great magnitude have occurred in each one of these ways, when the only cause was insecurity. Thus it is seen that losses, when they do occur, are frequently so disastrous that no degree of security in guarding against them seems excessive. As in business, so in trout raising, the magnitude of the risk calls for a corresponding degree of security.

3. The utmost security is also necessary in trout raising, because the dangers are so incessant and so constantly present. Plant your corn in the field, or turn your sheep out to pasture, and they are tolerably safe ; their dangers come seldom, and their enemies are few , but hatch your trout in the water, and not a moment, by day or by night, are they free from

danger, and there is not a moment when they are not surrounded by mortal enemies.

Frogs, lizards, land and water snakes, water-beetles, the caddis-worms, land-rats and water-rats, mice, minks, weasels, kingfishers, herons of several kinds, and even cats, are on the alert for them all the time, and, after they have once found them, will visit them every day or night as long as they last. The unprotected trout are like a flock of sheep in the haunts of panthers and wolves on the Rocky Mountains, and have about as much chance of surviving.

Their danger is incessant. It is not once a week or once a month that their enemies come for them, but every day and every night of their lives, if they are unprotected; and every week the number of creatures that feed on them will increase. It is surprising how fast kingfishers, . herons, frogs, and snakes will multiply around a well-filled and unprotected trout pond. Furthermore, there is the constant danger from the water itself which sustains them, either of its overflowing, or running short, or of getting too warm, or becoming unwholesome, — all which accidents are likely to happen and to be attended with fatal results. The constant presence of these dangers renders it doubly important to make security your first thought in raising trout.

4. This is not all; the sources of danger to which your fish are exposed are of the invisible, intangible kind, that keep out of your sight and out of your reach, and for that very reason security becomes tenfold more needful. Many of their dangers come when

they are least expected; they do their work unseen, often in the dark, and leave no trace of their presence.

For example, one or two of the fine threads in the screen of your hatching trough may be worn through, or there may be some small undiscovered crevice in a corner of your nursery, and day after day, for weeks, the little creatures may be slipping through and escaping, and an immense loss occur before you even suspect the cause of the mysterious waste.

Or the cover of your hatching trough, although to all appearances tight, may be loose enough to admit a mouse, and every night for a month he and his companions may come into the trough, and feed on your alevin trout in the corners, where they swarm by thousands; and yet, when morning comes, not a sign or a trace may you discover to show that anything has gone wrong, except that your fish are daily diminishing. Or it may happen that a muskrat, out of sight under the earth, is boring a hole that will let your fish out, when you think they are perfectly secure; or a mink, wholly unexpected, may have quartered himself in one of your ponds; or the invisible fungus may, without your knowledge, be gathering in the gills of your young fry, to their certain future destruction. Such is the occult character of many of the dangers which threaten the lives of your trout, and hence the need of extreme security in raising them is such that it can hardly be overestimated. Labor, patience, and constant care are required to be successful; but the one consideration which ranks above all others is to guard them from every species of insecurity.

Selecting the Water.

The first thing to do, in getting ready to raise trout, is to find suitable water. This is a very important part of your preparations, for it is the element that your trout are to spend their lives in ; and if there is anything wrong about the water, it will sooner or later show itself in fatal results.

In looking for suitable water, the following precautions should in no instance be overlooked.

1. Be sure that there will *always* be water *enough* for your purposes. To decide upon this, you must be guided by the amount of water flowing in the hottest week of the dryest time in the summer.

This is your guide : the stream or spring is worth no more than what it will do at its very warmest and lowest time. It seems like reflecting on the reader's intelligence to insist on this precaution, yet thousands and thousands of fish have been lost by neglecting it.*

Great care ought to be exercised to guard against being misled by deceptive appearances.

When you see a brook sweeping along in the spring at its flood height, it is extremely difficult to realize that the swollen stream can become, as it often does, a dry or nearly dry channel. Therefore, when you select your brook, either see it yourself in its dryest state, or take the testimony of some perfectly *reliable*

---

* I once received a letter from a man who wanted to know "what kind of fish he could raise in a brook which was quite large eight months in the year, and dried up wholly during the other four."

person who has seen it thus; and if from what you see or hear you are led to believe that it is *possible* for the supply of water to become insufficient, have nothing to do with it. Overcome all temptations to try it, and look elsewhere.

2. Be sure that no freshets which can carry away or overflow your works are possible. In deciding upon the character of your stream, in this respect allowance should be also made, as in the former case, for deceptive appearances, though in just the opposite direction. It is so very difficult to believe that the harmless little rivulet of August can become a resistless torrent in October, that many persons are apt to be misled by the deceptive appearance, and will actually go to work on a stream liable to freshets, and will build ponds, and will stock them, at great expense, with no guaranty whatever that the next fall or spring flood will not, as it generally proves, sweep everything away. Trust to no probabilities, but make *sure* that no freshets *can* come that can do you damage, or, at least, that no such freshet ever has come. If this is not made *sure* of, a single night will destroy the work of years.

Brooks subject to moderate freshets that can be controlled are not necessarily objectionable; they need not be given up, if the expense of carrying off the surplus water is not too great; but a brook where the freshets cannot be wholly guarded against is a delusion and a snare, and ought to be utterly avoided.

3. Be sure that the water does not heat up in the summer to an unwholesome point. Many brooks which have the appearance of being perfect trout

streams are worthless from becoming too warm in the summer. Here, also, the test should be the hottest day of the dryest time. For it should be remembered that one day of freshet, drought, or intense heat may do as much mischief, in taking away your trout, as six months of the same might do.

The waters otherwise suitable, which are most to be dreaded on account of their excessive heat, are outlets of ponds or lakes, and such as are at the fish preserves distant from their sources. These waters, though perennial and of even flow, and fed by springs, may yet, from too much exposure to the sun or air, be wholly unfit to keep trout alive, by reason of their temperature rising too high.

This objection is not always so imperative as the other two just mentioned, because there are two ways of obviating it to some extent, viz. : — 1. By putting ice in the stream. 2. By taking the water from near its source, through a pipe under ground. The first remedy often involves so much risk, as well as expense and necessity of constant vigilance in hot weather, that it had better not be contemplated, except in cases of great counterbalancing advantages. The latter remedy, however, when it will pay, is usually practicable, and will do if it can be made safe. But, at all events, make *sure* either that the water will keep cool of itself, or that you can and *will* keep it cool enough by one method or another.

Under this head it may be suggested that the quantity and force of current and vigor * of the water have

* I cannot exactly define the word " vigor " in its present ap-

much to do with the degree of temperature at which trout will live. For instance, when water does not possess much vigor, is deficient in quantity, and sluggish, it will not support trout life in so high a temperature as when it is vigorous, plentiful, and rapid. I think it is safe to say that sluggish flat water at 70° is dangerous, if not fatal, to trout; while they will live in vigorous rapid water which occasionally runs to 80°. I have found 85° to be fatal to them in all kinds of water.

4. Be sure that the water you select is intrinsically favorable to trout. Be very careful about using any brook or spring which can possibly receive the discharge of a tannery or mill, or drainage discharging any poisonous substance. The presence of some lime in the water naturally is not necessarily an objection; for trout do live in limestone regions, and in water having some lime in it. So of iron; but too much of either in the water will kill them. The best test of this point that you can possibly get is that the stream is a natural trout brook. On the other hand, if it is not a natural trout brook, or has not been one, be very shy of it; there is some good cause why trout do not inhabit it, and the cause is probably to be found in the unsuitableness of the water.

It is no objection to a stream where trout are *raised* that it is occasionally turbid, or even muddy. Such

plication, nor can I find a better word to give my meaning. In drinking water, we distinguish between that which is flat and that which is sparkling. What we call sparkling water, when we drink it, I mean by vigorous water in a trout brook. There are very great differences in this respect, as all are aware.

water, though injurious to eggs, is wholesome and beneficial to the fully formed fish of all ages.

It is always a good precaution, where a stream is used which has no trout in it naturally, to put in a few and keep them there the year round, and see how it suits them, before adopting it fully as a trout-breeding water.

There is some conflict of opinion about the comparative value of spring and brook water for raising trout. As a rule, I think generally, all things considered, that spring-water is best for hatching, and brook-water is the best for raising trout. It is said that brook-water is more natural for hatching ; that it hatches the trout out at a better time, namely, in the spring, and that the young fry, when they do come out, are uncommonly lively. It is not certain, however, that brook-water is more natural than spring-water for hatching, for in many brooks, and in most of those with which I am acquainted, half the fish lay their eggs in spring-holes, or so near the spring-sources of the stream that it is practically spring-water that they are hatched in. Then, again, it is a doubtful advantage, if any, to have them hatch late ; and lastly, they are not sure, by any means, to make better trout for being unusually lively in the earlier days of their infancy.

On the other hand, spring-water possesses, for hatching, the vast advantage over brook-water of being *safer*.

I think that in hatching, except in very rare instances, brook-water can have no advantages which can begin to offset this great counterbalancing advantage of safety. You cannot be too sure of the water which flows over your eggs. In most brooks you cannot be sure that there will not be trouble in the course of the winter from a stoppage of water, an overflow, sediment, or injury to the water above. At any rate, with a brook, your risk, on account of these dangers, is vastly increased. But with a spring there is an even flow, a steady temperature, very little danger of stoppage of the water or injury to it, and the whole thing is compact and well in hand.

These considerations will, in the long run, give the spring-water for hatching purposes a very decided advantage over brook-water.

Brook-water, again, is best to *raise* trout in. Spring-water, just emerging from the darkness of the interior of the earth, is cold, wholly free from animal and vegetable life, and deficient in that peculiar vitality which its flow through the open air and sunshine imparts to it. Trout will not grow fast, will remain small, and will develop small ova, in such water.

Brook-water, on the contrary, possessing the qualities which spring-water lacks, is much more nutritious, if I may use the word, will grow trout rapidly, will give them a good size, and will develop large eggs in the fish. For these reasons it is, if safe, better than spring-water for raising trout.

It should be mentioned here, however, that cold water makes a hardier and firmer-fleshed fish, and is less favorable to disease. It is consequently better, sometimes, when there is any tendency to disease, to keep the very young fry in the spring-water until they have acquired some firmness of bone and flesh.

The best water advantages of all are perhaps found

where *both* spring and safe brook water are at one's command, and either or both can be employed at pleasure.* The brook-water can then be used, if desired, while it is safe, and a mixture of spring and brook can be so graduated as to make the eggs hatch at any desired time between the minimum and maximum periods of incubation. In the long run, however, I think experience will prove that a large spring of even temperature and even flow is about as good as anything for hatching the eggs.

* This is the case at the Mirimichi Salmon-Breeding Works.

CHAPTER II.

PONDS.

THE first questions you will ask yourself, when you have decided that you have suitable water for your purposes, are, where shall the ponds be located, at what points on the stream shall the ponds be built, and how shall they be constructed ?

In answering these inquiries, a great variety of considerations of a special character will come in, such as the nature of the soil, the lay of the land, and your personal tastes, which you can best settle for yourself without help ; but there are other considerations of a general character which should be noticed here, and among them are the following.

1. The water you have is to be used for three distinct purposes, — for the hatching apparatus, for the nursery, and for the ponds of the mature trout, — and it should be borne in mind that the water which may be good for one of these may not be good for another.

For instance, the cold, barren water, just emerging from the earth, though just the thing for hatching eggs, is, from its cold and unnutritious character, poor water to fatten mature fish in ; on the other hand, brook-water, full of animal life, which is just the thing on that account for the mature trout, may, from its liability to sediment, or intractable character, or other causes, be extremely unsuitable for hatching. In locating your ponds, then, these three departments should be kept distinct in the mind; and it should be remembered that the works belonging to each should be so built in reference to their distinctive requirements, and also with reference to each other, that, when they are finished, each will have its proper water advantages, the precedence, when there is choice of water, being always given to the first two named, the hatching apparatus and the nursery. Nature has done so much in some trout-pond localities that very little foresight is required in this respect; but in many, especially where the water has to be used over once or twice, the exercise of considerable forethought will be well repaid.

2. Get your ponds, whenever you can without great inconvenience, either wholly or partly by excavating the earth, rather than by damming up the stream. This is for safety; with the bulk of the water above the level of the adjacent land, you are never secure. I never saw a trout-pond dam in my life that I considered absolutely safe.

Recollect that muskrats, frost, and decay are the active enemies of your pond walls, and their work is correspondingly mischievous in the degree that the ponds are raised above the level of the surrounding land. As I said, I never saw a trout-pond dam that was safe to hold trout in; but I have seen more unsafe ones than I can think of, that sooner or later led to disastrous losses by breaking away and letting out the fish. Excavated ponds are the only safe ones. Let your rule be, when possible, to excavate rather than dam up.

3. Build your ponds as compactly as possible. This might be said of your whole establishment also. Have all your ponds and works as near together as other more important considerations will allow. In rainy weather, and deep snows, and times of danger, you will appreciate this.

4. Build all your ponds small that mean business. Never break over this rule. Make your ponds for sport as large as you please, and I should say the larger the better; but when you mean business, build small. The greatest nuisance in the world, in a trout-breeding establishment, is a large pond, where the trout are out of control, and do as they please, and go as they please, wholly regardless of your convenience. This rule should always be observed, namely, never to let a trout escape to any place where you cannot get at it, observe it, and capture it at a moment's notice.

It is just as ridiculous, in the present stage of trout-breeding at least, to turn out your trout in a large pond, where they can get away from you, as it is to turn out your sheep or cattle in an unfenced mountain-pasture, where you will never hear from them again unless you fit out a regular hunting expedition to look them up. In course of time, when trout become as plentiful as the cattle and horses in South American pampas, this will do, perhaps; but now, when trout are as scarce as they are, and worth a dollar a pound, you want to have them where they cannot possibly get away from you, or even permanently out of your sight; consequently, your ponds should be built small. .

5. Have a fall, and as much of one as you can, at the head of each pond; this is not essential, but very desirable, as then the water comes full of air and life directly on your fish, which is worth a great deal. You can keep more fish in the pond by it, they will be healthier, and will grow better.

6. I think it is a good plan to locate your ponds far enough from the fountain-head of the stream for the water, by running through the air and sunlight, to have changed its character from cold barren spring-water to warmer and more nutritious brook-water. It will soon acquire this brook character, especially if it is spread out over considerable surface. Indeed, a pond having a *large* surface exposed to the sun, built directly over the spring, answers very well; but trout will not grow fast or fatten easily in a deep, small spring-hole or spring-water pond, not much exposed to the sun. Do not infer from this that trout need to be in the sun; it is not the trout, but the water that the trout live in, that requires the sunlight. Brook-water which has a good deal of sunlight in it is better for ponds than spring-water with none.

7. If your dwelling-house for yourself or keeper is built, then try to locate your ponds as near to the house as possible, within sight at least. If your house is not built, then build it very near your ponds. This I consider an important item, as experience is sure to teach.

You are never *entirely* safe from poachers, it is true, but your security is much greater for living near your ponds. Herons, kingfishers, minks, and other destructive animals, are also less likely to frequent your ponds if your house is near.

Then, besides the general advantages of always being near, and having your ponds in sight, you will many times, when a sudden shower comes up, or in some other case of need, go to the ponds, when, if you lived farther off, you would, perhaps, not think it worth the while. In the course of time the lack of this advantage will surely show itself in your record of losses.

8. You cannot exercise too much caution in making your ponds secure. To this end, I would recommend that every pond and every aqueduct on your place be built of two-inch plank. Had I followed this rule when I began five years ago, I should have saved thousands and thousands of fish. I have had all sorts of ponds and dams, and have had them built by experienced workmen, and warranted to stand twenty years ; but not a single pond has held, out of twenty-three that I have built, except my plank ponds. Some of them have stood for five years to perfection. Meanwhile, there has been no end of vexation, annual expense, and loss, caused by the other ponds breaking away ; and if I began over again, I would build everything from beginning to end, that the water flowed through, of two-inch plank. Stone, concrete, cement, and similar substances, may answer as well, perhaps, for single ponds ; but for a material to be used through-

out I prefer plank, because it can always be depended upon, repairs can be easily made, a screen can be readily put in anywhere, a tight joint can always be formed without trouble, tighter and more convenient connections can be made with the streams, and, on the whole, it stands the test of time and weather, and of both the routine and emergencies of experience, better than anything I know of.*

If you object to the want of durability of wood and its unsuitableness for fish, char the plank an eighth of an inch deep all round, and then you have both a durable and a suitable material.

I do not, however, insist upon the necessity of using plank, if you think you have something better. I only give the lessons of my own experience ; but, whatever you use, be *sure* that it is safe, that it will resist the muskrats, the weather, the frost, and the natural tendency to displacement, which, I suppose, all materials in the earth or on its surface are subject to.

If it is necessary to build a dam, I would recommend to the inexperienced to procure, by all means, the skill of an engineer, or practical dam-builder, who understands the nature of running water ; for to confine running water securely is an art in itself, and a beginner is almost sure to make a mistake somewhere, for which in the end he will pay a heavy penalty in losses.

Running water is the most treacherous of all things,

---

* These remarks are intended, of course, for business ponds. It does not matter much what amateur ponds are built of.

and is always seeking to run in a different channel from that artificially provided for it ; and if there is a weak spot anywhere about the sides of the dam or pond, the water will find it, and sooner or later, with the help of muskrats and frost, will bore a hole through it, and very likely this will happen in some place where you have never dreamed of its going. Once having gained an advantage, it never loses it, but will render your pond more and more unsafe, till you make an entire reconstruction of it or abandon it.

Employ an experienced man, then, to build the dam, if you must have one, and tell him to make it doubly safe; and even then, if your experience is like mine, you will be sorry you built it.

9. The shape of the ponds should be adapted to your water supply. If you have plenty of water at a low temperature, build the ponds of any shape you like so that they are not too large. If your water supply is small and cold, make your ponds narrow and shallow. If the supply is small, and liable to heat up, make them narrower still, and deep. Indeed, a deep ditch is the best thing where you have neither cold nor plentiful water. With average water, experience favors oblong ponds, not over twelve or fifteen feet in width, nor over three or four feet in depth, and of any desirable length ; these ponds can be easily inspected, easily swept with a seine, and will have no places of concealment for the fish to hide away in.

I think it is a good plan to have the ponds deepest

in the-middle, and to diminish in depth towards both ends, so as to grade off to nothing at the inlet and outlet. Such ponds keep the cleanest. If the pond is deep at the lower end, in the course of years a good deal of refuse and unclean matter will collect there, which you would rather have out of the pond, and which would have naturally worked off at the outlet if the bottom of the pond gradually shelved up towards it.

10. Always, if possible, have your ponds so arranged that you can draw off the water, if necessary. When you want to make repairs or changes in the pond, or wish to clean it out, this will be found a great convenience ; but it is especially serviceable when you want to use the pond for smaller fish than have been living in it, for it is never quite safe to put small fish in a pond which has been stocked with larger ones, unless it is drawn off.

Trout have such a wonderful faculty for getting out of sight, that even in the best-constructed ponds, where the water is not drawn off, they will often elude your search, and one or two fish may still be left in the pond after you have, as you believe, examined it thoroughly and taken them all out. I need not say how mischievous the mistake would prove. Instances could be cited of *hosts* of small fish having been destroyed by *one* or *two* large ones, left unwittingly in the pond. Therefore have your pond, if possible, so that you can draw it off if required, and always do so when you are going to substitute small fish for large ones in it.

11. Allow no hiding-places in your pond which you cannot remove at pleasure.   They almost always lead to mischief.   A dead fish, perhaps, will get in them without your knowledge, and foul the water ; or a mink will make use of them, and elude you for weeks, or, more likely than all, a large cannibal trout will hide there and prey on the smaller ones for months, undiscovered by you.   On the other hand, provide all the *movable* hiding-places within your control that you please, — the more, up to a reasonable extent, the better, — but never let them get out of your control, or exist without your having access to them.   The safeguards against outside dangers, which all ponds should possess, are very important, and would, perhaps, more naturally come in here, but they will be considered under the head of " The Care of Mature Trout." *

NUMBER OF PONDS.

There is no regulation number of ponds for a trout-grower to be governed by.   The best rule is to build all you want ; the usual number, three, recommended in books, being no guide to go by.   You will certainly want three, and probably several more.   I have often found ten quite few enough.   You may be sure of this, that you will in time have two sizes of young fry, two sizes of yearlings, and at least three sizes of older ones, which should be kept apart.

Besides the ponds for these, you will find a minnow-pond, a pond for rare fish,† and two or three experi-

* See pp. 227 – 234.

† At the Cold Spring Trout Ponds there is a pond twenty feet

ment ponds convenient. I should say, build all the ponds you please, if you have water enough ; you will not have too many.

SPAWNING BEDS.

The spawning beds consist simply of a long narrow flume, or raceway, at the head of the ponds, where the fish come up to spawn. They should be built at the very upper end of the pond, and should have a good current of water running through them. They are generally made of plank, and should be at least thirty feet long, with sides eighteen inches deep.

From the lower end of the spawning beds, the slope should be gradual to the lowest level of the bottom of the pond. If the slope is abrupt, the fish are not so likely to go up the races, and are more likely to spawn in the pond. The width of the spawning race will depend on the volume of the stream, it being an essential point to secure a lively current over the beds. Where there is plenty of water, the raceways should be four feet wide. If the water supply is small, two feet, and even eighteen inches, will do. There should be transverse bars placed on the bottom, across the whole width, high enough to make the water above them from four to twelve inches deep. The more water you have, the deeper you can afford to make the water in the beds, without dulling the current too much.

square, called the happy-family pond, where nine different kinds of large fish are kept together, including glass-eyed pike, mullets, black bass, and others. Although not profitable, I have always found it sufficiently interesting to make it worth while to keep it up.

In the spawning season, a layer of coarse clean gravel, three or four inches deep, should be thrown into these beds. They should be closely covered, and generally your whole force of water turned on.

The trout will come up here to spawn in preference to any other place in the pond, and it is here that they are trapped for the purpose of expressing their eggs.

The continued daily disturbing of them for this purpose will sometimes — and usually, I think — drive them down the stream a little lower, towards the end of the season.

It is therefore a good plan to cover and prepare only the upper half of the beds at first, and to trap the fish there at the beginning of the season, so that when they fall back, on account of being disturbed, they will not drop far enough down the stream to spawn below the lower beds, which, when the proper time comes, can be made ready and covered like the rest.

We have thus far treated wholly of the artificial method of taking the eggs. This method has two objections. It is entirely artificial, and it involves severe work, and exposure to water in the spawning season.

To obviate these two objections, Hon. Stephen H. Ainsworth conceived the very ingenious plan of making the fish spawn naturally, and at the same time of saving the eggs. This idea he carried out in what is now everywhere known as the Ainsworth Spawning Races.

The following description of this invention is by the inventor, Mr. Ainsworth.

AINSWORTH'S SPAWNING RACE.

This race may be built like the races made for the artificial impregnation of spawn used by nearly all trout-breeders to entice the trout up from the pond to spawn. It can be made of any length, from ten to fifty feet, and from two to six feet wide, according to the number of trout which are to use it and the amount of water for the supply of the pond. It should be made with plank sides and bottom, so tight as to keep out all sediment. Paving the bottom nicely with small stones will answer. The bottom, whether of plank or stone, must then be covered with a half-inch layer of fine, well-washed gravel.

When one has large trout to spawn in the race, the water should be two inches deep at the upper or supply end, and fifteen inches deep at the lower end, where it empties into the pond, with a gentle current throughout its whole length. This will give good spawning depth to the water for trout of all sizes from six to twenty-four inches long. Usually a race three feet wide, and from fifteen to twenty feet long, will be quite sufficient for a pond of one thousand or eighteen hundred trout.

The bottom of this race must be covered with fine wire-cloth screens, of about ten meshes to the inch, made of zinc or galvanized wire, so as not to corrode the spawn. Iron wire, *if painted*, will answer where zinc cannot be obtained. These wire screens must be nailed to wooden frames made of inch-square stuff, the frames to correspond in length with the width of the race, and to be as wide as the cloth will permit, — say two feet. Strips of ¾-inch stuff must be nailed to the bottom of the race for the screens to rest on, in such a manner that they will be raised a quarter of an inch above the gravel on the bottom. This is done to give good circulation to the water under the spawn as they fall on to these wire screens. These screens must be laid the whole length of the race, side by side, to catch the spawn as it is deposited by the parent trout.

Now, place over these another set of screens made of coarse wire-cloth, of about two or three meshes to the inch, so that the spawn will drop through easily. These screens must be nailed on frames of the same length as the others, but of two-inch stuff, and as wide as the cloth will permit. These screens must be strong enough to hold two inches of well-washed coarse gravel, from three quarters of an inch to two inches in diameter. They should be so large that there will be interstices between the gravel large enough to let the spawn pass down, if necessary, to the lower screen. The upper screens should have handles on each end to lift them by, as they will have to be taken out and replaced every few days during the spawning season.

When these two sets of screens are placed the whole length of the race, and all is complete, the water will pass over all, two inches deep at the supply end and fifteen inches deep at the lower end, with a moderate current through the whole race. The reader will perceive by the description and diagram that there is one inch of space between the two screens to hold the spawn as they are deposited by the parent trout, with a gentle current passing over and under them; and that the upper screen prevents the spawn from being destroyed by trout and insects, so that they are perfectly safe until removed to the hatching box.

When the trout is ready to spawn, she will enter the race from the pond and prepare her nest. This she does by whipping all the sediment from the gravel with her tail, and then she whips or digs a hole in the cleansed gravel about two inches deep, or down to the upper screen, and about four inches in diameter. She then bends herself down in this hole and presses her abdomen on the gravel, and forces out from one hundred to five hundred spawn, which fall to the bottom of the hole and down through the upper screen to the lower one. She then passes up the race, and the male trout attending her comes over the nest and spawn and ejects his milt on the ova; he then whips the water in the hole with his tail, sending the water and milt in all directions, so that the milt reaches all the spawn on the screen or in the gravel, and, as they are ripe and ready for the milt, impregnates every one of them. As soon as this is done, the mother trout returns and covers up the spawn and fills the hole, and soon digs another in like manner, and so on till she has deposited all her ova, which sometimes takes two weeks.

There may be from twenty to fifty trout in the race spawning at one time, and all, or nearly all, of the spawn will be found perfectly impregnated and fully matured, so that they will all hatch, if taken out every three days, or once a week, and placed in hatching boxes.

To take the spawn from the lower screens, first take out two of the upper screens with what gravel is upon them; then remove the lower ones, and wash the spawn off into a large pan of water carefully, and replace one set behind you, and then take up one set at a time and place back, until all are returned. Should any spawn remain in the gravel, by raising the screen up and down a few times they will drop down through the interstices. The race must be kept well covered during the time of spawning, all persons must be kept away, and the fish disturbed as little as possible.

By this method the spawn are all saved, are perfectly matured, are all impregnated, and will all hatch; the young will be perfect, few or none will die, as their sac food is complete, and they will be strong and healthy when they commence seeking food for themselves. It is much less work to take the spawn than by handling, and no parent trout are lost.

The spawning race above described answered its purpose perfectly in making the fish spawn naturally, and also lessened the work of getting the eggs.

The tending of the races, nevertheless, required considerable labor and exposure. This latter objection was ingeniously surmounted by Mr. A. S. Collins, the partner of Seth Green, in a modification of the Ainsworth Races, known by the name of the Roller Spawning Box.

I give a description below, written by the inventor.

Fig. 1 is a spawning box, with a portion of the side removed.

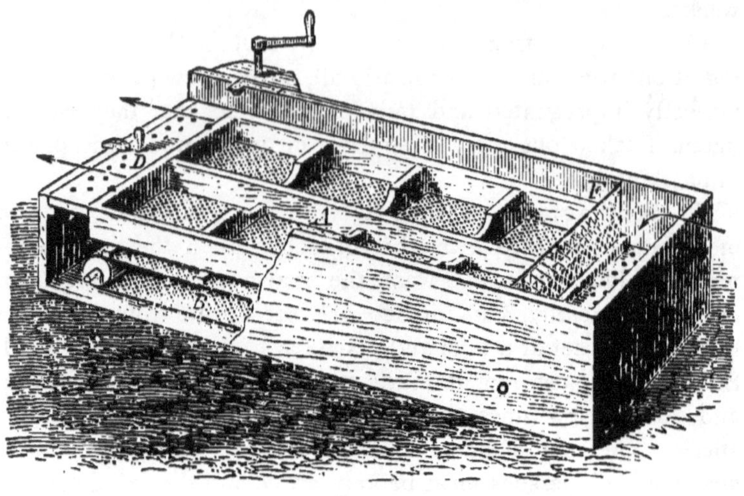

FIG. 1.

A is a double row of coarse wire screens; *B* apron of fine wire cloth; *D* a screen; *F* a screen.

ROLLER SPAWNING BOX.

For taking the naturally impregnated eggs of Brook Trout, Salmon, etc. (Patent of A. S. Collins.)

In the Roller Spawning Box the principle used is that of the Ainsworth Screens, and the improvement consists in a new and convenient method of collecting the eggs. A double row of coarse wire screens (three meshes to the inch), eight in number, each two feet square, are put together in one frame, eight feet by four. These screens are to be filled with coarse gravel, and the eggs pass through as in Ainsworth's Screens. Under these is an endless apron of fine wire-cloth, passing over rollers at the two ends of the box. This apron is about one inch beneath the upper screen, and is kept from sagging by small cross-bars, corresponding to the division of the upper screen.

These cross-bars are supported by, and, when the rollers are turned, slide on, an inch-square strip nailed to the side of the box. A similar strip, one inch above, supports the larger screens.

The cross-bars also keep the eggs from being carried down by the current. By using two small bevelled cog-wheels the front roller can be turned by a handle. As the roller is turned forward, the endless apron moves with it, and the eggs, as they come to the edge of the roller, will fall off. The pan is placed in front of the roller, and receives the eggs as they fall. The box need not be more than two feet deep; the depth depending upon the size of the rollers, which in a short race may be quite small, and the box not more than eighteen inches deep. The box is set directly in the raceway, and intended to fill it completely. The water may either enter with a fall over the top of the box, or the top of the box may be cut down until the water will enter on the level at which it is intended to stand over the screens.

Fig. 2 is an enlarged view of the front of the same box.

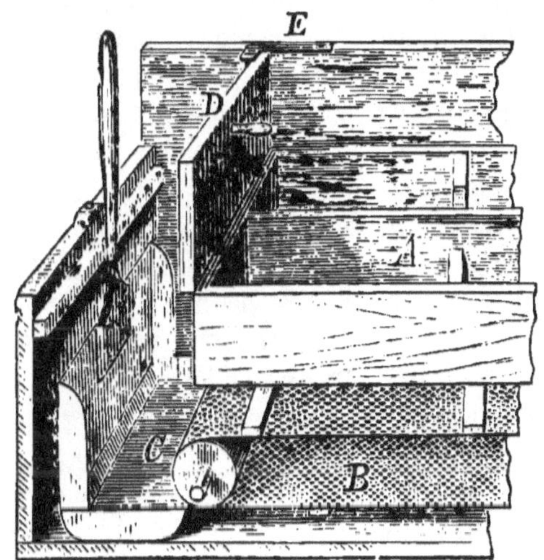

FIG. 2.

A is a double row of coarse wire screens; *B* apron of fine wire cloth; *C* pan to receive the eggs; *D* screen; *E* catch to hold screen *D* when raised.

A screen, intended to prevent the fish from running beyond the race or getting into the lower part of the box, may extend to the bottom, or be arranged differently ; a screen placed at the front of the box is also intended to prevent the fish from getting below. When the eggs are to be taken, this screen is raised on hinges to an upright position, and confined by a spring catch or latch. This confines the fish which may happen to be in the race, and none of them can get below. The pan is then lowered to its position, the roller turned, and the eggs taken. When the operation is finished the screen is again lowered, the button turned, and the work is done. If the box is wide, say four feet, it is more convenient to have the pan made in two or three sections, inserted in a light frame, as the eggs can be more easily carried in and poured out of a shorter pan. It is better, perhaps, to make the screen to open in the middle, having hinges at both sides. Then one half will keep the fish in the pond, and the other half the fish in the race, from running into the well. The box can be made of any length from four feet to forty feet, and of any width from two feet to six or eight. If it is made very wide, an additional longitudinal support must be provided for the revolving screen. We recommend the following dimensions for speckled-trout races: two feet wide, and from ten to twenty feet long; or four feet wide, and from twenty to forty feet long. The upper screens may be made in convenient sections, the whole width of the box, and six or eight feet long.

The end screens are so made that while a full current is permitted to flow over the upper screens, only a gentle current can flow through the under part of the box. This current is meant to be so regulated that when the pan is placed about an inch from the turning-roller, all the small stones which the trout may whip through the upper screen will fall short of the pan; the eggs, being lighter, will be carried by the current into the pan, while a great part of the dirt, etc., which may collect on the under screen will be carried up over the pan and entirely out of the box. The revolving screen *may* be made of tarred muslin or mosquito-netting. But wire-cloth (of ten or twelve meshes to the inch) keeps much the cleanest, and we are inclined to think it best for the purpose. I make my aprons half wire-cloth and half tarred muslin, furnishing the wire only with cross-bars, and always leaving it uppermost. This apron is fastened around the rollers by a lacing of cord. At the end of the season the water in the pond can be drawn down a foot, and everything taken out but the rollers. Give the screens a coat of paint or gas tar, and lay them away in a dry place until the next autumn. A stiff brush may also be placed under the forward roller, so that every time the roller is turned to remove the eggs the screen will be perfectly clean.

The box can be so arranged that the rollers also can be removed each season; and this arrangement on various accounts is much the best.

This box looks, at first sight, somewhat complicated, but is in reality very simple, and easier to make than to describe. Any one who has the knack of using tools can make one which will answer the purpose perfectly. The cost is very little more than that of the Ainsworth Screens (of the same area) as generally used. The cost for wire being the same in both cases, the lumber in the box itself being extra, and also the rollers, hinges, and cog-wheels (or windlass wheel).

A few of the advantages of the plan are as follows : Let us compare a double row of forty Ainsworth Screens, each two feet square and occupying a space in the raceway forty feet long and four feet wide, with one of the new spawning boxes of the same dimensions.

1st. By the old way it would take two men a good half-day to remove the screens singly, feather off the eggs in a careful manner, and return each (double) screen to its proper place.

It would take the new spawning box about fifteen minutes to do the same work with one man.

2d. The weight of the gravel which has to be lifted in the old way every time the eggs are removed amounts to many tons in the course of a season.

In the new box the gravel is not lifted at all.

3d. By the old way the operator's hands must of necessity be more or less wet during the whole operation. Now, as the trout and salmon spawn during the winter season, when the thermometer generally stands below the freezing-point, taking eggs in the old way is not only inconvenient and painful, but often impossible.

By the new way the hands are not made wet, and may be kept comfortably gloved.

4th. By the old way more or less of the eggs are lost by careless feathering, exposing the eggs to the freezing atmosphere, clumsiness in handling the screens (caused by cold fingers), tipping of the screens, wash of the current, etc., etc.

By the new way every egg is saved.

5th. By the old method every fish is driven out of the race when the eggs are taken. Some of them will not return, but will seek a spawning-place in the pond, and many eggs will be unavoidably lost.

By the new way the fish are not driven from the race. And as the boxes are always covered during the season, the fish will not even be disturbed. In fact, they may spawn *while the eggs are being taken,* and yet not a single egg be lost.

This Spawning-Box answers for securing the naturally impregnated eggs of salmon, salmon trout, speckled brook trout, whitefish, shad, etc. It is recommended by the leading pisciculturists of the country.

Mr. Ainsworth's idea was one of great value, and Mr. Collins's device an excellent modification of it, and I cordially recommend their methods to those who wish to avoid the labor and exposure of taking the eggs artificially.

No one who has not had experience in taking spawn by hand can conceive of the amount of labor and hardship which this beautiful contrivance saves. There is some difference of opinion as to the question which yields the most eggs, the artificial or the screen method, and the results of some experiments of Mr. F. Mather seem to be adverse to the Ainsworth plan. I will not express an opinion here on this point, but will say that the saving of exposure by the Collins Roller Box is worth paying a good many eggs for.

Inlets and Outlets.

12. The inlets and outlets of your ponds should be ample, and securely " jointed," if I may use the word, to the ponds ; that is, so joined to the side of the pond that no water will ever work its way under or around them. This is so simple and safe a process with the plank system, that the advantages derived from this alone would decide me in favor of the use of plank ponds.

The outlet is usually a plank trough, or bulkhead, with a screen to confine the fish, and the inlet is the same, except that one half the floor of the bulkhead is made to project over the pond, and is formed of hard-wood slats, laid longitudinally with the length of the bulkhead, and a quarter or half an inch apart. This is much better than a screen, because, while it answers the same purpose in confining the fish, it lets through all the food from above, and does not get so easily clogged up.

When a bulkhead inlet or outlet is made to a common earth pond, great care should be taken to have piling driven down to the hard pan below, and on both sides, for several feet ; and even then in some soils the water will work through it in the course of years.

Be sure to make the outlets broad enough to admit a screen of sufficient size to carry off all the water at its highest possible flood height, making large allowance, also, for the clogging up of screen. Always have a gate at the inlet which will wholly shut off the water in case of danger.

SCREENS.

Screens hold a very responsible position in trout culture.

All that separates your thousands of fish from the outer world, where they would be lost to you, is the twentieth-of-an-inch barrier of wire-screen. As far as their voluntary escape is concerned, the wire-screens stand in the place of gates, locks, bolts, and bars. It is obvious how responsible their office is.

All screens should be of copper or galvanized iron. Copper is best for fine-mesh screens, galvanized iron for large meshes.

Wooden slats answer very well for grown-up trout.

In using slats it should be remembered that a fish, by turning on its side, will go through a surprisingly narrow aperture, if it is long enough. A square mesh of iron will hold fish securely, when *slats* would need to be only half the width of the mesh apart.

The wire netting should be fastened on to firm frames, and the frames should fit tight in their place, especially at the bottom.

Thousands of fish have been lost by neglecting this simple precaution.

There should be eighteen threads to the inch for the very smallest fry, four threads to the inch for yearlings, and two to the inch for two-year-olds.

For placing the screens for the young fry, see p. 59.

If leaves or other *débris* coming down the stream make trouble by clogging the outlet screen, you can protect it by building out a board frame, say a foot deep, in front of the screen, with about eight inches of its width below the water and four inches above ; this will catch and retain the obstructions floating down, and the screen will remain comparatively clean.

Where it is practicable, it is a good plan to have all the inlets and outlets of the ponds of the same size, so that the screen of any one will fit all the rest. This secures uniformity of size in the screens, and is often a great convenience when it becomes desirable to move a screen from one pond to another.

When there is danger of too much water, have a side channel provided to carry it off. This channel should be considerably lower than the inlet to your pond, should be the channel the stream would naturally seek when shut off from the ponds, and should be very ample. I would have it, for safety's sake, double the capacity of any freshet that was ever known on the stream. For the want of this precaution, trout enough have been lost, within my own knowledge, to make a fortune.

It is usually the best plan to leave the natural channel of the brook for the surplus water, and to build your ponds on one side of it, and take off the water supply for them from the brook. This is the way the breeding ponds at the Cold Spring Trout Ponds are arranged, and it is the safest way in time of a freshet.

CHAPTER III.

BUILDINGS.

THE hatching house is the one essential building in fish breeding ; but a thorough trout-breeding establishment should have, besides the hatching house, several other buildings or rooms, as, for instance, a meat-room, carpenter's shop, and ice-house. It is not, of course, necessary to have a separate building for all these, but each one should have at least a separate room.

The reader inquires at once, I suppose, why the hatching house will not answer for all of these purposes, except, possibly, the ice-house. The reason is this ; if you engage in hatching on any considerable scale, you will have water running through the house in great quantities, half the year, and perhaps all the year round. The result will be that this house will be the dampest place you ever were in, and everything in it, that moisture can hurt, will be spoiled. Tools will rust, the firewood will not burn, the kindlings will be soaked, your scales, microscopes, matches, pails, pans, and papers, — everything, in fact, will become intolerably damp.

Then, again, the hatching house, being built for the use of water, should not contain anything that would restrict the most perfect freedom in its use. If it is essential to turn a stream of water over some fish, in an unusual place in the house, for a week or so, there should be no such obstacle in the way of it as the danger of exposing tools, or microscopes, or any utensils, to too much dampness. Therefore I would have the hatching house, or hatching room, devoted to the water, and have all other considerations so subordinate to this that you can deluge the house with water at any time you like, without doing any harm, and without any feeling of restraint, on account of things in it being injured by the dampness.

This is the reason why it is not best to use the hatching room for the other purposes mentioned.

The buildings or rooms which I would recommend are, a meat-room, an office, a storeroom and carpenter's shop combined in one, and an ice-house.

1. The meat-room. You should bear in mind that a stock of ten thousand large trout will consume at least forty pounds of meat a day ; this is over a thousand pounds a month.

This food must first be cut up, and some sorted out for the young fry and some for the old trout. Then the meat for the large fish must be run through a coarse meat-cutter, and that for the small ones through a finer one, and the meat must be kept thawed out in the winter, and fresh in the summer. This handling of the meat, sometimes a thousand pounds in a month, sometimes more, and keeping it in the right condition in all seasons, is no small task, and unless it has a separate room devoted to it becomes an intolerable nuisance, especially in the decomposing heat of summer.

I would then, by all means, have the meat-room by itself, and here in this room, and *nowhere else*, should be kept the two meat-cutters, with their stands, the meat-grater (if you use one) for the young fry, the meat-bench, the pails, pans, and baskets for holding and carrying the meat, the meat itself, and everything else, in short, that belongs to the commissary department, — in this room, and *nowhere* else.

The most disagreeable feature about trout-breeding is the commissariat; and the more you keep it by itself, and out of sight, and out of the way of everything else, the more desirable your place will be, and the better you will like your work.

The meat-room, like the other rooms, should have a plank floor, with a trap-door in it, should be well ventilated, should have a tank of water in it, supplied by a stream large enough to keep it from freezing in the winter and heating up in the summer, and arranged so that the whole stream can be turned on to the floor when it is cleaned or " swashed," — which should be *often*, — and whatever other conveniences may be desired.

The tank is not only to furnish water to keep things clean, but it will be found to be the best place in the summer to keep the meat, and the only place in winter. I have tried both the ice-house and the spring water for this purpose, but have found that the spring water answers much the best in practice.

2. The next most important room is the store-

room and carpenter's shop combined; these can be together as well as not. They are required, because a great amount of lumber, old screens and screen-frames, pails and pans not in use, and a thousand other things, will collect about the place, which you will want to have under cover and in a dry place. Then there is so much little work constantly to be done,—what is called in New England "puttering,"—that a carpenter's bench and tools are almost indispensable, the more so because what needs to be done must often be done at once, before one can send for a carpenter to come and do it.

3. An office is a very desirable thing about a trout-breeding establishment. It is almost as indispensable, in fact, as the carpenter's bench, unless your house is right on the spot.

The office will be your comfortable room, where you can keep a fire, can transact business, make your microscopic examinations, examine the progress of experiments, take notes, do your writing, receive orders, and keep your record-books and show-case of specimens. Indeed, so many things call for such a room that no establishment is complete, without it.

4. An ice-house is absolutely necessary, unless you can *depend* upon ice, whenever you want it, from outside sources; and even then it is desirable. In transporting live fish, young or old, you *cannot* do without ice, except in cold weather, and you may sometimes need it for the meat-house; you will frequently need ice unexpectedly, and you must have it for shipping your large fish to market. Have an ice-house, then, by all

means, and locate it near the hatching house, and where the fish are packed for market. A building of the size of an ordinary family ice-house will do.

5. Besides these rooms, there are at the Cold Spring Trout Ponds a bird-pen, made of plank, large and durable, and a fox-pen, also built of wood and of good size. The bottom of the latter, made of plank, is laid three feet under ground, and is covered with earth to this depth, so that the animals confined may have a good place to burrow in, without being able to escape by burrowing. These pens are desirable, because as you will trap more or less about your place, you will sometimes catch animals and large birds alive, which you may like to keep alive. There is also a roughly built shanty, with a stove in it, near the spawning beds, in which the spawn can be taken in stormy weather, which is also recommended.

The Hatching House.

The hatching house, or hatching room, is, of course, the central point of the whole establishment.

Here the swarms of young trout upon which the other departments depend for their supply are brought into being; the greatest care, therefore, should be exercised in having it just right.

It should in general be roomy, well lighted, firm, and durable. Such a one, however roughly made, will answer its purpose of hatching as well as a more expensive one; though if one's means are unrestricted, there is no reason why it should not be a handsome building, and an ornament to the place, like that of Colonel Thompson at Springfield, for instance.

The size of the hatching house depends on the amount of work to be done in it. A room thirty feet long and eighteen feet wide will have hatching space for one hundred thousand eggs, besides passage-ways between the troughs, or hatching-stands, and considerable spare room to keep the gravel-boxes, and to work in.

For more eggs you will of course need more room; but, whatever the amount of business you do, it should be remembered that it is far better to have too much room than too little. I know of few things more disagreeable than a cramped hatching house.*

The hatching house should be located near the spring or reservoir which supplies it with water; for the longer the aqueduct which takes the water from the spring to the house, the greater is the risk of the water going wrong. The house should also be placed, if possible, so that the water will enter it several feet above the floor. This will enable the hatching apparatus to be elevated to a convenient height for examining the eggs standing or sitting, which is a great advantage; and I think it is better, on the whole, to incur the risk of a longer aqueduct from the spring, if necessary, to obtain this advantage.

No fire is required in the hatching room, to keep the water warm.† That keeps warm of itself, and also keeps

---

* Our hatching-house at the Mirimichi Salmon Breeding Works is a hundred feet long.

† It is an addition to one's personal comfort to have a stove in the hatching house, though it may not be required to warm the water.

the house comparatively warm. There is often a difference of 30° between the outside air and the interior
of the hatching room in extremely cold weather.

It is a good plan to build the walls thick, and then
the water running through will keep the air not very
many degrees from its own temperature.

This makes a much more comfortable room to
work in.

The shape of the hatching house will be determined
almost wholly by local considerations.

It is becoming quite the custom now to admit the
light into the hatching room by large movable sky-
lights in the roof; this is optional, however, unless
sufficient light cannot be obtained otherwise.

I will only add that if the four rooms mentioned —
the office, storeroom, meat-room, and hatching room —
are included in one building, the first three should be
separated from the hatching room by a partition prepared with waterproof cement, or other covering,
impervious to water.

CHAPTER IV.

HATCHING APPARATUS.

THE hatching apparatus consists of the supply reservoir, the aqueducts, the filtering arrangements, the distributing spout, and the troughs, or hatching apparatus proper.

The Supply Reservoir.

The supply reservoir, which hatches the eggs, is the great motive power of the whole establishment. It is this which does the work of replenishing all the other departments of the trout farm.

On its steady, unfailing supply everything depends. If it should fail from any cause during the hatching season, the whole year's increase would be lost. It follows, then, from the importance of this agency, that it should be most securely guarded. You should, therefore, in enclosing the reservoir, make your work very firm and secure, especially the lowest parts of it, where there is the most danger. Leave nothing to *chance* in this work. Take no risk whatever, but guard it from the possibility of breaking away; and in doing so, do not forget that muskrats and frost will have no more consideration for your hatching reservoir — so important to you — than for any other body of water.

Make it as small as you can without sacrificing water. Cover it from dirt, leaves, and light. Keep it perfectly clean, and never put any fish into it under any temptation ; and finally, unless you are certain that you can make a very sure thing of it yourself, employ an experienced man to construct it for you.

HATCHING-ROOM AQUEDUCT.

One of the most important parts of the whole hatching apparatus is the aqueduct which takes the water from the hatching reservoir to the hatching room. It may be nothing but a simple short pipe or spout, but its office is nevertheless exceedingly responsible. Indeed, it is literally a *sine qua non* of a hatching establishment to have this aqueduct safe ; for if it fails for a night to fulfil its purpose during the period of incubation, that is the end of that season's operations, and unless you buy more eggs, there will be a gap of one year in your chain of fish broods that never will be filled up.

This aqueduct, therefore, ought to be made especially secure. To make it so, 1. Build it of 1½-inch or 2-inch plank, and fasten it firmly so that frost cannot heave it, and so that it cannot be displaced by any accident whatever. I have known serious loss to result from an aqueduct being simply pushed out of place by the foot.

2. Char the plank. This I consider very important indeed, if you use plank, for you cannot be certain, without charring it, that fungus is not being generated in it. Do not imagine that you are safe from fungus

because your hatching boxes themselves are well guarded from it. It may grow in the aqueduct and be borne down by the stream, and before winter is over, you may find, to your dismay, that it has fastened its fatal grasp on your eggs. If so, they are ruined. There is no remedy for fungus which will make healthy fish of the eggs attacked. They may hatch, but the young fish will be good for nothing to raise. Therefore begin at the beginning, and guard your eggs from fungus by charring the aqueduct.

3. As a rule, it is best to have the aqueduct covered, but beware of making the outlet end smaller than the inlet end, for then, if anything gets into the pipe too large to pass through the outlet, it will stop the water, and your eggs will be ruined. I have known great danger and actual loss to come from such a defective aqueduct. In one instance a frog got into the pipe, in another a muskrat, in another a cork ; each of which came very near shutting off the water altogether and doing very great mischief. For further safety, put a coarse, galvanized-iron screen over the end of the aqueduct which receives the water.

4. If you have a small stream, and must convey it a considerable distance, and want to economize any-thing in temperature, you can keep it a little warmer by boxing up the aqueduct itself. But as a general thing it is labor wasted. You will be astonished to see how little any considerable stream changes in temperature in passing through even a long closed spout.

At the writer's works at Charlestown, N. H., when

the mercury is 10° below zero, the water at the hatching house loses only two degrees in passing through one hundred and twenty feet of channel.

The Filtering Arrangements.

Next to fungus, sediment is the most dangerous enemy to trout eggs, and, like fungus, it is the more to be dreaded because it is invisible ; that is, as it is held naturally in the water. A stream or a spring may look to you as clear as crystal, you may examine most carefully and not find any traces of dust or foreign matter in it, yet the same water in running sixty days over any given spot will very likely deposit enough sediment to kill a million eggs. Some few springs are, I believe, sufficiently free from sediment to be used without filtering, but such springs are exceedingly rare, and are the exceptions. As a rule, all springs and streams, however clear they may appear, will in time deposit a fine layer of dust, or sediment, as it is usually called, which is sufficient to destroy or deform all the fish embryos that are exposed to it.

It is very important, therefore, to have this sediment kept away from the eggs ; and to effect this, the water is conveyed through a very efficient filtering apparatus. This usually consists of a large tank containing a series of flannel screens. These screens consist simply of light wooden frames, with flannel fastened on them, which are made to slide in grooves prepared for the purpose, on the inside of the tank.

The flannel should be drawn tight over the frames, and the frames themselves should slide obliquely into the tank at a very considerable angle, say 45°, with the lower end up stream.

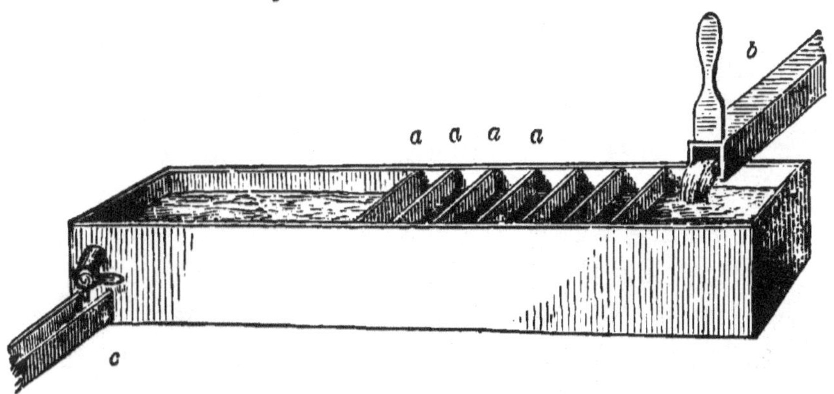

a Flannel filters.
b Hatching-room aqueduct or inlet.
c Outlet.

The tank should be built very solid, of two-inch plank, charred, and should be bound with iron bands, to prevent spreading. Its size will be governed, of course, by the amount of filtering required, a small or very clean stream needing less than a large or comparatively turbid one. But be sure of one thing, that the tank is large enough, no matter how large that may be, to arrest *all* the sediment, beyond all possibility of risk. Thousands of eggs have been lost by the filtering tank being inadequate. Better have it twice as large as is necessary, than to incur any risk of not stopping the sediment.

At the Cold Spring Trout Ponds there are two tanks for filtering, one containing eighty-one gallons and six filters, the other one hundred and sixty-eight gallons and seven filters.

I should say that it was better to have two medium-sized tanks than to have one excessively large one.

I should call the first of the two just mentioned a medium-sized one, and the second a large one, as large, perhaps, as should be made.

The outlet of the filtering tank should be at least six inches lower than the top of the tank, to guard against the water escaping over the top when the screens clog up. There should be two holes at least an inch in diameter in the bottom of the tank, to let the water off when necessary, and they should be plugged with very long stoppers, which will come nearly to the surface, so that they can be withdrawn without the arm being much immersed in the water.

The filters themselves may be made of any kind of strong, coarse flannel. White has the advantage of showing dirt best, and red, Seth Green says, will last the longest ; otherwise, one color will do as well as another.

These filters must be watched, and, no matter how often they require it, they must be taken out and cleaned as soon as they are dirty; but in doing this the rear one should be moved as little as possible. If you clean while wet, wash them under water, either with a brush, or a long-handled stick smoothed at the end ; the brush is the quickest method, the stick wears them out less. If you have a chance to dry them, the deposit on them can be easily brushed off with a dry brush. It may be necessary to clean the filters every day. If it is, do not neglect it. The tank is placed, of course, at the outlet of the spring aqueduct, which is usually at the head of the hatching-room, and no water should be allowed to pass over the eggs any length of time, without having first run through this tank. The tank need not be covered.

The Distributing Spout.

The next thing in order is the distributing spout, the office of which is simply to receive the water from the filtering tank, and distribute it into the various hatching troughs.

It joins the filtering tank, and extends, of course, either way, as far as the hatching troughs reach laterally, over which it is placed.

It is provided with an outlet at the head of each trough, and it will be found a convenience to have all these outlets levelled so as to each draw an equal supply of water when they are open. To secure this, the openings farthest from the inlet screen should be a little lower than the next, and so on, for the water at the inlet will be a little higher than the other end. If built of wood, the distributing spout should be of $1\frac{1}{2}$-inch plank, charred, and should be abundantly ample in width and depth for its purpose.

There should also be an aqueduct connecting the water supply above the filtering tank with the distributing spout, so that the water can be temporarily turned directly into the distributing spout when it becomes necessary to wash the tanks.

The distributing spout often has gravel placed in it for an additional filter. This is a good plan, because the gravel gathers up whatever fine sediment may have run the gantlet of the flannel filters, and any fine fibre of the flannel itself, which has become detached from the screens. But it is a better plan to have a special spout or aqueduct for the gravel filter, between the filtering tank and the distributing spout, and to have the latter free from gravel, on account of the gravel in it being often an inconvenience. The gravel should be coarse enough to let the water pass through it freely, the pieces being of the average size of chestnuts, or larger. There is usually enough of this coarse gravel sifted out when the fine gravel is being prepared for the hatching troughs.

If fine gravel is used, it will force the water to flow over it, and thus defeat its purpose.

Hatching Troughs, or Hatching Apparatus.

The hatching apparatus is of course the central feature of your whole indoor establishment, the part for which, indeed, all the rest is created. This is the fountain-head, from which all the other departments of the fish farm are furnished with stock. Here you intrust, for six months, the whole of your year's increase, and it occupies so responsible a place that no pains should be spared to get it right. Indeed, you cannot overrate the importance of having your hatching apparatus without a fault, especially as a single defect or neglect may cost you your whole stock of young fishes, — not merely part, but perhaps the whole.

Materials.

Various kinds of material have been used for hatching trout eggs, the principal of which are wood, soapstone, slate, pottery, metal, wood with glass lining, glass grilles, and charcoal, or carbonized wood. I think experience will finally reduce the number in general practice to two, namely, glass grilles and carbonized wood.

Wood in its natural state is out of the question, for the fungus that it grows wholly unfits it for hatching. I venture to say that hundreds of thousands of eggs have been destroyed by the fungus coming from wooden troughs. Metal, whether in the form of screens or anything else, will not do, because the absorbing power of trout eggs is so great, that, if placed in contact with it, they will in time absorb enough metallic matter to destroy them.*

Slate, pottery, and soapstone answer very well, but are all expensive; and if an expensive article is used, glass grilles, I think, have the preference over everything else.

For cleanliness, tidiness, and convenience they are not surpassed by anything. Their expense is their only objection. Charcoal troughs, on the other hand, are equally as effective as grilles, and infinitely more economical. They are also more accessible, more simple, and more durable.

In estimating their comparative merits I should say that the glass grilles are the thing for the rich man's experiments, and the carbonized troughs are the thing for business; I cannot but think that the carbonized troughs will supersede everything else, where trout-

* Fourteen trout eggs were placed on a copper-wire screen, in November, 1869, at the Cold Spring Trout Ponds, and in fifty days they had absorbed so much copper that they were of a dark brown tinge, and hard like peas.

breeding is carried on on a large scale, or where dura-bility, economy, or accessibility must be consulted.*

The comparative expense of the two methods may be estimated as follows : Glass grilles cost per tray $ 3.50 each, by the quantity.†   Allowing 1,250 eggs to each tray,† the apparatus for hatching 100,000 eggs, with glass grilles, costs $ 280.

The expense of the patent carbonized troughs, includ-ing cost of right to use them, is less than forty cents a foot, for one hundred square feet.   Allowing 1,000 eggs to the square foot, the apparatus for hatching 100,000 eggs, with the carbonized troughs, costs $ 40, leaving a balance of $ 240 in favor of the carbonized troughs.

Besides this, in the country, where most of our trout ponds are and will be, the wood to make the troughs, and also wood to char them with, is always plenti-ful and within reach, and, once prepared and placed, the carbonized troughs will last no one can tell how long.   The perfect freedom of charcoal from fungus, and its tendency to purify the water, will, I feel confi-dent, make it a favorite for hatching all eggs that are to be long under water.   The carbonized troughs were first experimented with at the writer's salmon-breed-ing establishment on the Mirimichi River, where they worked to perfection.   They have since been used at the Cold Spring Trout Ponds, and have given the most complete satisfaction. ‡

* See extract from Dr. Slack's Catalogue of fish-breeding apparatus, p. 65.

† See Dr. Slack's Catalogue, p. 4.

‡ The use of charcoal or carbonized wood for hatching fish was patented by the writer, June 20, 1871.

They seem to have solved the problem of obtaining a safe, economical, and durable material for hatching trout. I am aware that some of our largest operators have used wood loosely lined with glass, but it costs a good deal to get the glass, and it is also extremely unsafe when the young fry hatch, for they will get under the glass by thousands, and die of suffocation ; and finally it does not answer perfectly, as charcoal does, the purpose for which it is used, namely, to obviate the growth of fungus.

I would recommend, therefore, the use of glass grilles if you have the means and think they are better. Use charcoal or charred wood if you do not use grilles.

Placing the Hatching Troughs.

Having decided on the material for the hatching boxes, the next thing is to construct and place them. If you use charcoal or carbonized troughs, you should first send to the Cold Spring Trout Ponds, at Charlestown, N. H., and obtain the right to use them, they being patented, and the directions how to prepare them.

As to the size and shape of the hatching boxes or troughs, a great variety of opinion prevails. The following suggestions, however, may serve as a guide in making a selection. If you are limited in your supply of water, you should use long and rather narrow troughs, say twenty feet long by eight inches wide, and if you wish, you can have another trough of the same size below the first tier, using the same water over again, provided you have a fall between the two troughs of six

3 *

or eight inches. This second lower tier of boxes is, however, somewhat objectionable, because whenever the screens of the upper boxes are cleaned, or the water in them for any reason disturbed, the lower ones, in taking the washings from the upper, must suffer. This can be obviated, it is true, by cutting off the water temporarily, but this, again, is not only dangerous, but often inconvenient. It is best, therefore, not to use the water but once in hatching, if you have enough. Still it can be used twice, if necessary, without great injury. If you have plenty of water, I would recommend shorter troughs and more of them. There is no harm in having them twelve inches wide. I prefer ten or eight inches, however. They should be at least six inches in height in the inside, to guard against their running over, from the screens clogging up, and it is desirable to have them still higher, say eight inches, if you mean to keep the young fry in them any considerable time after they hatch. The troughs should be divided into compartments about one inch deep and fifteen inches long, by nailing charred cleats of the required depth transversely on the bottom of the trough, at regular intervals of fifteen inches. The head of the trough should be placed just under the distributing spout, from which there should be a fall of a few inches ; the trough should be high enough from the floor, if practicable, to be examined by a person standing. The troughs should be inclined, so that the water will make a gentle ripple over the cleats. A grade having a fall of one and one fourth inches to ten feet will do very well, but be sure to have enough slope to make the ripple, otherwise your fish, when hatched, will not be as strong as they might have been. At the lower end of the trough there should be a copper-wire screen of about eighteen or twenty threads to the inch. This screen should be very carefully fitted in, and should be made as tight a fit as human handiwork can make it, otherwise you cannot be sure that the young fry, when first hatched, will not slip through. In order to be perfectly sure to get this screen safe, first examine the place or bed that it fits into, with a strong light, and take care that every bit of sand or gravel is removed from it. Then put down the screen, having previously arranged a perfectly tight fit in the side cleats, and hammer it down.

This done, sift sand along the bottom and sides of the screen, bank up with gravel to the height of the transverse cleats, and sift sand about the sides again. You are then as safe as you can be with regard to the screen, and with these precautions you will be pretty sure not to lose many fish by this most common of all avenues of escape, — loosely fitting screens. Should any aperture be caused in the future by any springing or shrinking of the wood, or otherwise, calk the opening with flannel without delay. *Below* this screen should be placed what is called a trap-box, to catch any of the young fry that may escape through the screen above. This trap-box is nothing but a common box with a wire screen, which will let out the water, but hold the fish that come into it. I would have one at the end of every hatching trough. They are a very important safeguard, for they not only save all the fish that come through the screen, but will always tell you whether any are escaping, and also whether the screens are tight. If you do not provide this safeguard, thousands of fish may escape before you know it. It is a good plan also to have a larger box or reservoir, still farther down, on a similar plan, collecting the water from all the troughs, and arranged so as to detain everything that may have escaped, from any cause, from above ; and I think I may safely say that you will be astonished to find how often the young fry slip past places that you have considered perfectly tight. Having so far prepared the hatching troughs for action, and having tried them by running a stream of water through them, the next thing is

Laying the Gravel.

Gravel is used to hatch the eggs upon. This hatching gravel should be the size of half a pea, or less. Coarser gravel will not do, because the eggs will get into the chinks between the stones, and, being out of sight, will die without your knowledge ; and when they die, the dead eggs will certainly grow the fatal byssus, which will stretch its long arms out over other eggs above or near it, and destroy them. Coarse gravel is very vexatious on this account. Any clean gravel of the right size, free from rust, rotten stone, and the like, will do, and you will frequently find such gravel nearer than you suppose. It is therefore a good plan to try any high banks near by, before sending a great way for it. You may often find just what you want in a bank right over your brook. To prepare the gravel for use, you should have two screens, one to sift out the sand, and another to hold the coarse gravel. The residue which remains in the first and goes through the second screen is what you want for the hatching troughs.

Having obtained the right size of gravel, the next thing is to wash it. This should be thoroughly done. Then you can boil it, if you wish, to kill the insect larvæ in it ; and I would advise you to do this by all means, for the larvæ in unboiled gravel often produce insects that are very destructive to the eggs and young fish. It is not absolutely necessary to use gravel in charcoal troughs, as the eggs will hatch safely on the charcoal bottom. Twenty thousand salmon-eggs were placed directly on the bottom of the charred troughs, at the writer's establishment on the Mirimichi River, by way of experiment, and they did as well as the others hatched on gravel. A thin layer of gravel, however, is recommended. The gravel, if used, should be evenly placed in the troughs to the depth of about half an inch. According to the old method of hatching on wood in its natural condition, the gravel was placed an inch and a half deep, to prevent the fungus from growing up through it ; but in charcoal troughs, where there is no fungus, half an inch in depth, and even less, is sufficient. Be careful to level it off evenly, and leave no holes or depressions, or the eggs will surely collect in them deeper than they ought to.

There is always so much use for gravel about trout-breeding works, that it is a good plan to save all kinds, and what has been used once, and not washed, put away by itself. It is therefore a good plan to have four barrels or large boxes in the hatching house, — one for coarse gravel not clean, and one for fine gravel not clean, one for clean coarse gravel, and one for clean fine gravel. These boxes should be distinctly labelled, so that clean and dirty gravel will not get mixed ; and in course of time this little systematizing of the gravel will be found to be a source of great convenience, and economy also. A bushel of prepared gravel usually costs more than a bushel of grain.

When the gravel is laid in the troughs and the water is turned on, they are ready for use, with one exception, viz., —

THE COVERS.

I am firmly convinced that hatching troughs should be covered. I would not have *one* without a cover. Trout eggs and salmon fry are stronger and healthier for being hatched in the dark. It is more natural also. The fœtus, or embryo, of almost every creature — beast, bird, or fish, everything above insect life — is developed in the dark. The embryo of the trout is no exception to the rule. After the parent trout has deposited its eggs in the bed of the brook, the gravel with which they are covered, the stratum of water above the gravel, and the layer of ice and snow above the water, make it as dark, where the eggs are, as it is in the covered hatching-troughs.

Furthermore, the light seems to have a forcing effect on the eggs ; and those that I have seen matured in the light did not contain the dark, thick, firm, vigorous-looking embryos that are sure to develop in the dark. At all events, my experience has been decidedly to the effect that eggs hatched in the dark develop a thicker, firmer, and harder fish than those hatched in the light; and the first three months of feeding proves it. I am sure, at least, that no young trout.fry could be hardier or healthier than mine have been through their first six months, and all of mine are hatched in covered hatching troughs.

But even if darkness were not desirable, there is another reason of the utmost importance for having covers on the troughs. It is that you are not certain that your eggs are safe a single night in the open troughs. The enemies of trout eggs are legion. Mice, snakes, lizards, rats, weasels, and you know not what else, may be feeding on the eggs every night if they are not covered. I lost thousands of eggs and alevin trout in this way, before I began to use covers. At the Mirimichi Works, we lost at least twenty thousand salmon eggs, in the course of two weeks, by a weasel, before we began to suspect danger. There is no security without covers, at least in ordinary hatching-houses. On the contrary, when the covers are on and down tight, then, and only *then*, you *know you are safe*. And this is the only normal condition that any department of a trout-breeding establishment should ever be in.

The covers, for convenience' sake, should be made as light as possible. Half-inch pine, and even thinner, answers very well. There should be a piece cut out at the upper end to let in the water, and wire netting should be tacked over this opening, so that there can be no danger of anything getting in there ; and if the covers do not fit down tight, they should be hooked down, or caught with a spring. When the carpenter puts on the covers, examine them carefully, and see that there are no chinks to admit even a lizard. If there are not, then your hatching boxes are complete in every respect, and, if the previous suggestions have been carried out, will do their work to your perfect satisfaction.

I have proceeded thus far on the supposition that troughs of carbonized wood or other material are used. For the guidance of those who prefer glass grilles I quote the following remarks upon them from " Harper's Magazine "* and from Dr. Slack's Catalogue of fish culturist's apparatus.

" The Coste Hatching Tray (glass grilles) consists of a trough (made of earthen-ware, glass, or slate) about two feet long, six inches wide, and four inches deep. On the inside, about two and a half inches from the bottom, are small projections, upon which rests a glass grille, a species of gridiron formed of glass tubes. placed closely together, the ends being confined in a wooden rack. There is a spout on one side and at the top of the box to run off the surplus water ; at the bottom and below the level of the grille are two other openings, usually stopped, but convenient to open in order to remove the sediment which from time to time collects. In using these hatching boxes water can be supplied from a water-cooler through a filter,

* Harper's Magazine, November, 1868, pp. 728, 729.

and after passing through the box it can be caught and used over again. If water has been laid in the house, a constant stream of fresh water can be kept flowing with less trouble by using a discharge-pipe instead of a receiver. In one such box a thousand eggs — the product of a single trout — may be hatched. It will require no more attention than a globe of gold-fish, far less than an aquarium, afford a far more interesting study than either, and be quite as much of a parlor ornament.

" If it is desired to experiment more largely, this box may be duplicated interminably, as has been done by Mr. Coste, in perfecting his apparatus in use at Huningue. No greater supply of water and very little more room is necessary for a dozen than for one box on this plan. The advantages of this apparatus are : First, cleanliness, the sediment being easily removed without disturbing the eggs ; secondly, the eggs can at all times be readily examined ; and thirdly, the fry or young fishes can be removed from one box to another with facility, thus leaving room for more eggs in the first boxes."

These trays, invented by M. Coste, Professor of Embryology in the College of France, have been used during the past season at my ponds with perfect success, and it is intended in future to hatch all our spawn in them. The boxes are made of the best gal-vanized sheet-iron, and are coated inside and out with asphalt varnish. The grille is composed of strong glass tubes, firmly fastened in a frame of black walnut. This is so arranged that should any of the tubes become broken they can be readily removed and others substituted. Each box will hatch from one thousand to fifteen hundred eggs.

Prices of Coste Hatching Trays.

Single trays	$ 4.00
One dozen trays	45.00
Fifty or over, at the rate of	3.50
Extra glass tubes (each)	.05
" " " per pound	.75

FLIGHT OF TRAYS WITH STAND.

This is a neat and convenient form when several trays are required.

The stands are made of the best seasoned white-pine, neatly framed together.

Prices.

Flight of five trays and stand	$ 21.00
" three " "	13.50
Stands for five trays	2.50
" three "	2.00 *

There is another form of grilles used, which has stood the test of experience very well. It consists of very narrow strips of window-glass, laid side by side in the hatching-box, an inch or two from the bottom, and closely enough to keep the eggs from falling between them, but wide enough apart to allow the hatched fish to fall through. Each alternate strip is

* Dr. Slack's Catalogue of fishes, and apparatus used in fish culture, pp. 4, 5.

placed about an eighth of an inch lower than the rest. In this depression the eggs lie until hatched, when the young fish fall into the box or trough below. The advantage of this class of grilles over the last form is that they are cheaper. Another advantage is that they can be used in water where too much sediment would collect on tight grilles or in troughs, the sediment being easily washed off the eggs on the strips, and sinking down through the apertures out of the way.

CHAPTER V.

THE NURSERY.

THE next use for the water, after it passes over the eggs, is for rearing the young fish.

This department should be arranged with great care, as it is here that the trout pass through the most delicate portion of their lives, and require the most vigilant attention.   Hatching trout is easy enough, and so is the growing of them, after they are a year old.   But to bring them through the first year, and especially the first six months, is a more difficult matter.   This was the snag on which the earlier trout-breeding enterprisers were wrecked, and it is here that the greatest losses have occurred with most trout breeders at all times.   This has been the one weak point of trout-raising, and those who have succeeded in all other points have often failed here.   It is obvious, then, that it is very important to have this department just right.

THE WATER.

The water coming from the hatching-troughs should have considerable fall before it enters upon this part of its work, and the more the better, up to the height of three feet, especially if any young fish are still kept in the troughs.

If it is proposed to raise the young fry in a pond,

then nothing needs to be done with the water but to let it flow into the pond in the way most natural to it ; but if boxes or tanks are used to raise the young fish in, then it is desirable to collect together all the water from the various troughs into a common reservoir, or at least into a common aqueduct, from which to draw, in the quantities needed, for the supply of the rearing boxes.

Leaving the water here, we will enter at once upon the discussion of the methods of rearing the young fry.

The methods are two in number, — 1, By the use of ponds ; and 2, by the use of rearing boxes or nurseries. Of these two methods the rearing boxes are by far the safest for the first two or three months. I do not deny that satisfactory results have been obtained from the use of ponds at this stage, but I regard these as the exceptions. They were ponds peculiarly adapted to the wants of the young fry. As a rule, not one pond in ten, nor one in twenty, is safe for the very young fry.

Ponds, when contrasted with rearing boxes, present the following points of comparison.

1. As soon as the young fish are put into the pond they scatter to all parts of it, and cannot be brought together to feed. The consequence is that many get away into corners or holes, become weak from want of food, and die, while nineteen twentieths of the food fed to the fry in the pond is wasted, and only serves to foul the water. In rearing boxes the fish are all kept compactly together, where they are evenly fed, and where, owing to their being compact, almost all the food is consumed.

2. In ponds the young fish are exposed to all their enemies, whose name is Legion. Without enumerating them all again, it is sufficient to say that birds, frogs, and snakes will depopulate a pond of young trout with surprising despatch.

Rearing boxes being so prepared that when the lid is shut down nothing can get in and nothing get out, the safety of the fish is by this arrangement immeasurably increased.

3. In ponds the green *Confervæ* (frog-spittle) may grow. If it does, it will probably cost you a great many fish. It will not trouble you in the rearing box.

4. The comparatively still water of ponds is often unfavorable to the young fry inclined to be sickly. This objection is obviated in the rearing box.

5. In ponds there are likely to be unnoticed crevices, — at least, more than in rearing boxes, — where the young fry often escape without your knowledge. In rearing boxes perfect security can be obtained in this respect.

6. Dangers sometimes exist in ponds for weeks unnoticed. In rearing boxes the trout and the whole apparatus are so wholly under your eye that perfect security from this source, also, may be acquired.

7. When in ponds, you cannot keep account of the numbers of the fish without much trouble. When in rearing boxes, they can be taken out at a moment's notice, and counted.

Seth Green suggests that the hatching troughs be used until the fish are large enough for ponds ; this, he says, saves one removal. This may answer sometimes, but it is open to these objections : —

a. The hatching-house water is too cold and *earthy*, if I may use the expression.

b. If other hatching troughs work like mine, the screens will clog up, and call for extra watching.

c. The fish must be very much thinned out to make this method work, and in this case the one removal is not saved.

d. The fry do not do so well, in actual practice, in the troughs, as they do in the rearing boxes. I may also add that Green's partner, Mr. Collins, sent last spring for my rearing box to use at Caledonia.

My experience has all been one way in this matter. I have tried all kinds of ponds for very young fry, and in every instance have lost most of them, while in rearing boxes in most instances I have had surprising success, the loss having been very small indeed.

I am aware that the experience of others has been different, and that they have found ponds more successful than boxes ; but I repeat, that I think the ponds were exceptions, and that nineteen ponds out of twenty are not safe for the very young fry.

The use of rearing boxes is accordingly recommended, in preference to ponds, for the very young fish.

The principles of the rearing box will be described in the next few pages.

REARING BOXES.

A rearing box in its simplest form is *very* simple ; a common soap or candle box, with a wire screen at

one end, and some gravel on the bottom, with a stream
.of water running through, is a rearing box, and will
do, if only a hundred or two young fry are to be
raised.

A rearing box in its most perfect form is a more
elaborate and complicated thing, and should combine
these points,* viz. :—

1. A fall of water.

2. A current of water.

3. Protection against too forcible suction through
the outlet screen.

4. Security from overflow.

5. Absence of fixed hiding-places.

6. Compactness of fish themselves for feeding.

7. Protection against outside enemies.

8. Perfectly tight joints.

9. Protection against fungus.

1. *A fall of water.* The very young fry need all
the vitality and freshness which can be given to the
water ; and that imparted to it by a fall immediately
above them is too valuable to be disregarded. Experience has proved, also, that all trout do best just
below a fall of water.

2. *A current.* If you want to make hardy fish, give
the young fry a current to head up against ; this is not
only more natural, but it will keep them clean and
vigorous, while in (relatively) still water they will often
take on a fungus growth or fin disease, which will

---

* It should be added here, that ponds for young fry should, as
far as possible, be constructed on the same general principles that
are recommended for rearing boxes.

finally kill them. Again, by compelling the young fish to head up against a current, you not only keep them healthy, but can even sometimes save their lives when they have become sickly, and would otherwise have died.

The way to raise hardy, healthy trout is to put the young fry in a current, and keep them strong enough, by feeding, to make them feel like heading up against it.

3. *Protection against too forcible suction through the outlet.* If the pressure against the screen is too violent, the fish will be sucked against it, and cannot keep off. A very wide screen is the protection against this, or, if necessary, a dead-water board, nailed on below the screen.

4. *Security from overflow.* When sudden showers come up, especially in the early summer, the streams will collect so much fine floating matter as to clog up the screens very rapidly.

A very little of the green *Confervæ*, sometimes called frog-spittle, will give a great deal of trouble from this cause. Various other circumstances also make it important to take especial pains to guard against an overflow. This is accomplished by having deep sides to the rearing box, and by the use of wide screens. Sometimes, in order to obtain perfect security, it is found necessary to insert a long narrow screen in the side of the box, near the top, called a safety screen. This, with the regular screen at the outlet, will usually take the water off sufficiently fast when it rises to the safety-screen level.

5. *Absence of fixed hiding-places.* Such hiding-places are bad, because in general you do not know what the fish are doing in them. They may be dying there. They may be crowding in them too thickly. The hiding-places may conceal a snake, or a frog, or a cannibal trout, which is making deadly havoc with the small fish. The best rule for hiding-places is, not to have them fixed, but so that you can always remove the shelter, and look in if you wish; then you will know what is going on in them.

6. *Compactness of the fish themselves for feeding.* This I regard as a very important point. When the very young fry are scattered widely apart, you are obliged to feed them at a great disadvantage.

Only a few can be got together in a spot to feed. Sometimes they are so shy that they can only be fed at all with great difficulty, and, with the best you can do, nineteen twentieths of the food will go to the bottom. On the contrary, when the fish are compactly confined, their numbers seem to give them confidence, and they do not attempt to run away from the food. They will gather together to get it, instead of scattering as before ; and, being so thick together, they will consume nearly all the food given them, and very little will go to the bottom. The advantage gained by this is very great.

7. *Protection against outside enemies.* The necessity of this protection is obvious. It is obtained by attaching to the rearing box a wire-work lid, fitting down tightly, and provided with a padlock.

It is necessary to have even the opening where the water falls in protected by a wire screen.

One autumn I lost several hundreds of fine trout, three inches long, by something, I never knew what, entering the boxes where the water came in.

The cover can be made of wooden slats, if preferred ; but they should be very close, for snakes, which are very destructive to young fish when confined, will venture through holes which are big enough to admit their bodies.

8. *Perfectly tight joints.* Only a person who has had many years' experience in raising young fish knows the whole significance of this precaution. The knack which young trout have of going through very small crevices is almost incredible. I once made a solid bank of fine hatching gravel a foot long, to hold some young fry. In a week three hundred had found their way through it. I venture to say that there is not a trout breeder who reads this page, who has not lost more or less young fry, through some unnoticed crevice in their place of confinement.

It seems as if they had the gift of flattening themselves almost indefinitely. At all events, they will squeeze through a wonderfully small crevice, so that the only safe way is to examine the box or trough thoroughly and make every joint perfectly tight. If this cannot be done effectually with hammer and nails, the places should be calked with flannel, or something similar. The outlet screen should be as fine as eighteen threads to the inch. With anything larger than that, the fry will get their bodies through, and hang themselves by the neck.

9. *Protection against fungus.* Last, but not least, there should be no possibility of fungus getting on to the young fish. I wish I could find words to describe how infectious and how fatal this ubiquitous enemy is to trout. If they are exposed to it, it will attack their fins, gills, and every part of them, and, long before they begin to show it by dying, it may have spread over your whole brood, and rendered them past saving even when its presence is first discovered. I have known instances where persons have found their trout dying, and upon moving them to other places, and taking every pains with them, have wondered why they continued to die, with everything apparently favorable to their health, while the fact was that the fatal fungus had fastened upon them and doomed them to death days, perhaps weeks, before they were first moved. You cannot take too much pains to avoid fungus. The best way to do it — and it is a sure way — is to char the inner surface of all the woodwork leading to the rearing-boxes, and also the rearing boxes themselves. This is a sure preventative, and the only satisfactory one I know of.

The above points should be secured * in the rearing box for the young fry, and when they are so secured, if the water supply is right, the box may be regarded as a suitable place for growing them in the first two or three months, and much safer, as a general thing, than a pond. I should call the maximum water supply, just that amount which the fish will bear

* It was to combine these points that the rearing box of the Cold Spring Trout Ponds was contrived.

without being carried down with it. The minimum supply for very young fish is less than one would suppose.

A cold stream throwing one hundred gallons an hour will keep ten thousand alive, with a proper fall and current; but this minimum should not be resorted to except in cases of necessity.

If you have a large number of fry to raise in rearing boxes, build a platform where you want the boxes.

Make all the boxes of the same size.* Place them in a line, side by side, have your distributing-spout just over the upper end of the boxes, and draw the water from it just as you draw the water from the distributing spout in the house into the hatching troughs. This gives uniformity and system, and increases the convenience of feeding and taking care of the fish.

Place a layer of gravel in each of the boxes in such a way that the water will be deepest under the fall, and the bed of the boxes will slope up towards the outlet. Provide water-plants as freely as you please. Below the system of rearing boxes place a long trap-box, with a screen, which will catch everything that escapes from them by accident.

Then your arrangement for growing the young fish by this method will be complete.

If ponds are used, they should be shallow, narrow, very tight, and should be well stocked with water-

---

* Four feet long by sixteen inches wide and sixteen inches deep is a good size.

It is a good plan to widen the outlet and to admit a larger screen, say twenty-eight by sixteen inches.

plants,* which will improve the water and give 'the fish a chance to hide from their enemies, and supply them with a good deal of natural food.

The ponds should be also well provided with covers or rafts for shelter.

Even then I would have the ponds constructed on the principle of rearing-boxes, but I wish it distinctly understood *only for very young fry.*   I am myself in favor of turning the fish into safe ponds after they are two or three months old, but not before.

They are so small and frail at first, that it seems to me no better than destroying them by wilful neglect to turn them loose into ponds when they begin to feed.

* See Appendix III., pp. 274, 275, for list of water-plants.

PART II.

PROCESSES IN TROUT BREEDING.

PROCESSES IN TROUT BREEDING.

CHAPTER I.

TAKING THE EGGS.*

INTRODUCTION.

WE now turn from the construction of the works required by the processes of trout breeding to the processes themselves. The first in order of these is, taking spawn. This is a department of the trout-breeder's work which it is very important to understand thoroughly, for it depends on his success here whether he secures most of the increase of his breeding stock, or whether he loses most of it. A careless and unskilful person will not save over twenty per cent. A careful and skilful operator will not lose five per cent. The reader can see for himself what a vast difference this makes, when hundreds of thousands, or even millions, are the numbers dealt with.

This branch of the work is no child's play. It constitutes an art by itself, and requires, for its success, knowledge, proficiency, and skill. Do not neglect to give this department careful study. ·

* For description of eggs, see p. 106. For number of eggs, see pp. 267, 268. For spawning season of different fish, see pp. 270, 271.

PREPARATIONS FOR THE SPAWNING.

It is very desirable to have the preparations for the spawning season completed before the season begins, as it is often very inconvenient to attend to them afterwards. The hatching apparatus and experiment boxes, the filtering tank, and all the aqueducts above the hatching apparatus, should be thoroughly cleaned out and put in readiness. The spring or supply reservoir should be put in just the condition you mean to have it left in for the winter, for that often cannot be disturbed after the spawn are laid. The gravel for hatching should be obtained, sifted and washed and boiled, two sets of flannel filters made, and ready to place, and the outlet screens ready to drop in their grooves. A set of nippers and a bunch of feathers should be in their places, as also homœopathic phials for examining the eggs, the spawning pans for taking them in, moss to pack them with, and the tin boxes in which to send them away.

At the breeding ponds, the spawning races should be thoroughly cleaned out, and clean gravel put in, or the Ainsworth and the Collins apparatus * placed in readiness where these are used. A notice should be put up that visitors must not go to the breeding grounds till the season is over. The covers for the spawning beds should be ready and down. The nets and the rest of the spawning outfit should be at hand,

* For description of the Ainsworth and the Collins Spawning Apparatus, see pp. 29 – 36.

and yourself free to attend to the spawning as soon as the season begins.

THE SPAWNING SEASON.

As the cold fall days come on, the male trout take on brighter colors, the lower rays of the anal and ventral fins show brilliantly white, their bodies grow lank, their noses sharp, and there is an unmistakable air of expectancy in their whole expression, peculiar to this period. The females grow big with spawn, and lose some of the brightness of their color, though their forms still retain a grace which does not leave them till the eggs are deposited. You need not have any fear about telling the sexes apart. After a very little experience, you can hardly make a mistake in this particular, at this season. The brief description just given will be a sufficient guide.

Some time before any eggs are deposited, both sexes become indifferent to food, and work up into the shallow swifter water below the spawning beds, the males usually in advance. By the second week in October, and sometimes before, in the mean latitude of New England, a few stragglers, like advance skir- mishers, will get into the beds and begin making their nests. The exciting season of taking spawn is now close at hand, and as soon as you perceive that the fish on the beds have completed their nests, you may, if you adopt the artificial method of taking the eggs, proceed to try whether they are ripe.*

* For directions for collecting the eggs obtained by the "natural" method, see remarks about Ainsworth's Screens and Collins's Roller Spawning-Box, pp. 29 – 36.

· The method of capturing the spawning fish is as follows : A net of coarse bagging, six or eight feet long, is made. The edges of the upper end of the bag are fastened to a common wooden screen frame, which then forms the mouth of it. This frame fits into grooves made for it, at the lower end of the spawning beds. The other or closed end of the bag is made to taper somewhat, and an opening, say fifteen inches in length, is cut in it to let the fish through into the spawning tub. This is to avoid pouring them out from the upper end. This aperture is tied up with a string before the bag is put in position, and a large tub to receive the fish is placed on the ground close to the outlet of the spawning bed, where the bag will be placed.

Now, having brought spawning pans enough to take the spawn in, you approach the beds carefully with the bagging in your hands. You slip the frame at the mouth of the bag instantly into the grooves prepared for it, and the spawning fish are trapped. You now, with as little delay as possible, fill the tub half full of water. Keep the spawning pans perfectly dry, place them conveniently, and throw off the covers of the beds.

The fish, with a little urging, will rush down stream and hide in the bag. When they are all in, raise the bag up quickly but gently, drop the lower end into the tub of water, untie the string, and let them out. If you have many fish and an attendant to help you, it is a good plan to have two pails of water at hand, and to have your attendant, while you are taking the spawn, sort the males into one pail and the females into another, so that you can always lay your hand instantly on the sex you want. Having got everything ready and the fish into the tub, the next thing is to take the fish out and strip them.

The first point to learn about this is how to handle the fish. There are almost as many ways of handling them as there are persons who practise it. Almost every one has a way, or at least a peculiarity, of his own.

My own way is to close the left hand very gently over the face of the fish, and with the right grasp it just above the tail. It is now not necessary to squeeze the fish hard at all. She cannot get through either hand, because the body is larger in the middle than at either extremity. I then take the fish quickly out of the water, throw it over partly on its side, and holding it at an angle of about 45°, with the orifice near the bottom of the pan, press gently but firmly with the thumb of the left hand, on the upper part of the abdomen. If the fish is ripe, the eggs will flow at once, and then, by a peculiar bending of the body of the fish, together with a slight downward movement of the thumb, the eggs will come almost of their own accord. I use very little *force* indeed in pressing the eggs out. If they do not come almost spontaneously, with this method of handling, I let the fish go and try another. If any eggs seem to be left in the fish after the stripping just mentioned, I quickly change hands, and, grasping it firmly with the right hand, remove the remaining eggs by a gentle pass of the left thumb along the length of the abdomen.

This strips the fish completely, and it is ready to be returned to the water. I proceed in a similar way with the male, except that I exert the pressure lower down the abdomen than with the female. This method of handling does not hurt the fish; it seems to make the eggs flow spontaneously, the struggling of the fish only accelerates the flow of the eggs, it makes quick work and takes all the eggs. I do not claim anything for it, however, over other good methods of handling, and would advise beginners to try different ways, till they find the particular way most convenient for them, and adopt that.

Holding the fish is at first an awkward affair. It will seem to you, if you are a beginner, as if fish were never so slippery nor so uneasy, and never so liable to be squeezed to death before; but practice will make perfect in this as in other things, and you will at length feel as much at home with a pound trout in your hands as if it were a pet kitten.

I would, however, by all means kill and open a trout first, and see just how the vitals lie packed within, so as to know just where you can press without hurting it, and just where you cannot. This will give you confidence, and save the lives of many fish.

You can press quite hard on the face and head, and on the solid parts of the body, but be very careful of the gills and vitals. Do not ever press the abdomen very hard. If the eggs do not come with a light pressure, let them go till next time. You might not impregnate them all, if you took them. Do not press the female fish *at all* near the organ of exit, or lower part of the abdomen, except to push out the few remaining eggs, after the main part of the stripping is done. Let all the pressure at first be at the upper end, and always let the thumb *follow* the eggs, and never get in advance of them. Inflammation of the organs at the lower part of the abdomen is often produced by neglect of this precaution, the result of which is an entire stoppage of eggs and ultimate death from ulceration.

When the fish struggles, as you are taking the spawn, do not squeeze it any harder than you can help, but hold your left thumb firmly on the abdomen, just above the eggs, and the struggles of the fish will only help the flow of the eggs. Indeed, I usually try to make the fish really spawn herself.

You must keep your attention fixed incessantly on the fish in your hands, or it will squirm itself out of your grasp when you least expect it, and in a way that you cannot account for. You will probably drop a few fish occasionally, even after some experience, but it will do no harm if the fish does not fall into the spawning dish. This you must guard against, as a few lashes of its body then may kill a great many eggs. Be careful also not to let the trout in its struggles scrape the slime off its body; for this, especially in the first part of the season, will cause fungus to grow, and the end is death.

Impregnating the Eggs.

All fish eggs were formerly impregnated in water, a depth of one or two inches in the spawning pans being generally used. This was the universal custom in this country up to the last spawning season, that of 1871, in the summer of which year, through the efforts of Mr. George Shephard Page, the experiments of M. Vrasski, at Nikolsk, Russia, were made known in America.* By these experiments the very singular facts were discovered that fish eggs could not only be

* "In his experiments, M. Vrasski had followed the counsels given in French and German works on pisciculture; but the results obtained were far from being brilliant. In reality he obtained at each hatching but an insignificant number. 'From many thousands of eggs,' said he, in one of his letters, 'there were only some dozens of young fry. The rest of the eggs were spoilt and lost for want of having been impregnated. I have, however, observed with scrupulous exactness all the directions given by the manuals with a view to fecundation.' In the autumn of 1856, M. Vrasski was occupied with the microscopic study of the eggs and the milt, and kept a journal in which he registered the least circumstances and incidents relative to each fecundation that he effected. Two months of persistent efforts brought the desired results. The journal and the microscope proved to him that the cause of his failure proceeded precisely from the exact observation of all the counsels of the foreign manuals. It is necessary for fecundation that the spermatozoa of the milt of the male should penetrate the eggs of the female. In order to do this, the manuals recommended receiving the eggs in a vessel of water; afterwards, to receive in another vessel of water the milt of the male; and, lastly, to turn the diluted milt on to the eggs. By his journal, kept with scrupulous exactness, M. Vrasski convinced himself that the fecundation was so much the less complete according as the mixture of the milt and the eggs had been the most delayed. If ten minutes elapsed between obtaining the milt and the mixing of it with the eggs, the fecundation failed almost entirely. His observations and the microscopic researches of the eggs and the milt showed that first, when received in water at the instant of issuing from the fish, the eggs absorb the water and preserve the power of being

taken and impregnated safely in a dry vessel, but also that the *whole of them* could be impregnated in this way. Such marvellous success had never been reached before by any method, sixty-five or seventy per cent having been a large average of impregnation, in operations in this country, and Seth Green, who approxi-

impregnated only as long as this absorption is not finished ; that is to say, during a half-hour at the utmost. Once saturated with water, the eggs do not absorb any spermatozoa ; but if received into dry vessels on issuing from the fish, the eggs remain, on the contrary, for a sufficient time, in a neutral state, and do not lose the power, when once put into water, of receiving the spermatozoa. Second, the spermatozoa of the milt, in falling into the water, commence immediately, with much vigor and rapidity, to make movements, which only last, however, for a minute and a half, or two at the most ; when this time is elapsed, only in some few spermatozoa can there be seen particular movements and agonized convulsions. When, at the issuing from the male fish, the milt is received in a dry vessel, it does not change for many hours, and during this interval the spermatozoa do not lose the power of beginning to move when they find themselves in contact with water. Closed in a dry tube and well corked, the milt preserved its impregnating virtue during six days.

" From these observations, as also from the fact that the eggs, as well as the milt, are obtained slowly, their entire mass not being able to issue at once, M. Vrasski arrived at the conclusion that when they were received in water the greater part of the eggs attempted to saturate themselves with water, and the spermatozoa almost ceased to move before it was possible for the fish breeder to mix the eggs with the diluted water. M. Vrasski adopted then the system of dry vessels, and turned the milt on the eggs immediately he put them in water. The success was complete ; all the eggs were impregnated, without one exception." — " The Establishment at Nikolsk for the Rearing of Choice Fish." Review in New York Citizen and Round Table, May 27, 1871.

mated the method of the Russian by using a very little water, never claiming over ninety-five per cent for his best work. The result is that dry impregnation, or the method of taking the eggs in dry vessels, has in trout culture wholly superseded the old practice of impregnating the eggs in water, among all who have heard of it, the great gain in impregnated eggs being too much of an advantage to be sacrificed.

For the benefit of those to whom this part of the subject is unfamiliar, I will say that the milt, or seminal fluid, of the male fish consists of innumerable living microscopic organisms, called spermatozoa or zoösperms. These millions of infinitesimal creatures during their brief career in the outer world are endowed with great activity, and jump and plunge about among one another with a motion as ceaseless as it is rapid and vigorous. They appear all the while to be seeking something. At the same time, the eggs, when taken from the fish, exert a constant absorbing power, drawing towards them everything in their immediate vicinity. The eggs also possess on their surface a microscopic opening called the micropyle, which is intended for the entrance of the zoösperm. When, therefore, the spermatozoa and the eggs are brought together, the animalculæ seek the egg with all their might, and the egg draws them to itself with all its power. The consequence is that one (or more?) of the spermatozoa finds the micropyle of the egg and is drawn into it, and impregnation is the result.

When the egg has finished its absorbing action, or when the zoösperms have become inert, the power

to give or receive impregnation is at an end. The
time for it has passed. No human power can afterwards make milt or eggs anything but worthless.

It has been estimated that the absorbing action of
the trout egg lasts thirty minutes in water. The period
of the activity of spermatozoa in water has been vari-
ously placed at thirty minutes, fifteen, ten, two, and
one and a half minutes;* the last two estimates being
nearest the truth. As will be seen by reference to M.
Vrasski's experiments, this period of activity is vastly
prolonged by not diluting the milt with water, and the
chances of impregnating all the eggs are immensely
increased in consequence. For, according to the old
method of using water, either the spermatozoa died or
the eggs finished their absorbing process before there
was time for all the eggs to become impregnated;
while by the new method of not using water the milt
has ample time to come in contact with all the eggs,
during the period of the activity of the one and the

* The confusion on this point very probably arises from the
experiments being conducted in different temperatures of water,
the period of life of the zoösperms depending materially on the
temperature of the water. The zoösperms of trout milt do not
usually live over two minutes in water varying from 40° to
50° F.

Quatrefages's experiments showed that the activity of the spermatozoa of different fish diluted with water lasted in the case of
the

Brochet . . .	8 minutes,	10 seconds.	
Mullet . . .	3 "	10	" '
Carp . . .	3 "		
Perch	2 "	40	"
Barbel . . .	2 "	10	"

absorbing action of the other.* The consequent advantage is obvious.

This discovery being of great practical importance, perhaps I may be excused for quoting at length from my editorial on the subject in the New York Citizen and Round Table of March 9, 1872.

THE RUSSIAN OR DRY METHOD OF IMPREGNATION.

"The most important discovery of the past year in fish-breeding in this country was the method of the dry impregnation of the eggs of winter-spawning fish.

"Its importance consists in this, namely, that almost one hundred per cent of the eggs can be fertilized and hatched in this way, while hitherto, with the one exceptional instance of our great prophet, Seth Green,

* The following table shows the percentage of Salmon eggs impregnated by the dry method at the Maine State Salmon-Breeding Establishment, in 1871, under the charge of Commissioner Charles G. Atkins, of Maine.

When taken.	Estimated no. of eggs.	Percentage fecundated.
Nov. 2	12,500	100
" 3	11,500	94
" 6	9,500	92½
" 6	3,000	85
" 4	300	—
" 4	2,500	95
" 4	16,000	96
" 7	5,000	100
" 8	4,500	100
" 9	7,000	97½
" 10	85	100
" 10	50	100
" 10	365	100
	72,300	96

the percentage has ranged all the way from ninety and eighty to fifteen, and has probably not averaged throughout the country over fifty or sixty per cent.* The gain, of course, is enormous, as will be seen by the following table : —

The average yield of	By the old method.	By the new method.
1,000 eggs is	600	950
10,000 eggs is	6,000	9,500
100,000 eggs is	60,000	95,000
1,000,000 eggs is	600,000	950,000

"When to this is added the consideration that all the worthless eggs must be picked out one by one, by hand, in the coldest season of the year, and that to pick out three hundred and fifty thousand eggs (the difference in each million between the two methods) requires, in practice, at least thirty-five days of incessant and tedious labor, the immense advantage and importance of the new discovery becomes obvious.

"It will mark a new era, we are confident, in trout and salmon breeding, and will entirely revolutionize the system of impregnating the eggs of these fish. No one, hereafter, who has heard of the new method, will ever take the eggs of any cold-water fish by the old one. It is a very significant circumstance that Seth Green, with his wonderful insight, reached the same result nearly ten years ago by using a very small amount of water in the impregnating pan.

* There is not the same difference in impregnating the eggs of warm-water fish. Perch and shad, for instance, will yield nearly one hundred per cent good eggs taken in a pan full of water, the natural temperature of which, when these fish spawn, runs from a minimum of 50° F. with the perch to a maximum of 90°, and even more, with the shad.

"This was the mysterious secret of his success in impregnating trout eggs, which puzzled beyond measure everybody that tried to imitate him, which every one marvelled at, and no one could understand. Green used to tell everything about trout breeding except this, but this he kept to himself, and said it was as good as a patent right to him ; and so it was.

"The Russian or dry method of impregnating eggs consists simply in taking both the eggs and the milt in a dry pan. The pan will not, correctly speaking, be perfectly dry, for some drops of water will fall into it from the fishes manipulated ; but the pan should have no water in it to begin with. In reflecting upon this method for the first time, the objection rises instantly in one's mind that the eggs will all be killed by striking against the bottom of the dry pan ; but it is the very singular fact that though the same eggs would be destroyed at once by the same concussion a week afterwards, or even twenty-four hours afterwards, they do not suffer in the least from it at the moment of extrusion from the fish. These and the previous facts here stated were confirmed this last season by experiments of Commissioner Atkins of Maine, of Mr. W. Clift of Connecticut, and of the writer in New Hampshire, and are beyond dispute.

"At the last meeting of the Fish Culturists' Association, at Albany, we opened a box of about a hundred trout eggs, taken by us on the Russian plan last December, and gathered afterwards from the hatching troughs without our knowledge of the percentage of impregnation. Seth Green and others examined them, and only three were found empty. As less than two per cent had been picked out previously from the troughs, this leaves ninety-five per cent of good eggs.

"The explanation of the augmented impregnation seems to lie in the following facts:—

"The spermatozoa of the milt of the male are found naturally living in an alkaline fluid composed partly of phosphates and partly of other constituents which more scientific men know better than we do. This is their natural element, and, if it is not changed, they will live in it for several days after leaving the fish. On the contrary, if this liquid is diluted with water, as is the case in the old way of impregnating, the spermatozoa are killed ; they cannot live in the new element. Paradoxical as it seems, water drowns them.

"M. Vrasski says that he kept the spermatozoa alive six days in a corked-up phial just as they came from the fish, but that they died in two minutes when taken from the fish into water.

"With a view to testing these points, we tried some experiments with the milt of trout last fall, using a microscope that magnified a hundred diameters. The results were the same.

"Milt taken from the fish in a phial and secluded from the air and water remained unchanged for days. Carbolic acid killed the zoösperms almost immediately, and water drowned them in two minutes.

"The explanation, therefore, of the improved results of the Russian method, is plainly seen. The zoösperms reach the eggs in their natural element, and have time and vitality to impregnate them, while they are at the same time in vastly greater numbers to the cubic line than in the pan of water.

"The dry method of taking eggs was first discovered by M. Vrasski, a Russian, from whom it is called the Russian method. He experimented with the eggs of sterlits, we believe, at Nikolsk, Russia, and by careful and scrupulous observation with microscope and note-book solved in two months the mystery of the previous meagre impregnations, and made this most important discovery of which we are speaking.

"It is very singular that sixteen years should have elapsed before the knowledge of this remarkable discovery should have reached America. But sixteen years did pass, and many more might have passed had it not been for the enterprise of Mr. George Shephard Page, President of the Oquossoc Angling Association, who had the experiments of M. Vrasski translated into English, and who caused a review of his work to be printed in the New York Citizen of May 27, 1871, which we would recommend all practical fish culturists to read.

"To Mr. Page, therefore, belongs the honor of introducing into this country this discovery, second to none, in practical importance, that has been made in the art since its inception, and to the New York Citizen the credit of first making it public. We were very much surprised that the announcement in the Citizen did not make a deeper impression at the time than it did. Mr. Page was kind enough to send us a marked copy of the paper, and we wrote to him in reply that the statement of M. Vrasski, if true, would wholly revolutionize the present method of impregnating eggs ; but no one with whom we corresponded seemed to realize its importance, except Mr. Clift, President of the American Fish Culturists' Association, who wrote to us in very much the same terms that we used to Mr. Page. It was also by his recommendation, we presume, that Mr. Atkins adopted this method in taking his salmon eggs last fall. . We are satisfied, however, that the results of the investigations of M. Vrasski are of the utmost importance, and that the facts cannot make too deep an impression on fish breeders. We would advise them never to try the old plan again."

There are several interesting consequences resulting from the Russian discovery which seem to be worth mentioning.

One is that since the spermatozoa of the milt remain alive several days when kept from the air and water, a cross can be effected between fish living at long distances apart, without transporting the fish. For instance, a trout breeder in Kansas can bottle up some milt from his fish in a homœopathic phial, and send it by mail or express to a Massachusetts breeder, who can take a ripe spawner from his ponds and mix the Kansas milt and Massachusetts eggs in the impregnating pan, and so generate a cross between the two fish, as well as if the Kansas breeder had sent him, at a great risk, some male trout. The great ease with which this crossing can be accomplished may some day lead to valuable results.

Another consequence is that the old theory that a large proportion of the eggs ordinarily taken from the

spawning trout are immature, and therefore cannot
be impregnated, must be given up. I have opposed
this theory all through my trout-breeding experience,
and insisted that the trouble in poor impregnations
was not in the eggs, but in the milt, as it has now
turned out to be. But the immature-egg theory had
its advocates in high quarters, and has been very generally received. There, however, can be no question
about it hereafter. If ninety-five per cent of the eggs
are impregnated and hatched by the Russian method,
then not more than five per cent of the eggs are
immature, and we doubt if even this small proportion
are.

The Russian discovery also wholly sets aside the
question about which there has been such contradic-
tory opinions, as to whether the milt or the eggs should
be taken first. Under the old *régime* it was considered
an important matter, and so it was ; but now it makes
no difference which is used first, as, either way, both
the milt and the eggs will remain operative long
enough for all practical purposes of impregnation, and
in both cases the results will be the same.

In consequence of the discovery that all mature eggs
are impregnated by coming in contact with ripe milt,
the fish, both male and female, being taken at random,
we are compelled to admit, however unwillingly, that
the origin of fish life, in artificial impregnation at least,
is wholly a mechanical affair. The mere mechanical
mixing of the ripe milt of any male and the ripe eggs
of any female creates the germ of life, and perpetuates
the race, all previous considerations of pairing off

among the fish, or of this or that one selecting its mate, counting for nothing. The fish of either sex has no choice and no knowledge as to the individual through whom its progeny shall be generated. The female fish may become a mother without ever having seen her mate, and the male may become the father of innumerable offspring without ever having seen the mother. Whatever margin of uncertainty the unimpregnated eggs of the old system might have afforded for the conjecture that empty eggs were the consequence of mismating on the part of the fish, or rather of the manipulator, there is none left now. Mechanical contact of eggs and milt, indiscriminately taken, produces all the results that mutual affection and choice of mates could accomplish. There is now no possible place left for sentiment in the connubial relations of trout that are artificially spawned.

There are also two practical advantages incidentally connected with this Russian discovery, and with these I will close this discussion of its consequences. One of these advantages is that the operator need not feel obliged to hurry through the impregnation process, as he was formerly obliged to, lest the milt should become worthless before the eggs were secured, or *vice versa*, for by the dry method he can have time enough. And the other is, that when there is danger that the milt will run short on any day, the surplus milt of previous more favorable days can be bottled up and kept for the emergency, when the day's supply of milt proves insufficient.

Let us now return to the subject more particularly

before us, namely, the *modus operandi* of impregnating the eggs. The process is very simple. Having secured the fish and sorted out the ripe males and the ripe females, take a female and express the eggs from her into a dry pan, according to the directions on page 85. One layer is about enough for a pan. Then take the milt from the male. Shake the pan gently and tilt it at each end alternately, so as to mix the milt and eggs as thoroughly as possible. This will be easily accomplished, as the little water which falls from the fish into the pan, and the capillary attraction of the mass of eggs, will assist the dissemination of the milt.

After giving the spermatozoa and eggs time enough for thorough contact, but before the eggs set, pour on water to the depth of an inch or two. Stir well and leave till the eggs separate, which will be from fifteen to forty-five minutes, according to the temperature of the water, the eggs remaining set longest in cold water. When separated, rinse the eggs till they are perfectly clean. They are then ready to be placed in the hatching troughs.

How to tell Ripe Fish.

It is usually a very anxious question with beginners, how they will know when a spawning trout is ripe. I would advise those who feel this anxiety not to worry about it at all.

You cannot tell, the first time you try your hand at it; but follow the directions about trying them, and whenever the spawn does not flow easily, let the fish go, and try another. Do not urge the spawn too forcibly. This is the great fault of beginners. They are so afraid that the fish is ripe, and that they will not find it out, that they often kill it, if unripe, by using excessive force. Let me say that your danger, if you are inexperienced, is not half so much of losing the spawn as of killing the fish. I knew of a man who had thirty trout, and who killed them all before the spawning season began, without getting an egg, by trying to force the eggs. When the fish is ripe, the eggs will come : that you may depend on, in nineteen cases out of twenty. If they do not come and come easily in any instance, do not trouble yourself about that fish ; let her go. You will get her the next day again, if she is not quite but nearly ripe. If you have any doubt at all whether the fish is ripe, give the fish the benefit of the doubt. In time you will learn to tell at a glance, and patience and practice will soon bring that time to pass. To tell quickly and surely whether a fish is ripe, is something that cannot be learned from books.

There are certain signs, it is true, which usually accompany ripeness in a female trout, of which the looseness of the eggs in the abdomen, after they have left the ovaries, is the surest. There are others also, but the specific signs are all fallible, and what an expert tells by, is not one specified sign or another, but an indescribable ripe look, which is neither color, shape, nor condition of organs, but a something pervading the whole, a *tout ensemble*, which tells at a glance that the fish is ripe, as in a similar way you tell that a peach or a blackberry is ripe. This you must learn by practice. Books cannot teach it, but practice will.

FURTHER DIRECTIONS FOR IMPREGNATING THE EGGS.

The following additional suggestions may be of service to the beginner in learning to impregnate trout eggs.

1. *Use eggs that flow easily, and no others.* It is true that there will be some spawners which, from an exceptional construction of organs, will not give their spawn readily when ripe; but in nineteen cases out of twenty, when the eggs come hard they are immature; and the best rule to observe, at least in beginning, is to take only the eggs which come easily. Avoid all others. If the first half come easily and the balance less so, take the first half and leave the rest. When you perceive the eggs lying in rows under the skin, do not try the fish at all. The ovaries are not open, and she is certainly not ripe.

2. *Do not use too cold water.* The eggs begin to stick quicker, and remained stuck longer, in very cold water than in warmer water. The zoösperms of the milt also are less active and effective in very cold water.* At all events, my experience has been that very cold water is unfavorable to impregnation. In October the water in the brooks will do very well, but later, in November and December, it gets too cold, and the necessary exposure to the cold air while

* M. de Quatrefages says that the spermatozoa of trout milt live the longest at a temperature between 41° and 48° Fahrenheit; but that when the temperature exceeds these limits, the increase of the energy on the part of the animalcules compensates to a certain extent for the shorter duration of their vitality.

spawning makes matters still worse. During the latter part of the season, the water for the spawning pans should be taken from the spring, and, if necessary, kept at the spring temperature by artificial heat.

3. *Make quick work in impregnating the eggs.* Have everything ready beforehand, so as not to lose a moment's time after the fish are in the tub. Do not be over two minutes with any one pan, and take but one layer of eggs to a pan. By these precautions you will secure absorbing eggs and active zoösperms and a good intermingling of both, even at the minimum estimate of the period of their effectiveness. You will also thus avoid the reabsorption of milt by the males, which will sometimes happen when they are disturbed.*

4. *Stir the water well in the pans when first poured in, but not afterwards.* This precaution is, of course, to effect a thorough distribution of the spermatozoa through the water, to act upon the eggs. After the eggs begin to adhere, leave them perfectly quiet till they separate spontaneously. I have heard it said that the water should be stirred during the whole time of the adhering of the eggs, but this is a mistake.

5. *Allow the eggs ample time to separate.* It will do no harm if you leave the eggs an hour in the pan with the milt, but it *will* do harm to move them too soon. Some authorities say that thirty minutes is long

* Males having good and ready-flowing milt sometimes, when frightened, seem to reabsorb it into the glands, so that it cannot be pressed out naturally. By immersing the fish in warm water, however, say at 70° Fahrenheit, the glands will be relaxed so that the milt will flow copiously again.

enough to leave them, some say twenty minutes, and one late authority says one minute. I should rather leave them together forty-five minutes than less. It depends, however, very much on the temperature of the water, the adhesive period lengthening as the temperature decreases. You are more likely to err on the *safe* side by keeping them too long together, than by not keeping them long enough.

6. *Rinse thoroughly.* The eggs should be thoroughly rinsed before removal to the hatching boxes, for the effete milt clinging to them eventually putrefies and kills the eggs if left on them. They should therefore be rinsed till the water in the pan is perfectly clear. Some authorities recommend washing the eggs when first taken from the fish, to get rid of the mucus enveloping them, which is thought unfavorable to impregnation. There is no sort of sense in this.

7. *Practise to acquire dexterity in handling the fish.* Time is so valuable in impregnating eggs, that it is worth while to practise, as in any accomplishment, for dexterity. Dexterity, when acquired, saves time at the very moment when time is the most precious, and often secures the impregnation of eggs which would otherwise be lost. The difference between a skilled expert and a novice in this respect is astonishing. The former will run through a large lot of fish, and spawn them all properly in a time that would seem incredibly short to a bungler, who would very likely consume half a day on the same number. The results, also, of his manipulations, will present an equal con-

trast in the impregnation of the eggs. Acquire, therefore, as much dexterity as you can in handling the fish.

CLOSING NOTES.

The spawning season for brook trout in New England begins the first or second week of October. It is earlier north of New England, and later south of it. The length of the spawning period depends on the equability of the temperature of the water. In ordinary brooks, where the temperature of the water varies with the temperature of the air, the spawning is over by the middle of December, and often before.* In spring water, when the temperature is not affected by the air, the trout sometimes continue to spawn all winter. In Seth Green's ponds, the trout begin to spawn the 12th of October, and continue spawning till the 1st of March. At the Cold Spring Trout Ponds, they begin the same day, the 12th of October, and finish the first week in December.

All two-year-old trout spawn. Some yearlings do, and some do not. The main dependence of the trout breeder for eggs is on trout upwards of two years old. The eggs of the trout are large compared with

---

* I think it must be now admitted, in view of so much evidence, that individual members of the *Salmo* family spawn in the spring. How much is the rule and how much the exception we do not know. The Danube Salmon (*Salmo hucho*) all do. See Artificial Fish Breeding, Fry, p. 52. There is also a variety of salmon in the St. John River, N. B., that come up regularly to spawn in the spring. The same is reported of the British rivers Wye and Severn. See River Fisheries, "Land and Water," April 29 and May 20, 1871.

5*

those of most fish, except the salmon. They average about three sixteenths of an inch in diameter, varying very considerably in size, the very largest containing probably twice the bulk of the very smallest. They are sometimes colorless, sometimes orange-hued, and sometimes have a rich red tint.

The cause of the variation in the color of the eggs is not positively known. It has been thought to be hereditary.* It has also been attributed to the color of the flesh of its parent, and to the nature of the parent's food.†

A correspondent of Mr. Buckland says that the tints cannot depend on the color of the parent's flesh, because graylings' eggs have similar tints, and all graylings are white-fleshed.

The outer membrane of the egg is very elastic and tough. The internal structure of the egg is as follows. On the outside is the shell membrane, corresponding to the hard shell of birds' eggs. Inside of this shell, which is formed, as with birds' eggs, at quite a late period of the development of the egg in the ovary, is another membrane called the yolk membrane. This is very different from the shell membrane, and is quite delicate. This yolk envelope contains the yolk of the egg, in which are several drops of oil, which form the food that the young alevin absorbs in the yolk-sac stage. In the yolk also floats the germinal vesicle, which is a small cell, and which contains another set of minute cells called the germinative spots or points.

* Massachusetts Fisheries, Report, 1868, p. 31.
† Fish Hatching, Buckland, pp. 19, 20.

Here lies the germ of the egg, and the microscopic opening called the micropyle, through which the spermatozoa enter in the process of impregnation.

When the egg dies, the membranes let in water, which precipitates the contents of the egg in the form of a soft, opaque, white paste. It is this which gives the white appearance to the dead eggs.

The number of eggs to a fish is given as one thousand to the pound, but it is often more than this, and varies very much with the size of the eggs, those having small eggs yielding the most in number. I have taken eighteen hundred eggs from a pound trout, and once took over sixty eggs from a trout that weighed just half an ounce immediately after being stripped.

The Effect of the Weather upon the Spawning of Trout on Different Days.

Trout seem to feel the changes of weather quite as much as the air-breathing animals above water. Indeed, I have a theory that the various conditions of the atmosphere, which we describe by the words "raw," "chilly," "disagreeable," "pleasant," "agreeable," "delicious," are also shared by the water, — certainly the various electrical states of the atmosphere are, — and that the fish in the water feel the difference as we do. None know better than old anglers how much the weather affects the feelings of the fish under water, and I am inclined to think that most of them hold very much the same theory. It is at all events true, that in the spawning season the trout are very much influenced in their spawning by the character of the day.

An experienced breeder can tell in the morning, by the wind, the sky, and the state of the air, how his trout are going to spawn that day. Indeed, a person sensitive to the changes in the weather can tell by his feelings, with his eyes shut, whether it is going to be a good day for spawning. A warm rain is the most favorable condition for spawning. A sharp, frosty night, followed by a warm, bright, sunny afternoon, is the next best.* A warm rain, particularly, brings up the fish upon the beds in swarms.

This is partly owing to the increased volume of the water, for a freshet always calls out the instinct in trout and salmon to rush up to higher waters; but it is not wholly this, for the action of the pattering rain on the water hastens irresistibly their time of parturition, and they would spawn more in a warm rain, if the volume of water were not increased any. On these favorable days it is noticeable that the milt of the males is also much better ripened, as well as the eggs of the female.

A raw, chilly November day, when the air feels disagreeable, is the worst kind of weather for spawning, and in some of these days they will hardly come up at all.

An increased current and volume of water have an effect upon the spawning fish similar to a rain, perhaps from the same cause, namely, increase of friction in the water.

---

* Francis, I think, says that a cloudy day is best for spawning. My experience has been entirely to the contrary, unless it rained. The explanation may possibly be that he saw them best on a cloudy day, as they are less shy on such days.

At any rate, the trout come up better when the stream rises. This instinct the breeder can often turn to his own convenience. For, instance, if he must be absent a day, he can keep the spawners back by turning off the water as far as is safe ; or if he wants to hasten the spawning on any particular day, he can do so by turning on a powerful current.

The afternoon especially, whether rainy or sunny, I have always found to be the best part of the day for taking spawn.

To insure ripe eggs, I think once a day is quite often enough to manipulate the fish.

Spawning in the Pond.

In the course of a few weeks the daily disturbing of the trout on their nests will often, and I think usually, drive them farther down stream, and induce them to spawn in the pond. This of course results in the loss of the eggs, and must not be allowed. The best way to discourage it is, to throw in a shovelful of mud or earth, wherever you discover them making their nests.

At my own ponds I have two sets of spawning races, one below the other. I use the upper one only, to begin with, and when the trout abandon this, on account of being disturbed, they fall back to the second raceway, where they can generally be kept till the season is over.

The Spawning Pans.

The dishes for stripping spawn into are usually rectangular pans, or common milk-pans, with a rectangular depression of a quarter of an inch or so in the bottom. The object of this rectangular feature of the dish is to enable the operator to count the eggs, which of course is easily done for any one layer by counting the number in one row, each way, and multiplying them together.

It has been demonstrated that fish of the same family can sometimes be crossed. The Chinese have long been in the practice of crossing various breeds of the carp. Trout eggs have been impregnated with salmon milt, and hatched, and salmon eggs impregnated with trout milt have hatched.*

The question whether the progeny will ever reproduce, has not, I think, been decided by actual experiment : but science, popular belief, and analogy all bear uniformly negative testimony.

PLACING THE SPAWN.

This is a very simple process, After the eggs in the pan are thoroughly rinsed, take them to the hatching house, and set back the water in the hatching trough so that it will be about two inches deep. Then place one end of the pan below the surface of the water, and, drawing it slowly backwards up stream, gradually pour the eggs out under water. If you give the pan a

* "In 1869 I crossed the yellow perch *Perca* (*flavescens*) with the glass-eyed pike (*Lucioperca*), both percoids, using perch eggs and pike milt. The result was an embryo which continued to develop till the seventh day, when the development suddenly stopped entirely, although the embryo did not die. At this point it resembled the embryo of the same age of the yellow perch proper." — *Artificial Fish Breeding*, FRY, p. 52.

sort of sifting motion, it will distribute the eggs rather more evenly. When the eggs are all out, take a feather and separate and place them as you wish to have them remain. It is best, on the whole, in placing the eggs through the season, to begin at the bottom of the hatching trough and work up, because by this plan the shells and other waste matter coming from the hatched eggs are not carried down upon the others still hatching.

CHAPTER II.

HATCHING THE EGGS.

THE eggs being taken and laid down in the troughs, the next thing is to hatch them. This is a long and slow process, and coming, as it does, in the coldest season of the year, has, in the colder latitudes of this country, some hardships connected with it. For instance, the daily examination of the eggs in a house hatching a quarter or a half million is sometimes a long task of almost still work, usually in a room so large and damp that the stove has no effect on its general temperature ; and when the mercury is at zero or 15° below it, one can imagine what exposure this work in ice and water must be.

On the other hand, hatching the eggs is the very simplest and surest of all the branches of trout breeding. Any one can hatch the eggs with the knowledge now furnished from past experience, by simply following directions. It requires no skill or proficiency. It is mere clock-work routine when the hatching apparatus is properly prepared. When you consider that the eggs differ from the fish in these two points, namely, that they cannot move of themselves, and that they require no nourishment, you perceive at once how much the care of them must be simplified in consequence. Indeed, the eggs kept in clean running water will hatch themselves. Nature provides with the egg all that it needs for its nourishment, and what is required of the breeder is simply to see that nothing interferes with nature's work.

This negative task, however, of guarding the eggs from danger, though, with the present improved appliances for hatching, it requires no great skill, is not by any means a sinecure, but, on the contrary, calls for caution, vigilance, and labor, as will be seen by the following general remarks on hatching eggs.

.The main dangers to which the eggs are subjected are four in number, and are all fatal. They are, —

1. Alga (fungus).*
2. Sediment.
3. Living enemies.
4. Byssus (fungus).*

Carbonized wood is a protection against the first, fungus. The system of filtering is a protection against the second, sediment. Tight covers are a protection against the third, live enemies. The daily examination of the eggs is a protection against the fourth, byssus.

It follows, then, that the dangers are all guarded against by the provisions themselves of the hatching apparatus, in connection with the daily examination of the eggs.

It may be well here, however, to allude briefly to

---

* These are both fungi, but the first enumerated is usually called, in trout breeding, by its generic name, fungus, and the fourth by its specific name, byssus.

the character and effect of the four sources of injury mentioned.

1. *Fungus.** There is no word in the fish breeders' vocabulary that is so associated with loss and devastation as the word "fungus." There is nothing with which he has to deal that is so insidious and deadly as fungus. This silent, invisible foe is sure to come, if any door is left open for its entrance. It often fastens its irrevocable grasp on the eggs, without giving any sign of its approach. Once present in the water, it spreads over everything. It cannot be removed. It never lets go its hold. It is fatal in its effects.

Most of my readers know that fungus is a vegetable growth of a low order, which makes its appearance almost invariably where there is water, and especially on newly cut wood, on which it eventually becomes a mass of nearly colorless or milky slime.† What makes it so peculiarly noxious is, that each one of its cells, whether detached or not, is a reproductive seed, that is to say, a perfect reproducing plant in itself. Consequently, when it is torn up anywhere, or broken in pieces, instead of being destroyed, it only becomes more powerful to injure.

So where any fragment of fungus falls, however small, even if it is only one microscopic cell, it immediately proceeds to grow, and produce other similar

---

* "Fungus, a large natural order of plants, comprehending the microscopic plants, which form mould, mildew, smut, etc. The fungi constitute one division of the Linnean class of Cryptogamia." — *Webster's Dictionary*.

† On hard wood and knotty wood it is sometimes black, but the common form of growth is nearly colorless.

cells, and so on indefinitely. Therefore when it is torn off or broken in pieces, as it constantly is, by the action of running water, it is not destroyed, but rendered tenfold more capable of injury; for where one plant existed before, now there are as many plants as fragments. Thus having once found entrance, it spreads over everything, and its removal is worse than Hercules's task of killing the hundred-headed Hydra, whose heads grew out as fast as they were cut off.

This fungus, if once present in the hatching water, will certainly attach itself to the eggs, and when it does, their fate is sealed ; you cannot save them from its effect, as it never lets go its hold. It will surely eat out the vitality of the embryo within, and will either kill it wholly or will leave a puny, lifeless, transparent creature, which will in all probability never live to grow up. It cannot therefore be guarded against with too much care.

If the eggs seem to hang together, or stick to the bottom, or move about heavily, when they are agitated with a feather, you should be on the watch for fungus, for these are signs of it. It is detected for a certainty, on the eggs, by placing a few in a clear homœopathic phial, and holding them up to the light. If there is fungus on them, it will be seen as a collection of very fine, ethereal, colorless threads floating over the eggs like streamers. If you see this, the pestilence has come.

If it should by any accident form upon your eggs, shut out at once all light from them ; this will check its growth somewhat. Increase the current as much as you can safely, and make the water colder, if possible.   You can never make good eggs of them again, but you may arrest its spreading in some degree, and save the lives of some of the embryos.   An ounce of prevention is, however, worth a pound of cure, and in this instance it is worth a thousand pounds of cure.   Therefore char every box, aqueduct, and trough, and all the wood-work through which the water flows; then you will have no fungus.   It will not form on charcoal in the dark.

2. *Sediment.*   This is a danger of no small importance, but it is nothing like fungus in its destructiveness, for it can be removed, it does not spread, and it is not always fatal.   It is, however, a very bad thing, and sometimes very troublesome.   It consists of the very fine dust which is held mechanically in all running water.   As remarked in a previous chapter, it may not be discernible in the water when examined by the eye, but will show its presence after the water has run a certain length of time over a given place, by being precipitated as a light deposit of dirt or mud over the spot.   This fine layer of dirt, if it should settle on the eggs, would suffocate them in time, or if not in sufficient quantity to suffocate them would, by interrupting the processes of absorption and growth of the embryo at certain points, cause a deformity in the fish when hatched.   Many of the curved spines, hunched backs, and spiral bodies of fish newly hatched are caused by this partial suffocation of the embryo by the sediment.   The remedy for sediment, or rather its prevention, as before observed, is the system of filters.

These should be sufficient to arrest it effectively. If they cannot be made sufficient, then the stream is not worth using.*

If by any accident sediment should get upon the eggs occasionally, the method of removing it is so simple, that it need cause no alarm, if it is attended to at once. This method consists merely in watering the eggs with a common garden watering-pot, at the same time keeping the outlet screen clear, to let off the sediment as it floats down. This plan, though so simple, is very effective. It will remove every particle of sediment from the eggs, and leave them, as well as the bed of the hatching-troughs, cleaner than before the sediment was observed. The agitation also seems to do the eggs good in other ways.†

I should water the eggs occasionally, even if there were no sediment to be removed. The precaution

* When the hatching water has so much sediment in it that filtering cannot make it safe for the eggs in the common hatching troughs, the water can still be used sometimes with grilles, by washing off daily with the watering-pot the sediment which collects on the eggs. The sediment will fall through the openings between the grilles, and be out of the way of the eggs. The eggs can be safely hatched in this way, but the sediment must be closely watched and carefully kept off the eggs.

† "Une autre condition nécessaire au développement des œufs, c'est de les remuer souvent ; un repos absolu les tuerait nécessairement." — VÖGT, *Embryologie des Salmones*, p. 16.

It should be said, in explanation of the above note, that Vögt's experiments were not conducted in running water. This does not, however, invalidate his testimony as to the effect of agitating the eggs.

should be taken, however, to have the water about two inches deep, or the concussion of the falling water in the earlier stages of the eggs will sometimes be injurious to the embryo.

3. *Living enemies.* So much has been already said about this class of dangers, that I would pass them by here, if I had not seen so much carelessness on the part of trout breeders in leaving their eggs exposed to these enemies. I am convinced that persons generally do not begin to realize the danger from this source, and I have often wished, for their benefit, that a pic ture could be drawn, representing all the enemies to trout eggs directing their steps just after nightfall to their nightly feast in the hatching-house troughs. It is true they do not all come at once ; but if they did, there would be in the picture mice, rats, weasles, muskrats, minks, cats, frogs, snakes, lizards, evets, caddis-worms, water-spiders, boat-flies, water-beetles, and snails ; and then the picture would not include ducks, geese, wild water-fowl, eels, large trout, and countless other fish which would come in the daytime if they could get at them.

Yet persons imagine that, because they do not see these creatures feeding on the eggs or young fry in the morning when they open the hatching-house, they have probably not been there. But it is just the reverse. The probability is all the other way. It is even a certainty. Just imagine for a moment that a starving mouse has strayed into the house some freezing night ; it will not be long before he will find the eggs, and will make a feast on them. How can you suppose that the next night, when he gets hungry again, he will not return to where he left a rich supper the night before? Do you suppose there is one chance in a hundred of his not coming? There is not even that small chance. If the mouse is alive the next night, and has not been driven away, he will come back to his feast as sure as darkness comes on, and so he will continue to do every night of his life while the eggs last. And yet I hear people say, in the coolest way imaginable, of their unprotected spawn, "I guess nothing will come to take the eggs to-night." Why, not only is the warm hatching-house an attractive place to these creatures of prey in the winter, when the eggs are hatching, because of its comparative warmth, but they are every one of them impelled to these eggs by the strongest of animal instincts, namely, hunger. How, then, can the eggs escape, if they are exposed?

The only protection that I believe in is covers. Traps and poison may or may not remove the cause of loss before the loss comes, but tight lids make the thing sure. Have tight lids, fitting close, over all your troughs, and you may sleep in peace at night for all the injury that rats and mice and other outside enemies will do your eggs.

4. *Byssus.* This is also a fungus growth, like the other, but it comes from the eggs themselves, and not from external sources, and it is not so much to be feared. This plant is created by matter decaying in the water ; so that whenever a fish egg loses its vitality and begins to putrefy, byssus commences to grow. With trout eggs in water at 40° or 50° degrees Fahren-

heit it generally appears within forty-eight hours after the egg turns white, and often sooner, and the warmer the water the quicker it comes. It is never quite safe to leave the dead eggs over twenty-four hours in the hatching boxes. The peculiarity of byssus is, that it stretches out its long, slender arms, which grow rapidly, over everything within its reach. This makes it peculiarly mischievous, for it will sometimes clasp a dozen or even twenty eggs in its Briarean grasp before it is discovered, and any egg that it has seized has received its death-warrant. Like the alga before mentioned, every cell is reproductive; and it should, on that account be carefully handled. The remedy or protection is the daily examination of the eggs with feather and nippers. If this is faithfully performed, the byssus will never come.

This examination of the eggs is a very considerable part of the trout breeder's work in winter, and demands to be treated at considerable length, which I shall endeavor to do in this connection.

If your hatching streams would run just as you wanted them to, if the filters were all right and would remain so, if the eggs were all impregnated, this daily examination would be a very easy task ; but as this is too much to expect, you should be prepared to make quite a labor of this daily duty, and the following suggestions may be of some service in performing it. On entering the hatching house, look first at the *outlet* of all the hatching compartments. You will soon learn to do so instinctively. They will tell you whether the various streams are running right or not ; for if the outlet is running right, the inlet must be also, of necessity. If anything is wrong in the flow of the hatching streams, follow them up from the outlet till you discover the cause, and, when you have, remove it, and also, if practicable, the *possibility* of its occurring again. If the streams are running right, next examine the filters. If they are clogged up or too dirty for safety, take them out, change and clean them, according to directions given under the head of Filters.* Remove them carefully when they are taken from the tank, so as not to shake the dirt off the flannel into the water, and try to keep the rear one clean enough not to require changing at all; for when you remove that one, the sediment in front of it has free access to the gravel, and some of it may get through to the eggs.

The eggs claim your attention next; you proceed to them with feather and nippers. The feather you need to move the eggs with; the nippers you require to pick out the dead ones. A feather from a turkey's tail I like best for feathers. For nippers take a piece of flat steel spring, about ten inches long and not over an eighth of an inch in width; bend it exactly in the middle, spread the ends by hammering, and you have as good an instrument, I believe, as there is for picking out eggs. Other things are used, as, for instance, the bulb syringe, and a miniature spoon made of a concave coil of fine wire fastened into a wooden handle. These have the advantage over nippers for picking out *live* eggs, that they do not hurt the eggs;

---

* The tanks should be drawn off and thoroughly washed out, whenever much sediment begins to collect in them.

6

but for picking out dead eggs, there is, in my opinion, nothing better than the common steel nippers just described.   Nothing certainly can be surer and quicker in its operation in an experienced hand.

Your first question, when the eggs are to be picked over, will probably be, How can the dead ones be distinguished from the live ones?   But the anxiety which every new operator feels on this point is wholly needless, for you cannot mistake them.   The dead ones will turn as white as milk, and can be as easily told from the live ones as white quartz from gray pebbles.   You will even perceive the dead ones distinctly, as soon as you open the boxes.   You will at once remove them with the nippers.   To handle the nippers rapidly and safely is quite an art, and reminds one of playing at jack-straws.   But as the required skill will soon come with practice, I will say no more here, than that you should be careful at first not to touch the live ones with the nippers, and by all means not to bruise them by any pressure from above.   In time you will learn to hit the live ones, while picking out, without hurting them.   But till you have acquired this knack, you should be on your guard.

As it is only the unimpregnated eggs that die (except by accident), the amount of the work of examining the eggs depends almost wholly on the percentage of impregnation.   This is obvious.   If one hundred per cent were impregnated, there would be none to pick out, and the work would be nothing.   If ninety nine per cent were impregnated, the work would be very slight.   But if not more than fifty per cent were good, then the work would be increased fifty-fold. The difference in the labor would be very great, as this little estimate will show. Suppose half a million eggs are taken, and fifty per cent are empty. It takes about a minute to pick out twenty eggs ; then to pick out fifty per cent of five hundred thousand would take over twelve thousand minutes, or two hundred hours, or twenty days of ten hours each.

It is therefore very desirable to get a large percentage of impregnated eggs, if only on account of the work it saves, as well as for weightier reasons.

During the first few days after the eggs are placed, there will not be many white ones to pick out, unless they have been injured in being taken. You must not be elated at this, for it is no sign that the unchanged eggs are all good, or nearly so, for the empty ones will not turn white to any extent for two or three weeks, or more, and some will not die till all the good ones are hatched. But you are no better off for it. On the contrary, I think I have noticed that the better the impregnation of any lot, the sooner the empty ones of that lot died ; probably because the eggs were riper. Their turn will come, however, to all the bad eggs ; and when the time fairly sets in for them to die, then the work will begin in earnest, and unless you have a small stock or a very good impregnation, there will be work of no trifling character. To stand or sit in the damp, unwarmed hatching house for a long time in mid-winter at this still work, is in our northern latitudes a severe task, and trying to the hardiest constitution. It is to be hoped, however, that my readers will have few empty eggs, and a large stove near by, to warm themselves at.

The method of procedure in the daily examination of the eggs is, as before remarked, very much like playing at jack-straws. You begin first with the loose and uppermost eggs, then set more free by agitating the water with the feather, then pick out the loose ones again, then agitate the pile once more, and so on, till they have all been spread and all picked out in that lot. Leaving these evenly distributed, you pass on to the next, keeping account of the number you pick out, so as to know how many are left, and so on till all are examined. Strange as it may seem, this work, after all, has a certain charm about it, especially when you think what a vast wealth of life moves under the touch of your feather; and it, moreover, affords an excellent opportunity for quiet reflection, so that if you can pick over the eggs without suffering too much from the cold, it is not so unpleasant a task as it seemed before you began it.

The progress of the eggs in hatching will be watched with the liveliest interest. The simplest way to examine their progress minutely is to take out two or three eggs, and place them in a homœopathic phial filled with water. Hold the phial horizontally towards the light and above the eye. The contents of the eggs then become clearly visible, and can be examined at leisure, and a magnifying lens applied if desired. This is Seth Green's method.

Another way is to take a small pane of window-glass, and, by fastening narrow wooden sides to it, make a shallow box with a glass bottom. Pour in a little water, and put the eggs to be examined in the water; then by looking from above or below, but especially from below, you can see very distinctly what is inside the egg. This method obviates the distortion sometimes produced by refraction in the homœopathic phial.

You will soon be very anxious to ascertain how large a percentage of the eggs is impregnated.

It has been usually thought that the impregnated eggs could not be told from the empty ones previous to the formation of the embryotic line, which is the spine of the fish, and which appears when about one third of the period of incubation * is accomplished. This, however, is not strictly true, because there is a period, within forty-eight hours of the taking of the eggs, when the good eggs can be distinguished from the worthless ones. The distinction is this, that in the unimpregnated eggs a small annular disk, with a much smaller round dot in the centre, will be seen at the top of the egg, and will remain there until the eggs turn white, while in the impregnated egg the disk will disappear within twenty-four hours. The eggs, then, which after the first day present the disk, are unimpregnated. Those in which the disk is not visible are impregnated. The explanation of this is as follows.

* The word "incubation" from *in* and *cubo*, "to sit on," has been used in reference to the hatching of bird's eggs by steam, and seems to be equally allowable in this application for the hatching of fish eggs. There is no *sitting* upon the eggs in either case.

At the end of a few hours, more or less, according to the temperature of the water, the germ of the egg rises to the top in both the fertilized and the unfertilized egg, which look exactly alike. The germ in the unfertilized egg, however, undergoes no change whatever from this time, while in the fertilized egg a process soon begins which is called by the French embryologists " *sillonnement*," or furrowing, and by English writers "segmentation." This process begins by the sinking of a deep furrow through the centre of the germ, dividing it into two equal parts. This is followed by another, bisecting the first, and another and another, until the subdivisions have been continued indefinitely, when the germ again presents nearly the same appearance as at first. While this " *sillonnement*," or segmentation, is going on, the original disk formed by the germ in the impregnated egg disappears, and cannot be seen at all, thus distinguishing it plainly from the unimpregnated egg, which still presents the germ disk as clearly as ever. Therefore at this period the unimpregnated eggs can be told from the impregnated ones by the one presenting the distinct germ disk, while the other shows no trace of it.

The percentage of impregnated eggs can now be told approximately ; but as the light must be favorable in order to tell which eggs have the germ disk visible and which have not, and as it is not a good plan to handle the eggs too much at this stage, it is perhaps quite as well to be patient and wait till the tissues of the fish are firm enough to allow the egg to be handled, and the clearly marked eye-spots leave no doubt as to which eggs are impregnated and which are not, before attempting to decide with much exactness on the percentage of impregnation.

As remarked above, a fine dark line near the middle of the impregnated egg will be observed, on close examination, about the end of the first third of the hatching period. Soon the whole form of the fish will become cloudily apparent, and then the black eye-spots will appear, first one and then both. Now is the best time to tell what proportion of the eggs are impregnated. You can form some estimate, perhaps, before, by taking out a few in the phial, say ten, and counting the impregnated ones in it. If, for instance, nine are visible, then you infer that ninety per cent are good. But this method is very deceptive, and cannot be relied upon, both because the number is too small to base an estimate on, and also because the specific gravity of the empty ones being a little less than that of the full ones, it sometimes happens that a twirl of the feather will throw the empty ones together in a hole, and the impregnated ones together in another pile, on the mechanical principle which leaves sand, marl, and vegetable matter in a brook in different spots by themselves. In taking out three or four in a phial for examination, you may happen to hit upon one of these piles or the other, and so get a deceptive sample of the eggs in general.

The best way to get the ratio of the good to the worthless ones is to take out several hundreds or a thousand after the eye-spots show plainly, and pick out the empty ones. Count both, and add its proportion of previously removed eggs to the number of empty ones, and you get at the proportion of impregnated eggs. This, however, only answers for the particular box from which these were taken. To obtain the percentage of the whole season's yield, this operation must be repeated with each box or compartment. It will be well to observe here, also, that it is a good plan, as soon as the impregnated eggs are unmistakably distinguishable from the empty ones, to take them all out into pans, and remove all the empty ones before replacing them in the hatching-boxes. The work of picking over will be done much easier and quicker this way, and it has this great advantage, that it is done once for all, and you are for the rest of the season relieved of the burden of care which the daily necessity of removing the empty ones involves.

The time required for hatching depends chiefly on the temperature of the water. Seth Green's rule is that at 50° Fahrenheit trout eggs will hatch out in fifty days, and every degree warmer or colder makes five days' difference in time ; warmer water shortening the period, and colder water lengthening it. Green also says, that if the fish are hatched in fifty days, the yolk sac remains thirty more. If in seventy days, the sac remains forty-five days.

Mr. Stephen H. Ainsworth's table is as follows :—

Average temperature of water.	No. of days to first formation of trout.	No. of days to formation of eyes and red blood.	No. of days to hatching.	No. of days after hatching to feeding.
37°	43	81	165	
$38\frac{1}{2}$	29	64	135	77
39	28	62	121	
$40\frac{1}{5}$	27	54	109	60
41	21	49	103	
$42\frac{1}{3}$	19	42	96	
$43\frac{1}{3}$	17	37	89	46
44	16	34	81	
$45\frac{1}{2}$	15	31	73	
$46\frac{1}{2}$	13	29	65	
48	11	26	56	
50	10	23	47	30
52	8	18	38	
54	7	15	32	
Appearance of spawn as fig. 3.	as fig. 7.	as fig. 12.		

Although results somewhat varying from these figures will be obtained in different waters, they may, nevertheless, be regarded as a safe guide in general. I will only add that in my own experience I have found that the yolk sac requires more time for its absorption in proportion to the time of incubation ; I should say quite a third more.

As the development of the embryo advances, the care of the eggs will become more and more interesting. They will, however, lose their bright crystalline look, as they lie in the water, and will assume, collectively, a dull brownish hue ; but when examined separately, it will be seen that this does not arise from any unfavorable change, but from the embryo thickening and darkening in the shell. This development and the filling up of the shell with the embryo proceeds rapidly till about the same time has elapsed that was required for the eye-spots to appear, when the whole figure of the fish, thick and black and fully formed, will be seen, usually lying quiet and motionless, but occasionally stirring with a little spasmodic leap or wriggle. The time of their release is now near at hand, and you may expect to find a newly hatched trout or two in your earlier hatching boxes any day.*

An inexperienced person might suppose that all trout eggs will produce fish that are just alike when hatched. But this is very far from the fact. There is just as much difference in a brood of newly hatched trout as there is between the brawniest and puniest of a litter of pigs or brood of chickens. Some will be large, strong, and full of vigor ; others will be small, weak, and inactive. It is a desirable thing to be able to know how to tell a lot of eggs that will produce good fish from a lot that will produce poor fish, and it is very easy to learn. If the embryo in the egg is seen to be dark, firm, thick, clearly defined,

* As you will probably want to procure specimens of eggs and fish at different stages of growth, it is a good plan to have a set of homœpathic phials in readiness, and some alcohol. One part alcohol to three parts water is a good preserving mixture at this stage. This mixture will congeal, but will not expand in congealing sufficiently to burst the bottles. More alcohol with the water will destroy the delicate tissue of the embryo.

and heavy-looking, and hatches late, the egg will produce a healthy, hardy, broad-shouldered trout, and a
good feeder. If the embryo is seen to be thin, light,
transparent, and hatches before its time, it will produce a puny, weakly, thin-bodied fish, and a poor eater,
which has not five chances in a hundred of growing up.

Do not be anxious to have your eggs hatch early.
If they hatch before their time, it is a bad sign. If
the embryo remains long in the shell after forming,
and hatches late, it is a good sign. One sure consequence and indication of the presence of fungus is
the premature hatching of the egg, before the embryo
has become well hardened within the shell. Beware
of eggs that promise to hatch too early, for they are
very likely to be fungussy ; and out of a thousand fungussy eggs it is an even chance if one embryo lives a
year.

The microscopic changes in the eggs from day to
day are presented in the accompanying drawings by
Professor Agassiz.

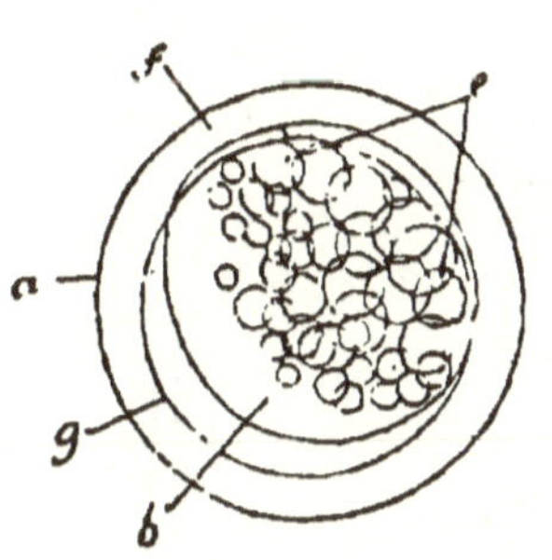

15

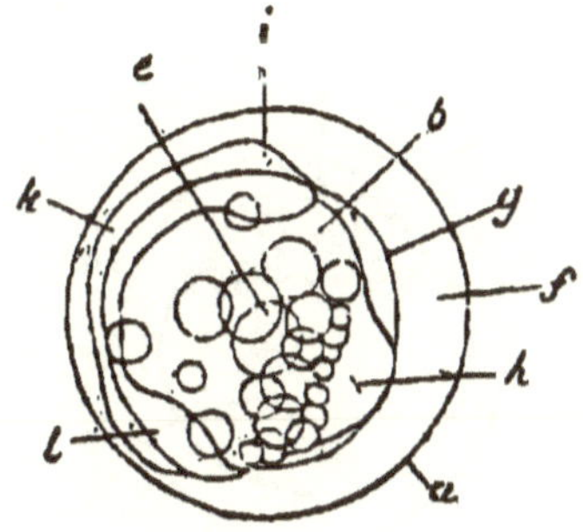

20

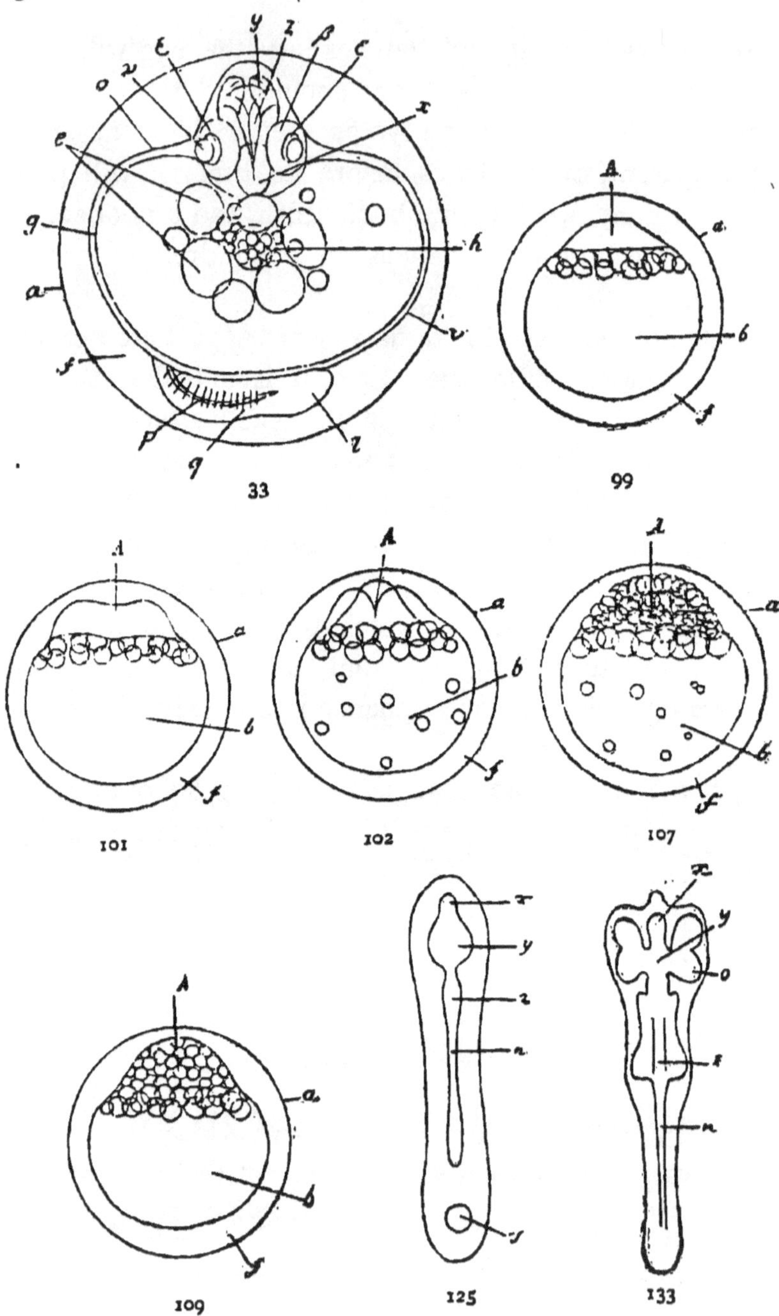

33

99

101

102

107

109

125

133

These plates represent eggs of the *Coregonus palœa* in different stages of their growth, as seen under a powerful magnifier.

No. 15 represents a spoiled egg.

No. 20. The embryo ten days old.

No. 33. Front view of embryo eighteen days old.

No. 99. An egg two days after impregnation.

No. 101. Appearance of first furrow second day after impregnation.

No. 102. An egg showing development of furrows.

No. 107. Mulberry form of the embryo.

No. 109. Embryonic germ immediately after the disappearance of the furrows.

No. 125. Projection of the embryo prepared with acid, 8th day.

No. 133. Projection of embryo prepared with acid, 17th day.

The letters denote as follows : —

a Shelly membrane ; *b* Yolk ; *c* Germinal vesicle ; *d* Yolk globules ; *e* Oil drops ; *f* Albumen ; *g* Yolk membrane ; *h* Yolk vesicle ; *i* Head of the embryo ; *j* Yolk cavity ; *k* Trunk of embryo ; *l* Tail ; *m* Dorsal keel ; *n* Dorsal furrow ; *o* Ocular lobes ; *p* Dorsal cord ; *q* Vertebral divisions ; *r* Sheath of dorsal cord ; *s* Cephalic bow ; *t* Nuchal bow ; *u* Trunchal bow ; *v* Epidermoidal stratum ; *x* Procencephalon ; *y* Mesencephalon ; *z* Epencephalon.

As too much caution cannot be observed in trout-culture, I hope the reader will pardon my repeating here the cautions already given : —

To keep the covers down carefully ;

To change the filters when dirty ;

To take out every dead egg once in twenty-four hours ;

To use the watering-pot freely, if sediment settles on the eggs ;

To guard everywhere against fungus.

TRANSPORTATION AND PACKING OF THE EGGS.

Transportation of the eggs. No one need have any fear about being able to transport trout eggs safely.

They have been sent to England and California without loss, and salmon eggs shipped from England have reached Australia alive. I have sent eggs to Kansas and Europe safely, and one hundred and seventy thousand salmon eggs from the writer's Salmon-Breeding Establishment on the Mirimichi came eight miles by private conveyance, one hundred miles by stage, one hundred miles by rail, two hundred miles by steamer, across the city of Boston by wagon, and one hundred and twenty more miles by rail before reaching their destination, where they were found, on opening, to be in good condition. Indeed, when trout and salmon eggs are carefully packed, they are about as safe in the moss which encloses them as they are in the hatching boxes, and the only risk to which they are exposed in transportation is rough handling; and I have observed that they will stand a good deal of that. A few, say a dozen in a thousand, will perhaps die on the way; but excepting these, they will, as a rule, arrive at their destination unhurt. Injury to any greater extent is the exception.

On the tag or label which accompanies them should always be distinctly written, —

That they are fish eggs;

That they should be handled carefully;

That they should be kept in a cool place;

That concussion will kill them;

That they must not be allowed to freeze.

Packing the eggs. It is a sort of paradoxical fact that fish eggs do not require much water for hatching, but, relatively, plenty of air. Consequently, when packed in wet moss, the conditions of hatching are supplied, namely, a little moisture and plenty of air. Moss is at the same time so soft that it will not bruise the eggs. Hence, wet moss is just the thing to pack fish eggs in. The moss containing the eggs can be packed in anything which admits air and is not injured by moisture.

For packing in large quantities, a basket answers very well. Fish eggs have sometimes been sent in small quantities in a perforated percussion-cap box, and in tin snuff-boxes. If sent by express without an attendant, the basket or box containing them should be packed in a still larger basket or box, containing hay or shavings or sawdust, to soften the force of accidental concussions, and to keep the temperature of the eggs equable.

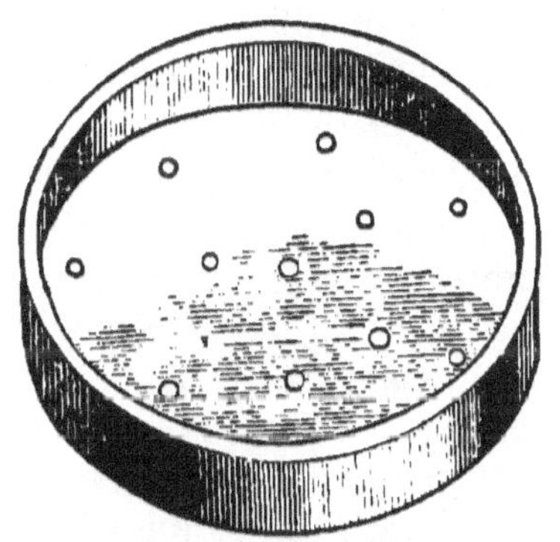 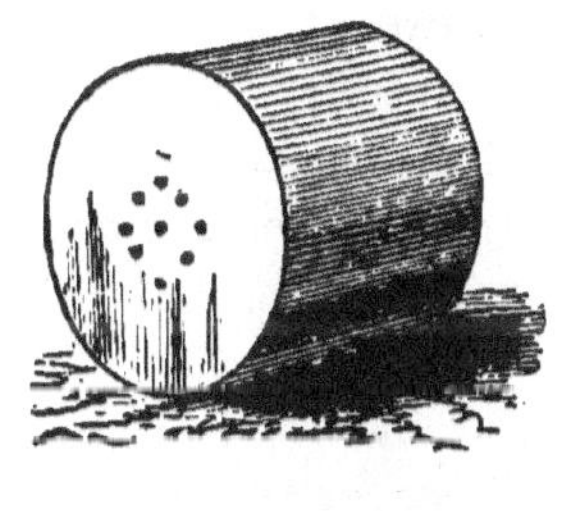

The usual way in practice to pack the trout eggs for transportation, with small quantities, is that adopted by Seth Green, which is to pack them in circular tin boxes, not over three inches in depth, with a perforated bottom to let the air in, and to pack the boxes themselves in a tin pail, somewhat larger, and to fill in with sawdust. This is a simple, compact, and safe way, and is the best now known, unless it is Mr. Wilmot's method.* The packing of the eggs in moss should be done as follows : Fill a large pan, a little deeper than the packing-box, with water. Make a bed of moss about half an inch deep on the bottom of the box, and sink the box in the pan of water. The bottom layer should be a single bunch of some kind of the finer common mosses, which are found almost anywhere in the woods. The subsequent layers should be the damp rank moss which grows in swamps, and is known by the name of Sphagnum.

Then take the required number of eggs from the

---

* Mr. Wilmot's method of packing fish eggs is a very excellent one. His apparatus consists of a cylindrical can of tin, say fifteen inches in diameter, having two walls or sides, one within the other, on the refrigerator principle. The annular space between the two walls is filled with sawdust, to preserve an even temperature within. The cylindrical space enclosed by the inner wall is filled with shallow circular trays about an inch deep, all of the same size, resting one upon another, and of a sufficient diameter to fit nicely to the inner wall of the can. Each one of these shallow trays or pans has a circular hole through the centre to admit a movable iron rod, which runs from the top of the can to the bottom of the last pan, to which it is fastened. The eggs are packed with wires in the shallow pans, and each pan as it is packed is strung on to the perpendicular rod, as beads are strung on a string. The first one, of course, going to the bottom of the can, the next resting on it, and so on till the top of the can is reached. The upper end of the rod now serves as a handle, by which all or any number of the pans can be raised at once out of the can, and by unstringing the pans, so to speak, each one with its contents can be examined.

hatching-troughs,* and pour one layer evenly over the moss.† This can be done with a spoon, or still better, perhaps, as Green suggests, with a ladle, the mouth of the ladle in pouring being made to rest on the rim of the box under water,‡ so that the eggs will not come to the air at all.

One layer of eggs having been placed, put in another thin layer of moss. This layer, as also the others succeeding it, should be carefully picked over, and all grass and roots removed, so as to make as soft and delicate a packing as possible.

After the second layer of moss, place another layer of eggs, and so on, alternating till the box is filled, taking care to keep the box and to conduct all the operations under water, for it should be always borne in mind, when fish eggs are moved, that the secret of moving them correctly is to keep the eggs *in the water*, where, of course, they ought to be.

After the top layer of moss is placed, take the box of moss and eggs out of the pan, and set it where the

---

* Any strainer of convenient shape will do to take out the eggs with. If they are much scattered, first collect them together in a heap with the feather. A skilful person will take them out safely with a large table-spoon.

† Theodore Lyman recommends placing each layer of eggs in a fold of mosquito-netting, to keep them from mixing with the moss, and so facilitate the unpacking of them. This is a great improvement. Stationary racks are also sometimes placed above each layer to catch the pressure of the supervening eggs and moss.

‡ All moving of eggs should be done under water when practicable.

superfluous water will drip out through the perforated bottom.   If the moss settles much with the escape of the water, fill up to the top again with moss.   Then, when the cover is soldered on in one or two places, to prevent displacement, it is ready to ·be packed in the pail of sawdust, the cover to which should be kept in its place by being well wired down.   When the label is fastened on, the eggs are ready to be sent off.

CHAPTER III.

CARE OF ALEVINS,* OR TROUT FRY WITH THE YOLK SAC ATTACHED.

SOME morning when you go to the hatching boxes with the nippers to look over the eggs, you will see a long, thin, dark object, like a little splinter of wood, lying among the eggs, which you will perhaps attempt to remove with the nippers, wondering how it came there in the night. The first touch of the nippers will show it to be a living creature, and you will experience, if you are a beginner, the exquisite sensation of knowing that your first trout has hatched. Soon others will follow, only one or two to the thousand at first, then more, till the hatching period reaches its culmination, when the eggs will hatch in great quantities daily, after which the number will decline again at very nearly an inverse ratio of progression. A warm rain will accelerate the hatching very much, as it does every other process of trout-life. More, per-

---

* I am aware that this French word, "alevin," means young fry; but as there is no distinctive English word to designate a fish during the period of the absorption of the yolk sac, and as the word has been employed by at least one English writer (Francis, Fish Culture, p. 99) in the present application, though not, I believe, by American writers, I take the liberty to use it in this treatise to distinguish the trout fry with the yolk sac attached.

haps, will hatch in one day, during a warm rain, than in the three subsequent days.

The newly hatched fish are about half an inch in length. The yolk of the egg is still attached to them, from which they are nourished by absorption till it is all gone and they begin to feed. The period of alevin life is about two thirds or three fourths the length of the period of incubation.

Its duration, like that of the egg period, depends on the temperature of the water, and it often happens, in water of a falling temperature, that the yolk-sac period lasts longer than it took the eggs to hatch.

On the contrary, with eggs hatched late in the spring, as in the natural brooks, with a rising temperature, the yolk sac remains on a very short period compared with the hatching of the eggs, — probably in some instances not one quarter of the time.

During the period while the young fish are breaking the shell, the bottom of the troughs becomes quite unclean from the collecting of cast-off shells and other causes, and it is a good plan to use the watering-pot freely at this time ; and as soon as it can be done without injury to the young fish, the bed of the troughs should be covered over with a layer of fresh clean gravel.

The alevins lie quite still the greater part of the time at first, sometimes on their sides, sometimes flat on the sac. Occasionally they vary the monotony of this quiet life by aimless sallies of a few inches through the water, apparently in great excitement, but with no particular goal in view. The exertion will soon bring them to the ground again quite out of breath, with their little hearts beating very fast, as is not surprising, considering their age, and that they carry about a burden twice the bulk of their bodies proper. They require no watching nor care of any kind for the first few days. They do not try to get away, they do not require to be fed, and if the hatching apparatus is well arranged, and throws a good supply of water over them, very few will die. Indeed, the yolk-sac period is one of the healthiest of the trout's early life.

They seem at first to be possessed of no particular instincts, but lie still near the spot where they were born, and do nothing. This, however, lasts only a few days.* They are soon seized, sometimes very sud-

* The following notes are taken from the writer's diary, January, 1869.

The embryos observed, were hatched from salmon eggs brought from the Mirimichi River. They were kept in a warm room, at a temperature that would probably make one day an equivalent of two or three days in the hatching trough at 45°.

First day. Eggs hatched to-day. Young fish quite vigorous. Yolk sac plump and full. Body proper, thin, and delicate, and with cloudy outline.

Second day. Change very slight. Outline a little more distinct. Body darker. Sac not quite so plump.

Third day. Changes of yesterday slightly intensified. Beating of the heart very perceptible. Main artery distinctly seen.

Fourth day. Form of yolk sac decidedly changed. Body firmer and darker. Eyes very clear. Motion of fins quite perceptible.

Fifth day. Fish much livelier. A new movement of the tail observed.

Sixth day. Yolk sac very considerably changed, and contracting towards a point at the lower end. Other blood passages clearly perceptible.

denly, with a singular and irresistible instinct to hide under something.   If they do not find anything in the troughs to get beneath, they all try to hide under each other.

From this moment they are never at rest day nor night, but, gathering together in large bodies, will seek some dark corner, and pass their whole existence in one incessant and ineffectual struggle to get under each other and out of sight.   In this struggle they crowd together in swarms, like bees.   I have often seen a solid writhing mass of them, over half an inch deep, which could almost be covered with the hand, and which could not have numbered less than ten thousand.*

This instinct to hide is so strong that they will dive head first, with all their might, into the gravel, and insinuate themselves into holes and chinks where you would think it impossible for anything to get, and where sometimes they can never get out again. Then woe to the little creatures if there are chinks

Seventh day. Bodies acquiring decidedly more solidity. Sac more pointed.

Eighth day. Fish decidedly harder, darker, and firmer fleshed. The herding-together instinct shows itself for the first time to-day.

* It has been thought by some that this crowding together is hurtful, but I never knew a single fish to be injured by it, though I have sometimes turned more than twenty thousand in together at this stage. Contrary to some authorities, I keep the alevins in shallow water and a strong ripple. If they were in deep water with a slow current, I think there might be danger of injury from excessive crowding.

or holes in the hatching troughs where they can so entrap themselves, for they will certainly do it. The instinct is so ceaseless that it seems to drive them on farther and farther, without any thought of turning back. I have seen a thousand at a time white and dead with suffocation under a pane of glass in the hatching trough, whither this instinct had pushed them on and on to this fatal termination. Here arises a serious objection to the use of hatching troughs with uncemented glass linings. The glass prevents the growth of fungus to some extent, it is true, but there is always danger of the alevins getting under the glass and becoming suffocated, as in the case just mentioned; and so invincible is their instinct to do this, that they will constantly try to return under the glass, even when they are just taken out white and almost dead with suffocation. If, however, the reader should happen to use loose glass linings, or any lining or hatching bed of any kind which the young creatures can get behind or under, he is here cautioned to examine every day, and see if any are hidden in dangerous places, and, if so, to liberate them at once It is true that after the eggs are all hatched the linings can be taken out, but as this is so difficult to do, without burying some of the fish under the gravel, and as it also releases the fungus behind the glass upon the young trout, the remedy is almost as bad as the disease; and besides this, it is no remedy at all for the earlier-hatched alevins, which must necessarily be exposed to the danger some time before the glass is ready to be taken out.

And while the patent charcoal troughs can be had,
it is not necessary. This irresistible instinct, which
drives the alevins past all obstacles to secure a hiding-
place, does not seem surprising, when we reflect that
it is the *only* instinct, as well as the only means of
self-preservation, which these very clumsy and perfectly
helpless creatures have to protect themselves against
their myriads of enemies.

Up to the time when the first half of the yolk-sac
period is passed, there is not much danger of loss,
except from the little creatures' getting suffocated as
just described, because they remain at or near the
spot where they were born, and do not roam about
much. But after the first half of this stage is over, a
new instinct makes its appearance, and it is accompanied with a new danger, which is both alarming and
insidious. This second instinct of the trout is to follow a current of water wherever they can find it;
usually, but not always, following the current up
stream, and diving into any corners, however small,
where their delicate perceptions detect the entrance
or exit of a current of water. Then woe to the trout
breeder if his troughs are not perfectly tight! for if
there is a loose joint in the box, or a nail-hole or aperture under or about the screen where water comes in
or out, these little creatures will be sure to find it,
and one by one will go through it in thousands, even
if the crevice is not much larger than would admit a
snow-flake. If a beginner were told how small a
crevice a six weeks' trout will go through, and has
gone through, he would say it was simply incredible.

Great vigilance is now required; and wherever there is a suspected place, a fine wire screen should be placed below it to catch any that escape. I once noticed a drop or two of water trickling from the head of one of my hatching troughs, and immediately placed a large screen under it. Two days afterwards I found nearly a thousand young trout on the screen, although I did not then, and could never afterwards, discover any hole for them to get through. The wire netting at the regular outlet should also be particularly watched, as the constant cleaning of the screen wears out the wire, and may make a fracture in it before it is suspected.

The trout at this age are the incarnation of perversity. They will go just the opposite way from which you want to have them, and if there is any place where you do not want them to go, they will be sure to collect in it in vast numbers, and when you try to drive them away they will dive their heads into the gravel and stick to the spot with a truly wonderful tenacity; or if you succeed in forcing them off a little way, they will return with redoubled momentum, and charge again and again, with a persistency which is as surprising as it is annoying. As the tissue of their structure is such an exceedingly delicate one that they cannot be pushed forcibly, even with a feather, they would be very difficult to manage if you wished to have them leave any particular spot where they had gathered, were it not for the knowledge of one instinct that they have. This instinct is to avoid agitated water. They have a great dislike to troubled waters, and will usually leave with one accord any spot where the water is violently disturbed, and if they have had a good stirring up will not generally return to it soon again. Therefore, when you wish to drive them out of a hole or corner, agitate the water violently with a feather, or, better yet, dip up a few cups of water and pour into the corner from a little height above. The effect will be magical. In a few moments the place which it might have taken half an hour to clear otherwise will be willingly deserted.

Though so very frail at this stage, the alevins will stand the cold wonderfully. I have frozen them several times so that they were glued tight on to the ice and could not stir, and in most instances it did not seem to hurt them at all. I have taken pains to keep these "frozen thaws" by themselves, where they could be watched for some weeks afterwards. In some instances they appeared as well as any trout of their age, and showed no signs of being injured by the freezing.

If, however, they are frightened while they are freezing in or thawing out, they will, in trying to extricate themselves from their icy fetters, tear themselves so that they will afterwards die.

Alevins will also live a long while without change or aeration of the water, if the temperature is low. A hundred young alevins will live a day or two in a gill of water at 34°, incredible as it seems. This is consequently a very favorable time to transport them. As they can stand the cold, you can, by reducing the water to a very low temperature with ice, send them a great distance in small bulk without change or aeration of water.

The alevins are also very hardy, as respects general causes of sickness or injury in their every-day life. If you have run a good ripple of water over the eggs when hatching, and have kept it up with the young fish after hatching, your loss in the yolk-sac stage will be very slight indeed, sometimes almost nothing.

A few will die in the act of emerging from the shell, and some will have what, for want of a better name, might be called the *blue swelling*,* which is fatal ; but with these exceptions you will lose very few indeed from disease during the yolk-sac period.

Some will be born with curved spines, or with two heads or two vertebral columns, but they are likely to live until the feeding period. It may be well to add here, that now is the time to collect any monstrosities that you may wish to preserve in spirits, such as double-headed fish, double-bodied fish, and the like. The perfectly formed fish are the most beautiful and most curiously formed in reality ; but you will probably want to preserve some of the misshapen freaks of nature, nevertheless, and now is the time to do it. In this instance there is no cruelty, in it, as these deformed creatures would all die a lingering death before long, if left to themselves. I never knew any of the misshapen fish to grow up, except those whose spines, after a curve or apparent joint, *resume*, or nearly resume, the original line of the vertebra. These will sometimes grow up and do well, even where there are two deflections or joints in the back. I sent one of that description to market year before

* Green calls it the " dropsy."

last that was three years old, which, from having a dark skin and a crook in his back, my friends had nicknamed the " Black Crook."

The alevin stage is, on the whole, the easiest time for the trout breeder of the trout's whole life ; and if everything is right at the outset when the eggs hatch, the alevins will be almost no trouble at all.

At this stage there are no eggs to pick over, no mouths to feed, not much care as to the amount of water supply, and none of the anxiety about their lives which comes a little later. This rest in the cares and labors of the trout raiser, however, is only the lull before the storm. No sooner is this stage over, and the trout get well to feeding, than work and danger begin again, as will be seen in the next chapter.

CHAPTER IV.

REARING THE YOUNG FRY.

Section I. — Progress of the Young Fry, and General Directions.

WE have now come to the most perplexing and the most inscrutable of all the branches of trout raising, namely, growing the young fry. How to hatch the eggs, which would hatch themselves if simply let alone by their enemies, was a problem comparatively easy in its solution, although this was a grand achievement at first, and reflects great credit on those who pioneered it through, the more because it was success in hatching the eggs that first popularized the art of fish culture and laid the foundations of the present wide-spread interest in it. But to make the young trout live, which have equally delicate and more complex organizations than the eggs, to find them the food which is wholesome for them, while it is wholly artificial, to anticipate wants which are not even known, to discover derangements of organs, when the organs themselves are microscopic, and to avert diseases without a glimpse of their causes, — in short, to make creatures live, so frail that a touch will almost kill them, and that seem to die without a cause, — this was a field of study apparently so obscure and intangible that it presented great difficulties.

Here the triumphant skill which hatched the eggs successfully was baffled; and it seemed for a time as if the wonderful art which had promised so much was to come to a stand-still at this gulf between the eggs and the yearling trout, a gulf which seemed as if it could not be bridged.

Those who made the earliest practical experiments in this country will undoubtedly recall, with me, the anxiety which was at one time felt lest the difficulties of bridging this chasm would prove insurmountable. This task has, happily, now been performed. Rearing young trout is no longer a problematical thing, it is a *fait accompli.*

The question is not now, Can young trout be raised? but How many can do it, and under what circumstances can it be done successfully?

As the yolk sac wears off, the dense masses of little alevins begin to separate, and assume a more individual existence. They seek to avoid, rather than to crowd, one another, and their fins being developed sufficiently, they can now rise and balance themselves in the water. The awkward, unwieldy body has acquired the graceful, symmetrical form of a fish, and each individual, taking a place for himself, heads vigorously up stream, and soon shows by his movements that he is on the lookout for food.

I have noticed that it is almost always a matter of anxiety to beginners how they will know when it is time to begin to feed the young fry. This anxiety is wholly unnecessary, because when the trout are ready to feed, they will let you know it plainly enough by taking the food which you offer them.

You need not give yourself any trouble about the matter, till you see them all up in the water, balancing themselves nicely, and heading bravely against the current. If you now throw in a little food, or any fine particles, indeed, of anything whatever, they will, if they are ready to eat, instantly turn out of line to seize the particles floating by them.

If they do this, you may know that it is time to feed them. If they pay no attention to what they see in the water, let them go for that day, and try them again the next, and so on, till they leave their places to snatch it, and from that time feed them regularly every day. Once will be enough the first day, twice the second, and, after that, four times a day for two months. From this time they should be fed two or three times daily until cold weather. I think the best food for them at first is liver, and curd made from sour milk, mixed in about equal proportions, or, still better, with two parts liver and one part curd. The young fish at this age, as may be supposed, can take only the finest particles of food. The curd, therefore, should be made as fine grained and moist as possible. The liver should also be reduced to the smallest possible particles. This is accomplished in various ways, but the way that I have found the most satisfactory and the most expeditious is to grate the liver on a common tin lemon-grater or cheese-grater. You must be careful to have the holes small enough at first to admit only very fine particles ; they should not be over one tenth of an inch in diameter.

The grater should be placed horizontally on a piece

of board or marble slab, and the liver grated on it; what goes through will for the most part be fine enough for the fish to eat. There are other ways of preparing the liver, I am aware; but you can prepare as much this way in ten minutes, as by any other method that I know of in half an hour. It was formerly thought best to feed the liver and curd to the fish through a small fine screen, so that no particles should fall to the bottom and remain unconsumed because of being too large, but since the discovery of the use of earth in absorbing the foul matter collecting on the bottom this precaution is unnecessary; still there is no objection to it, except that it is not so simple and makes more work.

The method of feeding adopted at the Cold Spring trout ponds is to mix the curd and prepared liver on a small paddle, say eighteen inches long and three wide at the blade, with a common case-knife, taking care to pulverize and separate the particles with the knife very thoroughly. The blade is then dipped in the water and the food moistened. It is then mixed and pulverized still more with the flat blade of the knife, very much as a glazier mixes putty, or a painter his paint, on a pallet. When sufficiently moistened and separated, to prevent any adhesion of the particles the paddle is again dipped in the water, and little by little the food is washed off, till the fish have had enough. When you first make your appearance, the fish, whether from playfulness or from actual fear, will dart away and try to get out of sight, but the presence of the food in the water will soon attract them again, and they will swarm around it from all quarters. If you have plenty of time and patience, and not too many fish, you can collect them all in one or two places, by waiting for them to come up; but if you have a great many and need to be expeditious, you will probably resort to feeding more rapidly and in several places. You can begin feeding, if you like, with the yolk of eggs, boiled a half-hour and pulverized very fine. This is sometimes more convenient and accessible, when you have only a few fish, than the liver and curd feed, and some persons continue to use the egg for several months; but this is not recommended. It is more expensive, it makes the worst possible corruption when it does sink to the bottom and foul the water, and I think it is not so wholesome or nutritious as a mixed meat and curd diet. Liver alone answers very well, but neither egg nor curd alone will do. It would be a great improvement, in the way of feeding the young fry, if you could prepare some self-acting contrivance, which would feed out the required amount of food gradually and continually all day, as, for instance, a closed box of fine wire netting, partly filled with food and placed under a fall, in such a way that the water will force out the food, little by little, all day. The box should be made so that it could be taken apart and the netting thoroughly washed and cleaned every day, as otherwise it would soon become so foul as to be injurious. Such a contrivance would save a great deal of time and trouble in feeding, and seems to be a more natural and wholesome way than to gorge them at intervals of three or four hours, and keep them in abstinence the rest of the time. When the young fry have eaten enough is a question not easily settled, although it has been asked very many times. I used to think that they would not eat too much, and I cannot now say that I ever knew of an instance of a death caused directly by over-eating ; and, as a general thing, I still think there is more danger of not feeding enough, than of feeding too much. On the other hand, overfeeding may *possibly* increase the liability to disease, when the fish are very much crowded. I do not believe that when there is plenty of room and water, they will ever eat enough to hurt themselves ; but when you have many confined in a small space, I would advise the exercise of some caution about overfeeding.

The most destructive instance of the ravages of disease in my experience was with the best-fed trout I ever had. The contents of two boxes, twenty thousand young fry, were attacked by parasites, which swept them all off in one week. On Monday morning they were the most robust and best-fed trout I had ever seen of their age, and on Saturday night the whole twenty thousand were dead. No others were attacked. I do not know that overfeeding had anything to do with the appearance of the parasites. I only mention the coincidence for the benefit of future observers, and would add that I think that over-crowding the fish had much more to do with their death than overfeeding. As a rule then, I repeat, you need not be afraid of the young fry's eating too much.

Their digestive organs are wonderfully active, and they will digest* almost as fast as you can feed them, and you will need a good deal of patience to feed till they refuse to eat. I never knew any healthy young fry of mine to decline eating but once, and then I had them fed incessantly for two hours, at the end of which time they gave up beaten. The young fry will repay you well for feeding them well, for there is hardly any creature which shows the effects of good feeding so quickly and strikingly as young trout. They appear sometimes to grow, almost like flies, on ample allowance, and one or two good meals will make a hungry young trout seem to double his bulk, and this is not wholly an illusion either. But although they are not likely to eat too much, they will not only at this age, but at all ages, take too large pieces of food at a time, and will sometimes kill themselves in this way. When you find a trout dead, with his head much swollen laterally, and both eyes forced outwards, you may know that he killed himself by bolting his food.

We have said nothing so far in this chapter about removing the young fry from the hatching troughs, and, indeed, this removal is not necessary for a week or two. The young fry will do as well in the hatching troughs, if the water is raised an inch or two, as anywhere else at first, but they must be *thinned out* very soon after they begin to feed. If you engage in

---

* Bertram compares the digestion of some fishes' stomachs to the action of fire. Harvest of the Sea, p.

Lyman says of pickerel, that they are " mere machines for the assimilation of other organisms." Mass. Fisheries, Report, 1871, p. 17.

the business of selling young fry, this thinning out will come naturally in the course of your sales, and will need no special attention; but if you do not sell them off, you must take out enough from each box or trough to leave only a safe number together. The number which it is safe to leave in a given space you must learn by experience, as so much depends upon the water supply, the character and temperature of the water, and other circumstances, that the number cannot be set with much definiteness for all places. You need not, however, be afraid to keep two hundred to the square foot, if they are shaded, till the first of May. By that time they will be ready for their summer quarters. You will notice that the young fry in the troughs, soon after beginning to feed, will seem to divide into two bodies, one consisting of the larger and stronger ones, at the head of the trough just below the fall, and the other consisting of the smaller and weaker ones settling down towards the outlet screen.

The division into these two classes will be maintained with more or less distinctness through the year and afterwards. The cause of the separation is, that some are really weaker and smaller than others, and these will avoid the more violent water and the presence of the larger ones, who would drive them away if they tried to stay with them. This division of the two classes becomes more marked as they get a little older, because the weaker ones are driven back and are obliged to take the food, the water, and the range that is left them by their superiors, who are all the time getting the lion's share of everything. The effect, of course, is to increase the contrast more and more every day. This effect can, however, be offset, in some degree, by taking pains to give better care and feed to the lower ones, and this should always be done. Indeed, by feeding the lower ones more than usual, and neglecting the upper ones, you can bring them somewhat together in point of locality, though never in point of size. I think that it is also a good way to take out all the lower division, and put them in an enclosure by themselves. They will never be as large fish as the others, but they will then, at any rate, be freed from the tyranny of the larger ones, and will improve correspondingly.

You may notice, too, that sometimes some of the lower young fry get against the screens, and perhaps die from the effect of it. *There is no need whatever of this.* If they get against the screens, it is because they are weak, and you may know that their weakness has come either from their being too much crowded, too little fed, or from being actually sick. The remedy for the first and second is obvious ; and the third case ought not to have occurred ; but in all three cases more feeding will bring them up. They are weak, and need to be fed to be made strong again. Therefore, when the little creatures get against the screens, or show a tendency that way, feed them more, and continue doing so till they come up strong again. Do not turn down the water, as is sometimes done, when they are weak and get against the screens, for this only makes them weaker ; but keep the water on, unless it was too violent to begin with, and make the fish come up against it by feeding, which they will do if not sick or too crowded.

There is a little trick which should be practised on them when they show this tendency to collect too much at the lower screen. It is well known that trout seek the deeper places and darker bottoms of any shallow stream. By taking advantage of this instinct, you can make most of your trout stay where you wish ; so when they collect too far down the trough, fill up the lower end about half an inch or an inch deep for a foot or so from the screen with light-colored sand. This will make the water more shallow here, and the bed of the trough of a lighter shade, and the fish will abandon it at once for deeper and darker places farther up stream. The force of the current is now, of course, increased near the outlet by this change, and an inexperienced person might suppose that if the young fry were collected down near the screen in slow water, they would be carried down much more by swift water. But this is an error. If the fish are not sick, their desire to get out of the shallow, exposed place will make them stem the current till they find a place above it less objectionable to them. The worst possible thing you can do, if you want to keep the young fry away from the screens, is to make the water slower by deepening it at the screen. It has just the opposite effect from that which is sought.

For the first two or three weeks after beginning to feed, — we are now supposing that the young trout remain in the hatching troughs, — the appearance of things is very bright. Indeed, there is no more hopeful time in the trout breeder's year than that when the young fish just get to feeding well. The dangers and hardships of the long winter's hatching are over. He has a fine lot of healthy, thriving trout. They feed well, they look well, and do not show a sign of a possibility of their dying. Everything goes on swimmingly, and unless he is more than human, or less, he will invariably draw the flattering picture to himself of what these thousands of tiny things will be three summers hence, each weighing a half-pound apiece or more. It is certainly an elating prospect.

But behold, at the end of about three weeks, an appalling change comes over this happy vision. It comes on very unobtrusively in the beginning, and the first sign of it which you discover is merely the gathering of two or three fish in a corner where the water is stiller than the rest. On examination, you observe nothing unusual about them, except that, to use an expressive Dutch-Americanism, they appear " logy,"* avoid the running water, and eat languidly, or perhaps do not eat at all. This seems a very trifling circumstance ; but to an experienced eye it is startlingly significant, for it is sure to be the forerunner of wholesale disaster. The next day the number of disaffected ones will be increased to a dozen, perhaps, and very likely some of them will be heading down stream. This number will steadily increase. Soon they will begin to drop down dead, by ones and twos

* From the Dutch *log*, dull, stupid.

at first, and then by dozens, then by hundreds, and, unless some remedy is applied, seventy-five per cent will die the next month, and perhaps all ; and many of them — we are still supposing that they have remained in the hatching troughs — will have a little round ulcer just on the top of the skull, which, when pricked, will discharge a thin, watery fluid. This is the stage, I take it, where Green's book says of their dying, that the cause is not known, nor the remedy. I must disagree with him. The cause is known, and the remedy is known also. The cause of this mortality is twofold. In the first place, the food which has been given them has to some extent, however carefully it may have been fed out to them, fallen to the bottom, and has formed a thin layer over the gravel, which has now had time to become putrescent and has fouled the water with its exhalations.

In the second place, the diet upon which the fish have been kept, although the best known and very nutritious, is deficient in some element indispensable to the health of the trout. It is like the experiment of feeding the dog wholly on olive oil, — the most nutritious thing in the world, — but which soon brings on an ulcerating disease that kills him in not many weeks. *The remedy for both these causes of disease is the free application of common earth, and it is a certain and effective one.*

I was led to this discovery somewhat in this way : I found my young fry dying by thousands, as just described, and those that were left losing their appetites and avoiding the current. I felt sure that the fine, thin film of mouldy matter which could be seen on the bottom was fouling the water, and I removed the fish to clean the troughs. This revived them somewhat, and they began to eat again, but they lacked their natural vivacity and looked lank and ill-favored. I then began to reflect carefully on the matter, and it occurred to me that their artificial food might be wanting in some tonic element, indispensable to health, and that liver and curd and nothing else might be to trout what olive oil and nothing else was to the dog. The symptoms certainly indicated it.

I might have got no farther, but I noticed that some of the young fry, which by accident happened to be where the mud was occasionally disturbed, did better and appeared thrifty. I also remembered that the wild trout in the natural brooks are never so lively and voracious as just after the streams have been muddied by a shower. Then it suddenly flashed upon me, that mud or earth, with its multiplicity of constituents, might possibly contain the deficient element. At the same time, I remembered the great absorbing power of earth, which might perhaps absorb the foul exhalations from the bottom, at the same time that it supplied the needed tonic.

I shared the common prejudice against muddying the water where the trout were ; but the crisis was an imperative one, and I determined to solve the problem. I poured in earth, enough to cover the bottom half an inch, making the water so thick with mud that every fish was obscured with it. I watched anxiously for the water to clear, to see how they came out of it.

K

The effect was magical. It had revived the mall. A change for the better was decidedly noticeable at once. In twenty-four hours the sick ones were nearly themselves again, and in two days they were all better fish than they ever were before.

On another occasion large numbers of my young fry had become sickly and were failing rapidly. They had begun to collect against the screens, and there was evidently a bad time coming very soon. This was on the 5th of March. This time they had been feeding only about two weeks. I applied the earth plentifully, with the same effect as before. On the 7th they were much improved. On the 8th they were all well again and off the screens. Earth or mud is the last thing one would suppose suitable for a fish, so associated in our minds with pure, clean water ; yet it is an indispensable constituent in the diet of young trout, and unless they get it, either naturally or artificially, they will not thrive. I repeat once more, we are supposing the young fry to be in the hatching troughs still, and supplied with water from the spring. Of course, if they are nourished with brook-water, which brings down more or less mud with it, this disease will not break out, and the fish will not require the artificial introduction of earth ; but they must get it in some way, and unless it is already in the water, it must be furnished artificially, or the fish will languish.*

I am not prepared to say what kind of earth is the

---

* I have sometimes found the stomach of a wild trout nearly half full of gravel.

best, but I think that the earth from just under a tolerably rich sod is as good as any, if not better. It is a very good way to put the whole sod in the trough or box. The fish will get off of it what they want, and the presence of the vegetable growth in the water is favorable to their health.

Muck I have sometimes thought the best, and it is said to be the most powerful of earth absorbents, but I have also had misgivings that the muck sometimes had something injurious in it. It may be only a fancy, however. At all events, the earth just under a fresh green sod answers the purpose, and is good and wholesome. The application of the earth should be renewed as often as the fish seem to require it, and, indeed, it is best not to wait till they show signs of wanting it, but to give it to them often, and keep sods in all the time; and whenever you perceive anything in the troughs that is likely to foul the water, throw a handful of earth over it.

If you have a pride in keeping a clean gravelly bed to your troughs, you can cover over the earth, after a day or so, with clean gravel, and it will look as well as before; but you must give them earth again soon.

As the spring advances the young fry will continue to grow, and one day's routine in taking care of them will be very much like another through the summer. This does not imply, however, that the work is monotonous or dull. On the contrary, it is exceedingly interesting, and the more closely you observe them the more interesting the care of them becomes. You will learn to distinguish individuals from one another, and to notice individual peculiarities ; and it will be a source of great pleasure to see them growing daily in strength and stature, and taking on by almost imperceptible degrees the ways and appearance of mature trout. Indeed, you cannot spend an hour or so a week more profitably than by studying the little fellows minutely, with your eyes as close to the surface of the water as you can get. This is the way to study them ; and if you want to obtain an insight into the nature of trout, and have signal success in raising them, this is the thing to do.

The young fry in their growth probably will not keep pace with your wishes at first. Still they are really growing rapidly, and if their apparently slow progress makes you impatient, take out one of them any time in the summer and compare it with one of your preserved specimens of a day old. You will be gratified with the contrast, and will see that they have doubled their size many times over, though they had appeared to remain nearly stationary. They are also getting their flesh hard and solid, as you may see by taking out a four weeks' trout on a piece of board or glass and letting it dry, and doing the same again in the summer with a six months' trout. The first specimen will leave hardly more than an impression of the fish's form, as thin as tissue. The second will show solidity as well as figure.

The young fry will continue to grow and require more food until winter sets in. In the mean while they will demand constant watching and care, the nature of which will be described more fully in the next chapter, and also in the one on the diseases of young trout.

Section II.—What to do to make Young Trout live.

1. *Have healthy, well-fed breeders.* When a young trout drops down dead during the first few months of his life, a beginner is apt to think that the cause originated the same day or the same week, which is as unphilosophical as to suppose that deaths among the human race, resulting from feeble constitutions or hereditary consumption, were caused by something that happened the day or the week on which the death occurred.

To discover and remove the causes of death among young trout, we must go back of the young fish's life, back of the eggs themselves, to the breeders which produced the eggs. This is self-evident, and yet it is often overlooked. In order to have healthy fry, you must have healthy eggs. To secure healthy eggs, you must have healthy, well-fed breeders. The progeny of puny, half-starved, half-suffocated fish cannot be as strong and healthy as those of well-grown, well-fed fish, with plenty of range and water. Therefore, if you want your young trout to live, give your breeders a good supply of water, feed them well and regularly, and keep them in good condition, especially from May to November.

Large eggs, on the whole, are better than small ones. They produce larger fish; and, other things being equal, the larger fry, it is observed, thrive better than the smaller ones.

Now the secret of getting large eggs is not to use large-sized breeders, for a two-pound brook trout produces no larger eggs than a half-pound brook trout, though they are more in number. Large eggs are the result of keeping the breeders in water that warms up in the spring and summer. It is true, if it becomes too warm, say above 70°, it is injurious; but water that stands at 65° in the summer will make larger eggs than water at 55°, and very cold spring water, say at 45°, will always develop small eggs. The reason is obvious. We know the rule is throughout the animal kingdom, that warmth, when not extreme, favors growth, and as the temperature of the fish's body corresponds to the temperature of the water,* it naturally results that the eggs developed in the warmth of 65° will be larger than those developed at the cold point of 45°.

2. *Develop strong and healthy embryos in the egg.* You must not suppose, when you find your trout dying in April and May, that the mortality is necessarily caused by something that has happened since they hatched. The causes may date back half-way through the period of incubation or more. I have seen trout embryos with the eye-spots just appearing, which I knew could not live three months after coming out, although they hatched like other eggs, and seemed like

* The temperature of the fish's body follows the temperature of the surrounding water, but keeps a little, perhaps two degrees, above it.

other trout for weeks. The reason was, that they were sickly and feeble embryos, which had not vitality enough in them to grow up.

In order to have strong and healthy trout that will live, you must have strong and healthy embryos to begin with. This is so obvious, that it seems trivial to mention it. Yet I have seen persons treat eggs in such a way that the fish from them could not possibly live to grow up, and wonder three months afterwards what made them die. To insure strong and hardy embryos, the suggestions in the chapter on hatching eggs should be carefully observed. The eggs should not be crowded too much. They should have plenty of water, though not too much, running over them. This water should be in constant circulation. The two kinds of fungus, alga and byssus, should be absolutely excluded. All sediment should be kept from the eggs, and, in the writer's opinion, they should be hatched in the dark. If you observe these rules, you will have strong and healthy trout from your eggs, and of these rules I should say that the most important are, to avoid fungus and still water.

3. *Provide a suitable place for the young fry when they begin to feed.* We remarked that the hatching troughs would do very well for the young trout for the first few weeks after feeding. This is true, if the fish are thinned out sufficiently, and a clean layer of gravel or sand put over the winter hatching bed ; but the hatching troughs are not favorable to growth, and usually are not so convenient for feeding as other places in which the fish might be kept. It is therefore

desirable to change them before summer, and it is very important to put them in a suitable place when they *are* changed ; and to effect this the following points should be secured, namely : —

The young trout, when removed from the hatching troughs, should be kept, —

Where they will feed well.

Where they will be safe from their natural enemies.

Where nothing can get in and nothing can get out.

Where no fungus can come to them.

Where the water cannot run over.

Where they cannot remain permanently out of sight.

Where the water supply cannot be cut off by accident.

Where the fish can have new, unused water.

Where they can find shade.

Where there is plenty of room.

The first six points were fully unfolded in the chapter on rearing boxes ; so I will here simply refer the reader to that chapter, and pass on to the consideration of the remaining points.

It is essential that the young fry be kept where there is no possibility of the water supply being cut off, even by the most unexpected accident. It is the *possibility* that you want to guard against, not the *probability*. My excuse for mentioning so obvious a principle is, that persons are so careless about this very thing. Though they may have expended hundreds of dollars to get their fish where they are, and have taken pains to have everything else safe, they will sometimes leave a faucet or a spout in such a way that it is quite possible for some accident to close the faucet or misplace the spout, and cut off the whole supply of water from the fish below.

I recall now several instances in which most disastrous results have been so caused. This point is the more important, because the consequences of neglect are so very fatal ; in the hot weather, when the young fry are being raised, two hours without change of water being often sufficient to kill a whole box or pond full.

They should be kept where new, unused water will run over them. This is very important. At first, when they begin to feed, the effete matter coming from them is very slight in quantity, and harmless ; but it rapidly increases with the growth of the fish, and becomes a prolific source of impurity and disease, as can be easily comprehended when it is considered what the amount must be from one thousand to ten thousand fish feeding almost hourly.

The water, therefore, that is used for the nursery, should be fresh from the spring or brook, and should not be that which has run over other trout above, un less the stream has run far enough to purify itself.

The place in which they are kept should be well shaded. Sunlight fosters the growth of fungi and confervæ, and predisposes the young fish to some of the diseases to which they are subject ; and when disease breaks out it makes bad matters worse. The young fry should be therefore guarded against it, as well as the eggs. Shade never killed a trout yet, young or old. Sunlight has killed a great many. It cannot be denied that trout often come out voluntarily into the sun, but they should nevertheless always be placed so

8

that they can take their choice, and not be obliged to stay in the sun because there is no shade.

Their place of confinement must not be too much crowded. Be very careful to guard against this, and do it in season. It is very injurious to keep young trout too close together. They will not grow as well. The water breathed over so many times becomes vitiated; the foul matter thrown off by the fish increases the evil; and in time disease will break out among them, and rage all the worse because of the very thing that caused it, namely, the overcrowding.

Anything which combines all the points above mentioned will answer for a nursery for the young fry, whether it is a pond, or trough, or rearing box, or what not.

I recommend the use of a rearing box, because it *does* embrace these points. Anything else that does will answer as well, but it will be a rearing box still, either on a large scale or a small one. It is the combination of *principles* which makes the rearing box, and not its name, or form, or material. It should be added here, that is a good plan to keep water plants* in the nurseries of young fish. I will not say that it is indispensable, but I think it is very important indeed.

Trout consume oxygen, and return carbon. Water-plants consume carbon, and return oxygen. By putting plants and fish together, therefore, we avail ourselves of one of nature's great universal agencies in balancing vital forces against each other, and main-

---

* For list of water plants suitable for trout ponds, see Appendix III. p. 275.

taining the equilibrium on which the continuance of organic life depends.* This is a good *a priori* reason in itself. Besides this, we have the facts that the plants do in practice improve the water, prevent disease, give shelter to the young fry, and furnish more or less natural food for them. They also absorb much of the feculence of the fish for nutriment.†

The larger the young fry grow, the larger the place they can be trusted in ; and it is never desirable to keep them in a smaller place than perfect safety requires ; for the more range they have, other things being equal, the better they will do. Accordingly, as they continue to grow, increase their range, and by the 1st of September or a little later, when they take their food like old trout, that is, spring for it from their lair and whirl, they can be put into a pond suitable for larger trout, and treated very much as the larger trout are treated. By this time they are much hardier, and less susceptible to invisible sources of injury ; they do not stay away alone and get lost, they are better able to take care of themselves ; you can throw them their food very much as you do the larger fish, and they can

---

* Self-preserving aquaria have been contrived by lining the sides and bottom of a tank with the most oxygen-giving water plants, so that the fish (*not trout*) confined in them have lived without a change of water. I am told by a gentleman who has had experience with Barnum's aquaria, that the fish kept in these self-preserving tanks without change of water thrived better than those in the ordinary tanks which had water running through them all the time.

† The introduction of fresh-water snails accomplishes the same end, but snails are destructive to fish eggs and very young fish.

be trusted in a trout pond proper. The pond, how-
ver, must be covered, and the fish must still be protected from rats, minks, snakes, and especially herons
and kingfishers, which will destroy great quantities of
them, if allowed to.

4. *Take good care of the fish.* Now, having bred
from a healthy stock, and having developed strong,
healthy embryos, and having provided a suitable place
for the young fry, only one thing more is required for
success, and that is to take good care of them.

If you take good care of trout, I think there are
ninety chances in a hundred that you will raise them.
I know that there is a good deal of scepticism (I beg
the reader to excuse the digression which follows)
about the practicability of keeping young fry alive
through the first six months of feeding, and I am
aware that some of the best authorities say that a considerable percentage will die unavoidably during that
time. Mr. Stephen H. Ainsworth, in a letter to the
writer, once said that a considerable percentage of the
eggs when impregnated were premature, and consequently produced an imperfectly developed fish which
could not live. Theodore Lyman, in the Report of the
Massachusetts Committee of Fisheries, 1870, says :
" All remained remarkably healthy till May, when a
certain number were observed to be weakly. It is
likely that they were *naturally* sickly, and, when the
yolk sac was gone, they had not enough vitality to
feed."* And Seth Green speaks in his book on trout
culture as if there were *necessarily* a great mortality

* Massachusetts Fisheries, Report, 1870, p. 33.

among the young fry, and says, " We don't know what is the matter with them, nor how to cure them."*

Now I wish at the outset to express distinctly my deference to authorities so high, — indeed, I know of none higher, — but I must, nevertheless, venture to disagree with them if they mean that there is any necessary inherent cause of death in the young fry which cannot be removed. Some will die, say five per cent, though it ought to be less than this, of weak constitutions. They are born into the world so weakly constituted that they cannot stand the wear and tear of life, and must die. I admit that there may be perhaps five per cent of these necessary, unavoidable deaths ; but that the rest come into being already doomed to premature death, or that young trout have any mysterious or *peculiar* inherent cause of death in them, any more than young calves, or pigs, or chickens, I do not believe. In the present state of information of the art, young trout fry may be more liable to accidents than other young domesticated creatures, and it may be more difficult to guard against their diseases ; but this is another thing. Careless breeding may, and careless hatching certainly will, produce a progeny of young trout of which ninety per cent will die ; but this is also another thing. Careful breeding and hatching will produce trout which are just as likely to live, in my opinion, as the same number of lambs or chickens ; and if the young fry die, it is not because of any mysterious, innate cause peculiar to them because they are trout, but it is because they

* Trout Culture, p. 42.

were killed, deliberately killed, by external causes, just as much as lambs or chickens are killed by storms, or by parasites, or from starvation or poison. It is true that they are killed from ignorance of their wants, and not from wilful neglect, but it is the same thing abstractly, — the cause of death is external and removable, and not innate and necessary. Their *wants* are peculiar, of course, and more occult and intangible than those of pigs and colts, and to a beginner it will sometimes seem as if they died without being diseased. But if they were as large as pigs and colts, and could be studied as easily, I do not think their wants would be found to be any more mysterious or peculiar ; and if the causes of disease could be magnified, so as to be observed and studied clearly, I think that no more trout would die when nothing was the matter with them.

I am furthermore convinced that study and experience will eventually clear up this subject, notwithstanding the difficulties which surround it, and that at some time it will be known how to raise trout, and make them live, as well as it is known how to raise turkeys and chickens. I believe that there are energy and intelligence enough now interested in the cause to accomplish this end. I take this ground, partly because any other is unphilosophical and uncomplimentary to the intelligence of those who are studying the art, and partly because the facts of experience confirm it. Who that sees the healthy young fry and yearlings and two-year-olds in Dr. Slack's ponds in New Jersey, or at Mr. Dexter's at West Barnstable, or Mr. Furman's on Long Island, can doubt that others can raise them in other places and make them live.

The beginner may accept these axioms in raising trout : —

1. No trout dies without a cause.

2. The causes of death are discoverable.

3. They can, in most instances, be removed.

My own experience has invariably been to confirm these principles. I lost in my apprenticeship days as many young fry as any one else ; but with every death, say over five per cent, there appeared a distinct assignable cause, present or remote, which could be removed or avoided next time ; and the more I lost the more I became satisfied that the causes of death among the young fry could be discovered and avoided.

My later experience has added confirmation to this opinion. And now, since I have used charcoal troughs and tanks altogether, deaths among the young trout have been, among some lots, rare occurrences, and in general have been no more frequent — over the five per cent weak ones — than among the yearlings and breeders.

In one charcoal trough, in particular, containing over five thousand, there was, in the season of 1870, less than one per cent of deaths from all causes in three months. It has been the same this year (1871). In one box of a thousand I have not taken out ten dead ones in three months. I attribute this in a great degree to the use of charcoal in hatching, but it confirms the theory just advocated, that the causes of death can be removed.

This has been a long digression, I know. I beg the reader to excuse it. I was saying that if you took good care of the young fish, hatched and provided for them as has been suggested, there were ninety chances out of a hundred that you would raise them. This remaining contingency, however, of *taking good care* of them, is no trifle. It involves constant vigilance and a very faithful attention to all the conditions upon which the life and growth of the young trout depend.

As any further directions as to the care of them would be a repetition of what has already been written, I will merely advise the beginner to be always on his guard against accidents and dangers ; to visit the fish the first thing in the morning, and the last thing at night ; to carry out Macbeth's resolution, " to make assurance double sure," even if it seems like taking a "bond of" *certainty*. And now, hoping that the reader will have the best of luck during this delicate period of the trout's career, let us pass on to the consideration of the unpleasant but important subject of the diseases of young trout.

SECTION III.— DISEASES OF TROUT FRY.

We are now come to the department of trout culture which is the least known, namely, the diseases to which young trout are subject. This is an almost untrodden field of study,* where little is known, and

* The art of raising horses and other domestic animals has

still less recorded. It is important, however, that this department should not be overlooked, partly because no art which has for its object the cultivation of any creature can be considered perfected without a knowledge of its diseases; and, especially, because the diseases of young trout are often clandestine in their operation and epidemic in their effect, so that, when the ravages of disease break out, they are peculiarly widespread and fatal, and rapid in their work.

I therefore venture, though with some timidity, to give the reader the little knowledge which I have gathered on the subject from observation of the trout under my care, with the hope that others will follow in the same path, and supplement my scanty notes with more valuable information; and I wish to say that I claim neither appropriateness in the names of the diseases mentioned in this chapter, nor perfect correctness in the diagnosis. I only give the plain result of my incidental observation, without pretending to great thoroughness or scientific knowledge of the subject.

The diseases and causes of death which have come under my notice among young fry are as follows:—

1. Fungus on the egg.
2. Partial suffocation of the embryo.
3. Strangulation of the embryo in hatching.
4. Seth Green's dropsy, or blue swelling.

books on their diseases, and we know where to go to find horse-doctors and dog-doctors and the like; but no book has been written on the diseases of young trout, and I suppose there never was in all the world such a thing as a fish-doctor.

5. Deformity at birth.
6. Fungus on the surface of the body.
7. Constitutional weakness.
8. Emaciation.
9. Starvation.
10. Ulcers on the head.
11. Animal parasites.
12. Fin disease.
13. Black ophthalmia.
14. Irritation of the optic nerve.
15. Inflammation of the gills.
16. Black gill fever.
17. Fatty degeneration of the vitals.
18. Spotted rash.
19. Strangulation by food.
20. Cannibalism, nibbling.
21. Overheating.
22. Suffocation.
23. Paralysis.

1. *Fungus on the egg.* This is the most insidious, the most devastating, and the most obnoxious of all the diseases of young trout, and the first in order of the causes of death. It blights the embryo in the egg. Once present in the water, it spreads unseen over all the eggs, and is sooner or later fatal. The effect of fungus has been already described in the chapter on Hatching the Eggs, p. 115. We mention it here again among diseases of trout fry, because it sometimes does not *kill* the eggs, but causes them to produce prematurely a weakly young fish, which usually dies before summer.

For causes, signs, and remedies of fungus, we refer the reader to the chapter on Hatching the Eggs, pp. 115, 116.

2. *Partial suffocation of the embryo.* It sometimes happens that the embryo will be partially suffocated a short time before the egg hatches, so that, although the embryo will be born alive, it will die soon after. The cause of this, of course, is not giving the eggs air enough, either from overcrowding them or not having enough circulation in the water. The remedies are obvious.

3. *Strangulation in hatching.* Sometimes the embryo dies just in the act of hatching. I have attributed it to the strangulation of the embryo by the shell of the egg. It may be from other causes. There is no remedy that I know of, and the instances of death from this cause are not numerous enough with trout to make it a very serious matter.*

4. *Seth Green's dropsy, or blue swelling of the yolk sac.* This is a very noticeable disorder among the alevin trout, and, being an affection of the yolk sac, is of course confined to them.

The sac becomes swollen to three times its usual size. The outer membrane shows very thin and transparent, is seen to be filled with a bluish liquid, and, when punctured, discharges a thin, watery fluid. Seth Green's book calls it the dropsy; it affects only a

* Mr. Parnaby, of Troutdale Fishery, England, says he has noticed this cause of death particularly in the char (*Salmo umbla*), and he attributes it to the tough shell of the char egg and the peculiarly round and full form of the yolk sac, which makes it more difficult for the char to liberate itself from the egg than for other fish.

few fish and is not contagious. I know of no special cause and *no* remedy. Green says the fish can be sometimes saved by tapping the sac and letting out the dropsical matter; but I doubt it, and think the disease is always fatal.

5. *Deformity at birth.* Some trout are born with curved spines, spiral spines, double heads, and with bodies more or less imperfect. The proportion of these to the whole is generally small, though the number of deformed spines will be made considerable by careless hatching. Unless the deformity is slight, the fish will not live long after feeding, although a double fish, with two distinct vertebral columns and separate tails, and united only at the sac, will survive for some time. If the deformity is trifling, they sometimes live. I have killed several grown-up trout with somewhat bowed and crooked backs. Careful hatching is the remedy for deformed spines, or rather the preventative.

6. *Fungus on the surface of the body.* This cause of mortality is distinct from fungus on the egg, as it attaches itself to fish hatched from perfect eggs. The fish usually get the fungus on them when quite young, by rubbing it off the sides of the box or pond in which they are confined. It sometimes floats down with the water and gets in their gills. It is always fatal, and usually very destructive. It cannot be too carefully guarded against. There is no remedy for the disease after it attacks the fish, unless it is salt water.* It can be prevented only by shutting off any possibility of

* See Appendix I.

fungus growing in the hatching troughs or coming into the water. This can be done by the use of carbonized troughs and aqueducts throughout.

7. *Constitutional weakness.* This is an evil which is the necessary lot, we suppose, of a certain proportion of all domesticated creatures that are born into the world. This proportion, in the case of domesticated trout, can be reduced very much by careful breeding and hatching; but there is, nevertheless, a limit as with other creatures, beyond which the causes lie too deep and too far back to be controlled. What the limit is with trout is not known. I think Mr. Ainsworth's opinion is, that the percentage of loss from this cause is very large with artificially taken eggs. I think it is much less, and with care in developing strong and healthy embryos need not be over five per cent. The constitutionally weak ones may be distinguished from the rest by being at birth thin, puny, undersized, and looking as if they never would come to anything. There is no help for them, but the number of them can be much reduced by care in the development of the embryo.

8. *Emaciation.* Many of the young fry are usually observed to wear away without any visible cause. They do not wholly decline food, but grow thinner and thinner every day, till at last they die.

This emaciation, although the *effect* of disease, is classed here among diseases, because the causes are not known. If sufficiently studied, the disorder would probably be found resolvable into some of the other diseases here mentioned. These attenuated fish may not always die, but I do not think them worth the trouble of raising. The best thing to do with them is to turn them out into a natural brook, and let them shift for themselves. They may come to something there. They never will in the nursery.

9. *Starvation.* This, Seth Green thinks, is a prolific cause of death among the very young fry, and it does not follow that they will escape because their keeper takes pains to feed them ; for, if confined in ponds of considerable size, they will often wander off where they can find no food, and from shyness and ignorance will not come up to take it when offered. The consequence is that they are soon carried against the screens, or drop down dead from exhaustion, forty-eight hours of fasting being enough to reduce very young fry to a state of extreme weakness.

I have often thought also, that, when very hungry, they will eat things which do not agree with them, and so hasten their death.

The remedy for the danger of starvation is to confine the trout where they will take their rations regularly and feed them faithfully. Then you will not lose any from this cause.

10. *Ulcers on the head.* This disease has already been mentioned in the chapter on growing young trout. It usually attacks the fish, if at all, when they are young, and always comes when the water gets foul from decaying food, and when the fish have no earth. Great numbers died of it before the use of earth as a remedy was discovered. As this disease progresses, the fish becomes lank in body, its head

swells and grows soft, and an ulcer appears on the top of the skull, which discharges a thin, watery fluid when punctured. It is not contagious, but always fatal. The remedy is found in prevention. It is to keep the water pure, and give the trout plenty of earth.

11. *Animal parasites.** This is a very alarming and destructive cause of death among the young fry, and all the more because the parasite attacks the best and fattest and healthiest fish. They come suddenly and unexpectedly, sometimes as early as the 1st of May, and first show themselves as a little bunch of whitish jelly-like matter on the back or sides of the fish, in most cases not far from the dorsal fin. At first the fish does not appear to mind it much, and feeds and remains in good condition for a day or two. But soon after he seeks an eddy where the water is still, refuses food, and dies within a week. This disease is fatal, and whether contagious or not, it is certain that whole boxes are attacked at once, and in the instances within my experience every fish was destroyed in ten days, none escaped; it is the most fatal and insidious disorder that I have encountered in raising young fry. The microscope which I used for examination revealed nothing but a gelatinous protuberance on the body of the fish. I have supposed it to be the eggs of some water insect floating in the water, but provided with the power of attaching itself to whatever it fell upon, like the eggs of perch

* See Appendix I. for account of another class of animal parasites, not discovered when this chapter was written.

and other fishes. I have therefore called it an animal parasite, though future observation may prove this to be incorrect. At first sight one would take it for the fungus, which is so common among injured fish ; but a little examination shows it to be quite different, affecting the fish differently, and, what is the worst feature about it, attacking perfectly healthy, uninjured trout; the largest and most promising being among the first of its victims. In my experience, the parasites have not, I think, originated always or usually in the enclosure where the fish were, but somewhere above in the stream, where they are generated, and whence they float down to where the fish are which they fasten upon. The fish that are affected cannot be saved, but the spread of the disease may be checked by prompt measures.

Therefore, as soon as the presence of this disease is discovered, take out the affected ones and throw them away. Then change all the others to a new place where you can depend upon the water, and lose no time in doing it.

12. *Fin disease.* At all stages of growth during the first six months, the fins of the young fish may sometimes be observed to be mutilated. Occasionally as many as one fourth of them will be found to be so affected. Sometimes the fins will be simply a little frayed at the edges, at other times the fin will be seen to be nearly gone, and will present a fungussy edge. The affected ones will usually gravitate towards the outlet screens, and will be the weaker and smaller ones of the lot, but occasionally a large and vigorous

one at the upper end will have a fin or two half gone. This disorder is not always fatal, by any means, for some will recover; but if either of the pectoral fins are nearly destroyed, or if fungus has set in, the trout will probably die.

One cause of this disease is the biting of other fish. Young trout, like cub bears, are irritable in their nature, and do not like to have others come too near them, but will snap and bite their companions when they show a disposition to crowd. The result is that their fins frequently get mutilated, and present the appearance just described. They show this irritableness especially when they are left unfed for a while and get very hungry, the hunger, perhaps, having a double agency in making them bite at each other. This unnecessary cause of the evil should at least be avoided. When you discover any young trout with injured fins, take them out and put them by themselves, where they have plenty of room, plenty of water, and plenty of. food. Some will die, perhaps half. With the others the fins will grow out again, and the trout in a few months be as well as ever.

13. *Black ophthalmia.* This is a strange disease. You sometimes observe a fish becoming very black and inclined to separate from the rest. He is somewhat emaciated, refuses food, and is less easily frightened than the others. If you examine his eyes, you will see that the tissue of the pupil is more or less destroyed and his eyesight much injured, which is the cause of his not being frightened at your approach.

The emaciation continues, the blackness of the skin increases ; the fish finally becomes totally blind and dies. I know of no cause or remedy, though I have noticed that more cases occur where the water has become somewhat foul, and once I thought a fish affected with this disorder recovered on being removed into better water, but I do not feel certain of it. The disease attacks young and old alike, and is not contagious.

14. *Irritation of the optic nerve.* Fishes, as is well known, have no eyelids to protect their eyes from excessive light. It is therefore a very serious thing to young fry, that have been used only to the dark, to be suddenly exposed to the glare of the sun ; and it sometimes happens that when they are so exposed, and cannot escape from the sunlight, their brains become hurt, they assume most unnatural positions and movements, and after darting about frantically, like crazy creatures, for a few moments, they die. I have supposed that the unaccustomed light produces an irritation of the optic nerve, and have so named it.

15. *Inflammation of the gills.* This corresponds to inflammation of the lungs in animals, and it is the result usually of crowding too many trout into too small a space, without a sufficient change of water. Their gills or lungs have too much work to do, and this, with breathing over the impure water, produces inflammation. It is a lingering disorder, more in that particular like consumption in higher orders. The affected fish may contrive to live for some time, and eat the same, but will not grow any ; they will become attenuated, and

finally die. I am inclined to think, however, that the disease is not always fatal, but that a change to pure water and plenty of it will often effect a cure. The application of earth in this disease seems injurious, rather than beneficial, probably owing to the irritating action of the sandy particles on the inflamed tissues. You can detect the disease before death by looking directly down on the fish from above. In a perfectly healthy fish the gill covers completely cover the gills, and shut down closely over them. In a sick fish the gill covers do not wholly conceal the gills, which are visible through the whole respiration of the fish, and appear swollen and inflamed. After death the fish looks so much like a perfectly healthy fish, that an inexperienced person would say there was not a mark of disease upon it. Deaths from this cause are very provoking to beginners, for the fish seems to them to die without any cause whatever.

16. *Black gill fever.* There is another disease of the gills, which is more rapid in its action, and to which I have given the above name because it seems to resemble a fever, and because the gills of the fish turn black. I have not had many cases of it myself, but I believe it is usually fatal ; others who have observed it think that it is contagious. I know of no remedy.

17. *Fatty degeneration of the vitals.* Sometimes when you examine a young trout that has died without a visible cause, you will find an abnormal accumulation of fat about the vitals, and nothing in the stomach. This is probably the cause of its death. There is, as

is well known, a corresponding disease among higher orders, called fatty degeneration of the heart. Dr. Slack of the Troutdale Ponds speaks of this disease among trout, and says that a constant diet of curd will produce it.

18. *Spotted rash.* I once gave an abundance of water-cresses (*Nasturtium officinale*) to a lot of young fry that had been kept wholly without vegetable food. In forty-eight hours their bodies were covered with brown spots, and within the next forty-eight hours most of the fish died. I cannot say for a certainty whether it was a rash coming from within, or a parasite coming from without. I have called it spotted rash for want of a better name, and have noted it for future observers. Whatever it is, it is certainly very fatal.

19. *Strangulation by food.* Trout of all ages will sometimes take too large pieces of food, which they cannot disgorge, and which they cannot swallow, and therefore get choked to death. You will see them in the pond with their eyes protruding, and head very much swollen laterally, and the offending morsel sometimes projecting from the mouth. The situation is usually fatal, but not always; they will sometimes recover, after having had a frightfully swollen head and eyes; sometimes you can save them by pulling the piece of food out of their throats.

20. *Cannibalism, nibbling.* This is a frequent cause of death among the young fry. Trout are cannibals; they will always eat each other, if they can, when they are hungry; and this can be taken as a rule, that a trout of any size, if hungry enough, will eat a trout of half its

length. A trout a foot long will eat a trout of six inches, or a trout two inches long will eat a trout an inch long. Cannibalism is something, too, which grows on trout; and after having once tasted flesh of their own kind, they, like human cannibals, prefer it, and, refusing their ordinary food, they will lie in ambuscade in holes and corners, where, feeding on their weaker fellows, they thrive and grow better than the rest. This makes the evil doubly mischievous, because from their new habit of hiding they are less likely to be discovered, and their increased rate of growth is daily putting a greater difference in size between them and their companions, and making them more formidable. Careful sorting is the remedy, together with regular feeding. If these rules are observed, there will not be much trouble or loss from the trout *eating* one another. But there is another form of cannibalism, which, though less repugnant, is more injurious, namely, nibbling. The young fry when they first feed are very voracious, and will nibble at the tails and fins of those in front of them, and, if allowed to get very hungry, will often do a great deal of injury in this way, especially if much crowded. The younger they are, the more they are given to the habit, but they finally outgrow it. The remedy is to give them regular feed and plenty of room.

21. *Overheating.* This simply means being kept in water that is not cold enough. As summer advances and the weather grows warmer and warmer, the water in your brook sometimes grows too warm for the trout to live in. If that is your coldest brook the

consequence is inevitable. The trout must die. This cause of death is trying, because you can see the trouble and know what is coming, but cannot help it. If you have colder water, remove the fish to it without delay, and take the first hours of the morning in which to do it, when the water is coolest; use ice in conveying them. If the heat is only exceptional, you can do some good by the use of ice placed in the inlet. I have saved some in that way; indeed, as long as the ice lasts you are safe, but it wastes very rapidly in running water, and therefore is often unavailable. The dangerous point of temperature lies somewhere between 70° and 85° Fahrenheit. I have known water to be fatal at 72° or 73°, and I have known trout to live in good vigorous water at 78°, but danger is near when the mercury begins to be above 70°.

22. *Suffocation.* This is simply the result of want of air, from the water having been breathed over too much. The cause and remedy are obvious. I will only say that the colder the water the slower trout breathe.

In case of suffocation, the fish should not be given up because it *appears* to be dead, for suffocated trout are often restored, even after life seems to be entirely extinct. The way to do this is to aerate the water in which they are contained as vigorously as possible. The effect is often very startling, as well as gratifying, in bringing to life fish that appeared dead.

In concluding this chapter on the diseases of young fry, I would recommend to the trout-breeder to examine his trout carefully every day, and to be always on the watch for the appearance of disease, and, when he detects its presence, to act promptly on the maxim in the beginning of Seth Green's work on fish culture, " Never put off till to-morrow what you can do to-day." The progress of disease among young trout is often so rapid, and so epidemic in its character, that you cannot be too vigilant in discovering it, or too prompt in suppressing it. I would add, also, that you must not suppose because none of your fry are dying that no disease is in progress, or that disease has just set in when the fish begin to die. On the contrary, in some instances the disease or offending cause may have been at work for weeks before the first fish actually dies from it. Therefore be vigilant and prompt in guarding against the first approach of evil.

23. *Paralysis.* There is still another disease to which young fry are subject, and I should call it paralysis if I thought that fish were subject to this disorder. It attacked one lot, and only one, of my alevin trout. They had been hatched about a month, and the yolk sac was nearly half gone. There were, perhaps, about two thousand in the compartment. Sixty or seventy were attacked. The first time I discovered that anything was wrong was one morning when the water was being agitated with a feather. The well ones immediately headed with all their might against the current as usual, while a few, only fifteen or sixteen at first, were observed to lie perfectly motionless, and to move unresistingly with the current, and finally to collect in a heap in the centre of an

eddy.   On examination they appeared to be perfectly lifeless ; but they did not — and this is the singular part of it — they did not change color, as dead fry of this age invariably do.   The next day, and for two or three days, they continued to look like live fish as they lay still in the water, and to appear like dead fish when more closely examined.   After three or four days one or more white spots were seen near the heart, and these finally extended all over the body ; but the entire white change did not come on for a number of days, and always began internally and worked outwards.   Sixty or seventy were affected in this way.   All 'died ; but the others in the compartment did not seem to suffer at all, and remained alive and well.

Section IV. — Filling Orders for Young Fry.

Filling orders for young fry in the spring is part of the trout-breeder's business, and promises to continue to be, on the principle that people will buy their young fish to save hatching them, as people buy young cabbage-plants and tomatoes to save starting them.

A few words about sending off the young fish may be of service to the beginner.

The first thing to do in preparing to fill an order for young fry is to arrange temporary boxes to put them into after they are counted.   These boxes should have a stream of water running through them, should be provided with an ample screen for an outlet, and should be light and portable, so that they can be lifted, and the fish and water poured from them when wanted.* The boxes should be perfectly clean, so that there will be nothing but the fish and the water to pour out. The next thing is to count them. To do this, net out a quantity from the hatching-troughs into a pan of water. Place this pan side by side with a large can or pail of water. Then take a dipper and dip up a few fish from the pan and pass them over to the pail, counting each dipperful as it is passed over. You had, perhaps, better begin with only four or five in the dipper at once, but with practice you will be able to count seven or eight or more at a time as you pass them over. It takes from half an hour to an hour, according to your dexterity, to count a thousand. It is a good plan to score every hundred, so that, if you lose your count, you will not have to go back far to recover it. It is very easy to forget your count, and very provoking to be obliged to count over again two or three thousand because of forgetting the exact number ; but if you score every hundred there is no danger of being driven to this. The temporary box for the night should be in place when you begin to count them, so that the counted fish will not be obliged to stay long in the pail or can. If there is a large number to send off, they should be counted the day before, and placed in the boxes, fed well, and covered over for the night. They will then be in good condition to start the next day, which is a very important point.

* In transferring young fry from one receptacle to another, it is easier and safer to pour them over, water and all, than to net them out. If the fry are very thick, it is sometimes best to transfer part of them with the net, and pour over the rest.

In the morning feed them again, and when it is time to start, transfer them to the tank or can which is to carry them.   For small quantities, say 1,000 or 2,000, I use a twelve-gallon tin can.   For larger quantities, say 5,000 or more, I take a seventy-gallon tank, a drawing of which may be seen in the Massachusetts Report of the Fishery Commissioners for 1868, Plate III. Fig. 6. The tank has a pump attached ; but this is not worked when small fish are carried.   I use also a hundred-gallon tank for moving still larger quantities.

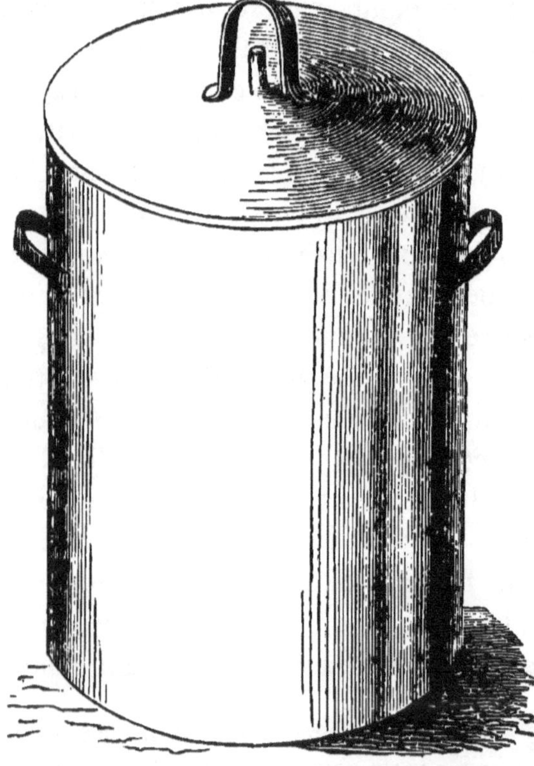

Tin Can for the Transportation of Young Fry.

The tank for carrying fish, when filled with water, is very heavy, and should have four iron handles on the sides to facilitate moving. It must not be made too large round, or it will not go into the door of the express-car, which would be found to be a very serious difficulty.   In travelling long distances, I take, besides the tank,* a water-pail, a bag of ice, tin dipper or bellows, and a sponge. The ice will be all needed before night, if the weather is warm. The pail is a convenience in various ways, the dipper or bellows † is for aerating the water, and the sponge is for the floor of the car, if the water slops over. Be careful to have plenty of help when you load into the car, and also at every change of cars, for, different from other merchandise, an upset is often a total loss. ‡

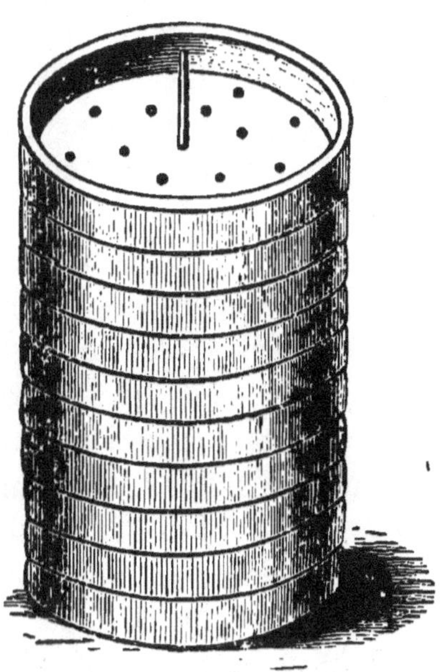

The Strainer on which the Ice is placed.

Keep the temperature of the water very low all day with ice, — using large pieces when standing still, and small pieces when in motion, as the large pieces are then apt to bruise and kill the fish. Do not change the water *en route*, but give it a thorough aeration once in half an hour. The aerating will be sure to keep them alive, while

* The Troutdale Transit Tank is recommended as an excellent thing to carry live fish in. See Dr. Slack's Catalogue of fish culturists' apparatus. A common flour-barrel, well soaked, with floats on the top of the water to prevent slopping, is a very good impromptu affair for carrying live fish.

† A common hand fire-bellows is as good an extempore aerating machine as can be found.

‡ See Appendix II., on Journeys with Live Fish.

there is always a risk of killing them by using water with which you are not acquainted.

It is best, I think, to accompany the fish all the way, and see them safely in the hands of those to whom they are consigned, though, where there is no change of cars to the end of the route, I sometimes leave them the last fifty miles, with a small fee, in the hands of the express messenger.

Alevins require less air than older fish, and no food, consequently more can be taken in less water than when older, and the risk of loss is correspondingly less, making the alevin stage the best time for transportation. But, as you cannot sell all your fish at the alevin stage, you will probably have occasion to transport the young fry at various ages. This is always practicable; only it should be remembered that the older they are the more water they require.

A thousand alevins can be carried in a gallon of water, kept very cold. At the age of three months I allow a gallon of water for each two hundred feeding fry.

In brief, then, when you transport young fry, count them the day before, start them in good condition, go with them, keep the water very cold with ice, do not change it, aerate it regularly, and do not upset the tank, and you will find the fish will do almost as well on a journey of twelve or twenty-four hours as if they were at home in the stream. I have carried ten thousand young fry, four months old, all day in hot weather, from 5 A. M. to 6 P. M., in fifty gallons of water, without change, and with a loss of only seven fish out of the ten thousand. See Appendix, on Journeys with Live Fish.

CHAPTER V.

GROWING THE LARGE TROUT.

SECTION I. — TROUT IN GENERAL.

*Scientific Description of the Salmo Fontinalis. By David Humphreys Storer.**

SALMO FONTINALIS. Common Trout. Mitchill, Trans. Lit. & Phil. Soc. of N. Y., I. p. 435.

Salmo nigrescens. Black Trout. Raf., Ichth. Ohien., p. 43.

Red-spotted Trout. Doughty, Cabinet of Nat. Hist., I. p. 145, Pl. 13.

Salmo fontinalis. Rich, Fauna Boreal. Americ., III. p. 176, Pl. 83, fig. 1., Pl. 87, fig. 2, head.

Salmo fontinalis. Common Brook Trout. Storer's Report, p. 106.

Salmo fontinalis. Speckled Trout. Kirtland's Report, pp. 169 – 194.

Salmo fontinalis. Brook Trout. Thompson, Hist. of Vermont, p. 141.

Salmo fontinalis. Brook Trout. Dekay's Report, p. 235, Pl. 37, fig. 120.

Baione fontinalis. Spotted Troutlet. Dekay's Report, p. 244, Pl. 20, fig. 58.

* A History of the Fishes of Massachusetts, by David Humphreys Storer, 1867, pp. 322, 323, 326.

Salmo fontinalis. Brook Trout. Ayres, Bost. Journ. Nat. Hist., IV. p. 273.

Salmo fontinalis. Common Brook Trout. Kirtland, Bost. Journ. Nat. Hist., IV. p. 305.

Salmo fontinalis. Common Brook Trout. Storer, Mem. Amer. Acad., new series. II. p. 444.

Salmo fontinalis. Common Brook Trout. Synopsis, p. 192 ; Cuv. & Val., Nat. Hist. de Pois., XXI. p. 266.

COLOR. — The upper part of the body is of a pale brown, mottled with darker undulating, reticulated markings ; the sides lighter, with a great number of circular yellow spots, varying in their size from a small point to a line or more in diameter, and many of them having in the centre a bright red spot ; sometimes, the yellow color surrounding them having partially disappeared, they seem distinct from the circular spots, or are surrounded by a dull bluish halo ; these red spots differ exceedingly in number in different specimens, in some three or four only are observable, and those are situated below the lateral line ; in others, twenty or more are seen, scattered above and below the lateral line indiscriminately, presenting a beautiful appearance. The body beneath is white, yellowish-white, slightly or dark fuliginous. Head above darker than the back of the fish. Gill-covers golden, and fuliginous. The dorsal fin is yellow with irregular transverse black bands. The first ray of the pectorals and ventrals is white, the second dark-colored, the remainder of the fin is red. The first ray of the anal fin is white, the remainder generally red. The caudal fin is of a dirty reddish-brown, mottled with black spots.

DESCRIPTION. — Body elongated, compressed. The length of the head is about equal to one fifth the length of the fish; the top of the head is flattened; the snout is obtuse. The eyes are large and circular. The distance between the eyes is equal to one fifth the length of the head. The jaws are equal in length; the gape of the mouth is large; the teeth are sharp and recurved; the teeth on the tongue are larger than those of the jaws; there are teeth also on the palatines and romer. The scales are very small; those on the lateral line, which pursues a straight course, are larger than those on the rest of the body.

The quadrangular dorsal fin is situated upon the anterior half of the body; the adipose fin is quite small, and near the tail.

The pectorals arise in front of the posterior angle of the operculum; their length is equal to one quarter of their height.

The fan-shaped ventrals commence opposite the middle of the dorsal fin; when unexpanded, their extremities together form a sharp point.

The anal fin arises in front of the adipose fin, and is higher than it is long.

The caudal fin is deeply emarginated.

The fin-rays are as follows: D. 11, P. 13, V. 8, A. 11, C. 19.

Length, eight to twenty inches.

Labrador: H. S. Storer. Maine, Massachusetts: Storer. Connecticut: Linsley, Ayres. Vermont: Thompson. New York: Mitchill, Dekay. Pennsylvania: Dekay. Ohio: Kirtland. Lake Huron: Richardson.

General Remarks about Trout.

The trout has always stood at the head of the fresh-water game fishes in the popular estimation. The fickle public may change its favorite some time for a more admired successor, but up to this time the trout has distanced all rivals. This honorable place he has gained and held, not by accident, but by merit. He deserves to rank by himself *first*, for where has the trout his equal? There may be fish of nearly as fine flesh as the trout, but they have a repulsive coat, like the pout; or a coarse appearance, like the bass; or a disagreeable one, like the mascalonge; or are full of bones, like the shad; or have no game in them, like the mullet; or fail somewhere to match the excellent points of the trout. There is not one of them that for perfect faultlessness can compare with the trout. This is his special peculiarity. He is *faultless*. He surpasses all other fish in grace of form, in beauty of coloring, in gentleness of expression, in fascination of manner, in gameness of spirit, in sweetness and firmness of flesh, and in general personal attractiveness, and to excellence in these points he also combines faultlessness in all others. Hence it is that he is the favorite among fishes, and deserves to be so.

Trout are peculiarly suited to domestication, being very hardy, easily tamed, conveniently confined, satisfied with plain food, well adapted to artificial breeding, prolific enough to increase rapidly, and having a sufficiently high value as live game, or as a table luxury, to make it worth while to raise them. I will not attempt any exhaustive description of these beautiful fish here, as they are so well known, and have been so thoroughly described in books on angling and on fish in general, but will confine myself to the few general remarks which follow.

The vision of the trout is incredibly sensitive to motion and to colors, but not to distinctions of form.

As to their sensitiveness to motion, it may be safely said that a company of soldiers standing motionless on the bank of a trout brook would not frighten the trout in it so much as the moving shadow of one of them across the water.

Their sensitiveness to colors is seen every week at the ponds where trout are domesticated, especially when their keeper changes a dark coat for a light one, or leaves it off altogether. The appearance of the un-accustomed light coat or white shirt will often frighten well-tamed trout into a panic.

Trout do not appear to see their food at any great distance in clear water, — I should say not over a rod, and in roily water but a very short distance, some-times not a foot. Trout can see somewhat in the night, but I think not in as dark nights as some writers have stated. If the sky be clear, they will detect an object on the surface of the water, projected against the sky, better than in the water, projected against the banks. A moving light above the water in the night will frighten trout; a stationary light in the water will attract them, and apparently stupefy them, for they are easily captured while staring at it.

The eye of the trout has very convex lenses, and is not provided with lids or any other shield whatever from the light. This makes bright sunlight sometimes fatal to young trout which have passed their embryo period in the dark. The eyes are situated above the line of the widest part of the head, and are a little protuberant, thus enabling them to see above, before, behind, and around, but not below them. Hence they cannot feed off the bottom, except at random. They will dart at a piece of food on the bottom, hit or miss, if they have seen it fall; but you can see that they feel for it with their mouths, rather than catch it with their eye, and their movements are also then very bungling compared with their swift, certain aim at anything above them in the water. They will sometimes poke the food off the bottom with their noses high enough to see it, and then they will take it as well as ever.

The peculiar position of the eyes of the trout has been sometimes overlooked in the controversy of fishing down stream *versus* fishing up stream. But it is, nevertheless, not true, as advanced in the argument against fishing up stream, that the angler must necessarily throw his line over the fish's head to attract his notice to the bait, and so be liable to frighten him; for the trout can see the bait if above and considerably behind him, and will whirl and take it so placed, if disposed.

Opinions are divided about the sense of hearing in trout. I think that there never was a controversy in the world in which assertions on the subject were more positively made on the one side, or more flatly denied on the other. Scott says, very decidedly, in his Fishing' in American Waters,* "Fishes hear; of this I feel quite sure," and quotes instances of fish coming to be fed at the sound of a bell. Seth Green says, in his Trout Culture,† that trout cannot hear, and that "they will not stir a fraction of an inch at the sound of a gun fired one foot above their heads."

I will not say that trout cannot hear; but this I will say with the greatest positiveness, for I have tested it repeatedly, that they are not frightened at noises, however loud, nor do they pay the slightest attention to them. You may place your mouth directly over the trout in a pond, and if they do not see you, you may scream with all your might, or ring a bell as loud as you please, and the trout will not move a fin to show that they are either frightened or attracted, or that they have in any way noticed it. You may even fire a revolver, or, as Green says, a gun, very near them, and if they do not see the flash or feel the concussion they will not notice it any more than if they were stone-deaf.

On the other hand, if you are in the habit of calling the trout with a bell to be fed, and have found that they come at the ringing of it, go to the pond some day at feeding time with the tongue taken out of the bell, and shake it as usual. The trout will come to be fed exactly the same, though not a sound is made.

* Fishing in American Waters, p. 38.
† Trout Culture, p. 58.

The nerves of smell in trout are large, and the sense of smell is probably well developed. Hence the use of fragrant oils and strongly scented bait in fishing for trout.

HABITAT.

Brook trout abound chiefly in cold, swift-running gravelly brooks ; but they thrive in all pure cold waters which contain sufficient air. Hence *brook* trout are found in many ponds and lakes, which apparent contradiction of terms has frequently led to confusion among those unfamiliar with fishing. I may be, therefore, excused for saying, by way of explanation, that the name " brook trout " is not confined to trout caught in brooks, but applies to all of the varieties of *Salmo fontinalis*, whether found in brooks, ponds, lakes, or rivers. Their range is very extensive, covering a wide belt from one end of our continent to the other. In phrenological language, their *locality* is very large, which gives them a strong attachment to places. In brooks, certain individuals will take up particular holes or rapids for their abode, and occupy them for months, and sometimes, I am inclined to think, for years.

In lakes and ponds, the shoals of trout have, like perch and other fish, particular resting-places, where they stay regularly. This is one reason why a person acquainted with their haunts will go out and catch a string of trout, while others, with better tackle and equal skill, will fish a whole day for them in vain.

The largest trout in brooks are found in the deep wide pools in the warmer waters. The smallest ones are found in the cold, narrow mountain rivulets near their source. The largest brook trout of all are found in large lakes, where range, space, feed, warmth of water, and perhaps inherited tendencies, all combine to produce a large race.

Trout, like other fishes, have small brains compared with the higher animals, and are very slightly sensitive to pain.

They have a rapid digestion, which, though not equal to that of a pickerel,* and some warm-water fishes, makes them susceptible to very quick growth indeed under favorable circumstances. Trout have this peculiarity also, that they vary from one another in their personal appearance to an endless degree. No two trout are alike. Every trout has its individual markings, as much as human beings, which distinguish it from all other trout. A mullet caught in a lake looks like all the other mullets of the lake, so with the white-fish and others ; but each trout has its individual marks which distinguish it from all others. The trout also of different brooks and lakes all differ from one another, so that the streams in which they are caught can frequently be told by the looks of the fish. Their different localities in the same stream also affect their appearance. Over a light gravelly bottom the trout grow light-complexioned, and they vary through all shades of complexion, from this to the dark slimy trout, almost as black as a bull-head, which

* Most fish have a rapid digestion. Bertram compares the digestion of some to the action of fire. Harvest of the Sea, p. 4.

is caught in shady places over black, muddy bottoms. And what is still more remarkable, trout have the chameleon gift of almost instantly changing their tint within certain limits.* ·

They do not, strictly speaking, change their color, because a black trout will remain a black trout and a silvery trout will remain a silvery trout wherever you expose them; but a complete change comes over their whole complexion, so to speak, as if the light to which they are subjected were diffused through them, so·that, in passing from a dark, muddy bed over light gravel, they will in less than a minute take the general hue of the gravel, and *vice versa* in passing from gravel to mud.†

The natural food of trout is very various. They are carnivorous from choice, though omnivorous in emergency. Their food, when wild, consists chiefly of water insects, smaller fish, larvæ, fish eggs, crusta-,cea, and the flies and insects which fall from the air into the water, — all of them together forming an astonishingly extensive variety. They also eat each other, and there are some individuals which adopt cannibal habits altogether, and remain hidden, like spiders, in dark holes and corners, and only emerge to. devour their like.

The quality of their food affects the growth and appearance of trout, and it is even thought that the dif-

---

* The black bass and some other fish have the same power to some extent.

† This change takes place, not in the scales, but in the skin underlying the scales.

ference in the color of their meat is sometimes caused by certain kinds of feed ; the fresh-water gammon or polex being supposed especially favorable to the production of red-meated trout.

It is certainly true that their growth depends very much upon the nature of their food. Francis, in his Fish Culture, mentions the following experiment, of which he says he once heard.*

" Equal numbers of trout were confined for a certain time by gratings to their several portions of the same stream. The fish in one of the divisions were fed entirely on flies, in another upon minnows, and in the third upon worms. At the end of a certain period, those which had been fed on flies were the heaviest and in the best condition, those fed on minnows occupied the second place, while those fed on worms were in much the worst order of the three."†

The age to which trout live is not known. Seth Green says that twelve years is probably about the average age, and that they are in their prime between the age of three years and ten years. I am inclined to think that they live to a greater age than this. Other kinds of fish in parks in the Old World are known to have attained enormous ages,‡ and to have

* Francis on Fish Culture, p. 113.

† The result of these experiments should be received cautiously, as it is doubtful whether all the other modifying conditions were so exactly alike that the results were wholly due to the difference of food. For illustration, a considerable difference in *temperature*, or in the *quantity* of food, would affect the condition of the fish more than the difference in the nature of the food.

‡ Pike and carp in artificial ponds have been repeatedly found

been equalled only in their longevity by the human race before the flood. Why should the trout be so short-lived?

Mr. Lancaster, of Oxford, in a memoir published last year, says that fish have great tenacity of life, and mentions a carp that reached the age of 150 years, and a pike, 19 feet long, that lived in a fish-pond in Germany 267 years.* He says whales are believed to live one or two centuries.

The size to which brook trout may grow is very uncertain, and when we come to the question of the size of those that have been actually caught we are on mythical ground. The trouble is, as Green mentions, that many of the "fish stories" which are told are so incredible † that they throw discredit on even well-authenticated cases.‡ I am fortunate enough, however, through the kindness of George Shepard Page, President of the Oquossoc Angling Association, and B. F. Bowles, Esq., a member of the same Association, to cite three instances of unquestionable authenticity, of

with gold rings in their fins, and other kinds of labels, on which were found dates that proved conclusively that one hundred years had elapsed since the inscription was made. — JOE SMITH, *Nat. His. Mass. Fishes*, p. 57.

* The greatest wonder about such a fish, if he were in this country, would be that he had escaped the poachers so long.

† A famous fish-story teller once said that he cut a hole through the ice at Lake Erie, not more than two inches across, with his pocket-knife, and presently pulled out a mascalonge that weighed a hundred pounds. On being asked how he drew so large a fish through so small a hole, he replied that he had not thought of that.

‡ Trout Culture, p. 45.

trout (*Salmo fontinalis*) actually caught, which weighed between 9 and 10 pounds. They are as follows. In September, 1867, Mr. Geo. S. Page caught at the outlet of Rangeley Lake, Franklin Co., Maine, two male trout, one weighing 10 pounds, the other 9½ pounds. In June, 1871, Theo. L. Page, Esq., caught a trout in Mooseluc Maguntic Lake, in the same county, weighing 9¼ pounds. These are the largest brook trout in regard to which I have succeeded in obtaining well-attested statistics, after making inquiries in various directions; and I think it is safe to venture the assertion that these trout, if not the largest individuals ever caught in this country, are representatives of the largest type of the *Salmo fontinalis* in the United States.* The weight of trout is very deceptive. There is no safe test but the scales. The length is no guide, for his depth and breadth will often in a short trout more than compensate in weight for what is lacking in length, and then again a lean trout in poor condition sometimes actually does not weigh more than half

* The following letter gives a fuller account of the large trout caught by Mr. Page : —

10 WARREN STREET, NEW YORK, August 14, 1871.
LIVINGSTON STONE, ESQ.

DEAR SIR : In reply to yours of the 5th instant, making inquiries with regard to brook trout, I have much pleasure in mentioning three, caught in September, 1867, by the subscriber at the outlet of Rangeley Lake, Franklin County, Maine, — this lake being the head-waters of the Androscoggin River : —

One 10 lbs. male,
One 9½ lbs. do.,
One 8¼ lbs. female.

The first and last were transported alive in a box of water, what he would when fat and in his best condition. This is a great difference, it is true, but it is a fact. It is said by medical authorities that a man cannot lose over three eighths of his weight and live. It is not so with a trout; he can lose full fifty per cent and live.

Section II. — The Commissary Department.

The question of food for trout is a very important one, and I think, as a general thing, a very simple one too, though some printed remarks on the subject have made it appear complicated.

The one correct thing to feed trout on, as a rule, is the heart, liver, and lungs of animals killed for market. These combine the three desired points of trout food. They are cheap, nutritious, and accessible.

They are Cheap,

averaging in the country about thr e cents a pound. It is true that liver in thickly settled places costs ten cents per pound, and if you should feed the trout entirely on liver in those places it would be very expen-

aerated by an air-pump, to my pond in Stanley, Morris County, N. J., but afterwards died in consequence of too high a temperature in the water. The first weighed ten (10) lbs. by steelyard within a half-hour after death. It is now in a glass case in my office in New York. The $9\frac{1}{2}$ lbs. trout was sent to General Grant.

Two of the trout from these waters I have sent to Professor Agassiz, in 1863 and in 1867, and in a personal interview he pronounced them real Brook Trout (*Salmo fontinalis*).

Faithfully yours,
GEO. SHEPARD PAGE,
Pres't Oquossoc Ang. Ass.

sive feeding. But the lungs are quite as good food for trout as liver, and better in some respects. The lungs can be bought in any community for two cents a pound. Sheep's and lambs' plucks can also be bought for the same. As a general thing, in the more thickly settled places the lungs and sheep's plucks are cheaper than in the country, because of the greater number of animals killed in such localities. While food can be bought at these figures, trout can be profitably raised at half the present market-prices. *This kind of food is accessible.* Wherever there is a community of any size, cattle and sheep are killed for its support, and wherever these are killed the plucks may be procured. This class of food can always be obtained also at the great cattle markets, like Brighton and Cambridge in Massachusetts, where it can be bought so low, that, with a hundred miles' express-charges added, it will not cost over the average price in the country of three cents a pound.

THEY ARE NUTRITIOUS.

The plucks of animals, being solid fresh meat, are the most nutritious food in the world for trout, and cannot be objectionable in this respect. This food, I should say, then, should form the chief reliance of the trout-grower.

To prepare it for the fish, run it raw through a common sausage-grinder, and it is then ready to feed to them.

Various other things can be used for food, and the best among these are : —

1. Other kinds of meat.
2. Live minnows.
3. Fish-flesh ground up.
4. Sour-milk curd.
5. Worms and insects.

1. *Other kinds of meat.* Trout, being carnivorous, will always thrive on meat. Therefore, any kind of meat, whether raw or boiled, which is cheap enough and convenient enough, makes suitable food for them. Horse-flesh,* young calves, and scant sheep would answer for trout-food, and are also cheap.

2. *Live minnows.* These unquestionably form a very desirable article of food for trout, and should be given them when they can be afforded.   They are natural food, and at the same time furnish a wholesome change from the usual meat diet. In some favorable places they can be obtained in vast quantities, and are the cheapest food that can be had. These are exceptional localities, it is true ; but in almost all brooks they can be collected in considerable quantities by shutting off the stream above, and netting them out of the little pools in which they are trapped by the receding water.

The use of live minnows in large ponds has been objected to on the ground that minnows, living on the same insects and other food as the trout, rob the trout of what they would otherwise get themselves. This objection has some weight, it is true, in itself; but it is more than offset by the value of the minnows to the trout. The minnows more than compensate in themselves to the trout for what they

---

* Paris lived on horse-flesh ; why should not trout ?

eat. I would give the trout all the minnows I could get.

There is another objection which deserves more consideration, and this is that in amateur trout ponds, where large and small trout are kept together without sorting, the habit of feeding on minnows may encourage the bad habit, in the trout, of feeding on each other. In this case I would take a day or two for the work, and sort the fish thoroughly, and then let them have the minnows; but if this cannot be done, perhaps the objection against the minnows holds good.

3. *Fish-flesh ground up*. This is undoubtedly good food for trout, and in some districts fish are so plenty that it is the cheapest and most accessible food. For instance, on the Mirimichi River, where smelts are used to manure the land, or on the Missisquoi, where a large sturgeon can be bought for a dollar, and perch for nothing, these or other fish, killed and run through a mill such as is used for grinding mackerel bait, would answer quite as well as meat. Trout like meat best, but thrive well on fish food.

4. *Sour-milk curd*. This makes very good food for trout, though they do not like it as well as meat. It is easily prepared by pouring boiling water on bonny-clabber and straining out the whey. What remains in the strainer is the curd. When milk is plenty, this food is very accessible, and also not expensive, and makes a very good occasional substitute for meat; but an exclusive diet of curd is thought to be unhealthful.

5. *Worms and insects*. These, of course, with all

other natural food, are good for the trout. Give them all you can get, which, after all, will not be much, compared with the rest of their food, if you have many trout. You can, however, breed maggots for them in considerable numbers by hanging the meat over the ponds and letting the flies work in it. This is called a maggot factory, and, though a good food-producer, especially for yearlings, is to my mind very objectionable about a domestic trout pond. If you have a pond at a distance which you seldom visit, a maggot factory will do very well ; but where you go every day, it is a nuisance. If you do use one anywhere, contrive to cover the meat with a box. This softens the objectionableness of it somewhat.

A few words more should be added here about the care and preparation of the meat, where trout breeding is practised on a large scale. At a trout breeding establishment in full operation there are three distinct sets of fish, the young fry, the yearlings, and the large trout, and there should be a dog. These three sets of trout require three different preparations of meat. For the young fry the liver is used, and is prepared by grating it on a cheese-grater, as described in the chapter on young fry. For the yearlings the heart is used, and is cut up in a meat-cutter, which will cut it finer than the sausage-grinder. For the large trout the meat that is left is run through the sausage-grinder, except the coarser parts, which are given to the dog. The heart is used for the yearlings, simply because it will cut up better in the cutter.*

* The cutter used at the Cold Spring Trout Ponds is Star-

Starret's American Chopping Machine.

When, therefore, the meat is brought to the ponds, it is first sorted ; the liver is cut off and laid aside for the young fish, the best part of the heart is cut off for the yearlings, the coarser pieces are saved for the dog, and the rest is run through the grinder for the large fish. This systematizes the whole thing, and disposes of all the meat.

In the spring and fall you will have no trouble in keeping the meat ; but in the summer and winter it is different. The meat freezes solid in winter, and spoils quickly in summer, and in the exceedingly hot weather it is sometimes very troublesome. Your great protection against these evils lies in the spring water. Keep the meat in the cold spring water, and it will not spoil in the summer within a reasonable time, nor freeze in the winter. It is true that remaining under water does

ret's American Chopping Machine, and the sausage-grinder is Perry's Patent No. 4. Both answer their purpose very well.

not improve its quality ; but the other advantages are more than sufficient, at extreme temperatures, to offset this objection. Do not feed spoiled meat to the fish. If you ever have any on hand, bury it in some place set apart for that purpose.*

The trout feed differently at different seasons of the year. In the spring, when the water begins to warm up, they are most voracious, and will eat a larger daily allowance for their weight than at any other part of the year. During the first half of the summer their appetite does not diminish much, except when the water gets heated. When this occurs, they do not care so much for food. Mr. Ainsworth found that his trout in New York stopped eating at 70°. Mine continue to take food up to 75°. Above that they are more or less indifferent to it. As the spawning season approaches, the trout care less and less for food, and just at their spawning time, and a week or two previous, they avoid it, and go without eating entirely. When their spawning is over they eat again, and are quite ravenous on warm days, and where the temperature of the water does not alter much they feed well all winter ; but in brooks or ponds where the water cools with the season their appetite falls off, and when the water drops to 36°, or less, they either scarcely notice the food or take it very languidly. At this degree of cold they are in a torpid condition, and there is about as much difference between their spring and elasticity at this time and in the summer, as there is between the

* This place at the Cold Spring Trout Ponds has been nick-named the "Potter's Field."

movements of a mud-turtle and a Scotch terrier after rats. On mild days in winter when the sun warms the water, or after a warm rain, they will wake up from their lethargy and eat as they do in summer. These are the times when they will indulge their cannibal instincts if they are not fed, and you should be prompt on such days to anticipate their unusual appetite with proper food.

Trout feed differently at different times in the day. In the winter the favorable time is the warmest part of the day. In summer they take their food best about sundown ; they are very lively then both in the spring and summer, and will leap out of the water and lash the surface with their tails in a way that is very exhilarating to see.

When the keeper approaches to feed them, they will come towards him, or will collect in their accustomed place of eating, if they have not been disturbed ; but if they have been molested they will fly about in all directions, stir up the gravel, reject their food, and act as if they were crazy. This is a bad sign, and when you see it you may know that it means that they have been molested and frightened during the night, probably by minks, herons, or men.

Once a day is sufficiently often to feed the large trout. They will keep fat and grow rapidly on one feed a day ; but I think they would grow somewhat better if fed oftener and less at a time. There is not much danger of their eating too much. Feed till they decline the food, then stop. They will sometimes take too large pieces, and so choke themselves to death, and they will perhaps eat enough in the excitement of feeding time to feel uncomfortably afterwards ; but they are usually not gluttons enough to *gorge* themselves to a fatal repletion.

Experience will teach the trout grower how much to feed daily to a given number of trout. This quantity varies with the season, the quality, the quantity, and temperature of the water, and other circumstances, and cannot be stated definitely. Green says five pounds of meat a day for a thousand three-year-olds, three pounds for a thousand two-year-olds. I should say this would be an average feed through the year, but in summer my two-year-olds and three-year-olds eat much more. I think it is safe to say that under favorable circumstances large trout of any age will eat one fiftieth of their weight in the summer, that one per cent of their weight a day will keep them in good condition through the year, and that they would do very well on half that allowance. I have also observed that with two-year-olds and three-year-olds five pounds of meat food is an equivalent for one pound of trout growth.

Section III. — How to secure the Large Trout against Loss.

There is no domesticated creature in the world that can be kept with so little loss as large trout, if carefully protected. Indeed, the loss is almost nothing. The large trout keep healthy and vigorous at all seasons, and very rarely die if properly cared for ; though if they are carelessly exposed they will waste away like dew before the sun.   If you observe the following directions, many of which are only repetitions of what has been previously said, I think your trout will be safe : —

1. Guard against freshets.
2. Avoid overstocking.
3. Guard against heated water.
4. Handle carefully.
5. Keep the trout well sorted.
6. Never let the water get foul.
7. Protect from natural enemies.
8. Protect from poachers.

1. *Guard against freshets.*   So much has been said under this head in the chapter on suitable water, that we will merely refer the reader to that chapter, saying, *en passant,* that the danger from this source cannot be overestimated, and that the losses, when they do occur, are usually overwhelming.

2. *Avoid overstocking.*   There is no indiscretion in the world so easy for a trout breeder to fall into as overstocking his ponds when he has many fish and not much water *; but I need not say it is a fatal mistake. There is usually a very dry hot time in the summer, which, if not a fiery furnace, is, at least, a watery furnace for the trout to pass through ; and it is often hard in the fall, winter, or spring, when the deceitful water is cold, and there is plenty of it, to realize what the inexorable exactions of this ordeal will be ; and almost without knowing it the trout breeder will sometimes get more trout into his stream than it will carry through the summer.   Therefore the beginner cannot

* See remarks on water supply and droughts, pp. 11 – 12.

too carefully impress on his mind the simple truism that no stream can be relied on for more than what it will do in the hottest and dryest day of the hottest and dryest season of the year, and this principle should be acted upon. If, however, you ever happen to have on hand more than you know you can summer in your stream, there is a very simple way to get over the difficulty, and one which I have often resorted to, namely, to turn some of the trout out to pasture through the dry time. I mean by this to carry them off to some neighboring brook where you have provided a temporary enclosure for them through the dangerous crisis ; this is not a difficult matter, and if you want the spawn from them in the fall it is expedient to do it, taking the precaution to remove them on cool mornings when the transportation and handling will not be likely to hurt them.

If you have too many on hand in the spring, and have no means of pasturing them, then kill and sell them for what you can get while they are in good condition ; it is better than to have them die of the heat. If you know of no one that wants them, then pack them in ice, and consign them to some good firm in Fulton Fish Market, New York City, to sell on commission. Fresh brook trout are always in demand there.

But if the dry time comes suddenly, and you are caught with too many trout on hand and a short supply of water, you have two remedies. One is to use ice ; if you are not in a very bad predicament, a moderate quantity of ice, used three hours a day, — the hot

interval between 1 P. M. and 4 P. M. being the worst
time for the water,—will often save them.   The other
remedy is to reservoir part of the water in the stream
above the trout during the cool of the night, and let it
on by degrees in the hottest part of the day; this will
answer to some extent, when the days only are hot.   But
if the heat and drought are extreme and long continued,
and nights and days are both hot, then neither ice nor
reserves of water will save your trout in an overstocked
pond, and you must lose them.   I will merely add that
a plethoric condition of the fish, and an uncleanly pond,
increase very much the dangers of the dry season.

3. *Guard against heated water.*   This point is somewhat related to the last, inasmuch as the water is usually the hottest at the dryest time, and the warmer it
is the less stock it will keep.   But there is also danger
of the water heating up enough to kill the fish, even
when there is plenty of it and the season is not particularly dry.   This point has also been discussed on
page 12, to which the reader is referred.   I will repeat here that the extreme limit of danger is variable,
depending upon the quantity, quality, and rapidity of
the water, and also upon the degree of exposure to
the sun, and the condition of the fish.

The trout exhibited by the writer at the Mechanics'
Fair, at Boston, in 1869, appeared easy with a medium
supply of water at 68°.   At 70° they were a little distressed, at 73° much distressed, and breathing at the
rate of 100 times a minute.   Mr. Stephen H. Ainsworth,
in a letter to the writer, says that 68° is the highest
temperature that his trout do well in, at 70° they stop

eating, at 75° begin to die, at 80° die faster, and at 90° all die. Seth Green's book says that trout will die at 68°.* This may be the case in New York, but it is not so in New England. Trout in our vigorous swift running water will sometimes live through 75°. Still I consider 75° very dangerous, and anything over 70° unsafe.

There is no remedy for the water heating up, except artificial cooling. If you have ice enough, you can do something in that direction in a small stream as long as the ice lasts; but it is a forlorn hope. However, if you find the water heating to a fatal extent, and think it worth while to try to save them with ice, first diminish their rations or stop them altogether, make the current as swift as possible, and then do what you can with ice. You will probably save some, if the heated term does not last too long. But if your brook heats up so as to require the application of ice, in any but very exceptional instances I should say select another place for your operations. Ice may save the fish, but it is paying too dear for the whistle, and it is coming a little too near danger to be desirable.

4. *Handle the fish carefully.* Handle the fish carefully when you have occasion to handle them at all, which will not be often, except in sorting, in moving from one pond to another, and in spawning. It makes a great difference in handling and carrying trout whether it is hot or cold weather. In winter you can do almost anything with them, short of using actual violence, without killing them; but in very hot weather

* Trout Culture, p. 52.

in summer, when they are fat and the water is warm, they actually seem to die before they are hurt.

Rough handling is very often the cause of death; but it is a very unnecessary and inexcusable cause. All the handling that needs to be done can, ninety-nine times in a hundred, be done without hurting the fish. The suggestions given in the chapter on spawning trout will perhaps be a sufficient guide on this point. I would by all means dissect at least one fish, and find where the vitals lie, and just how the viscera are packed together inside. You will find you can, by practice, squeeze a fish very hard, if you know where the vitals are, without killing it. Always be careful not to scrape off the slime from the skin, for where the slime is off fungus will grow, and the result is death.

5. *Keep your trout well sorted.* I know that it is often said, " Feed your trout well, and they will not eat each other." Perhaps they will not, *but it is not prudent to trust them.* It is a risk, to say the least of it, to keep fish of different sizes in a herd together, and, being a risk; it ought to be avoided on principle. If any one doubts whether actual mischief is done by it, let him put five hundred trout of different sizes in a pond for a year, and take them out at the end of that time and count them over again. I think he will be convinced. This is something that some trout growers are altogether too careless about. They would not think of keeping foxes and fowls together, even if the foxes were well fed, yet they run equal risk with their trout, and think nothing of it. I have seen more than

one trout pond where it was only a question of time about one half of the fish going down the throats of the other half. The fact is, trout are by nature incurable cannibals, and they *will* always gratify their natural instincts, to some extent at least, and will sometimes carry them to a very destructive length.*

My advice is, where you have different-sized trout confined, to draw off your pond, or, if you cannot draw it off, sweep out all the fish with a sweep seine, and sort them thoroughly at stated intervals. In sorting, it is well to remember that there is six times as much mischief from having one large one with six small ones than six large ones with one small one, because the one large one will eat up all the small ones, while the whole of the other six can eat only the small one. The most dangerous times, when the trout are not kept sorted, are just after a rain in the spring or summer, and when the weather suddenly moderates in the winter. In the first case the disturbed water prevents their taking their regular feed, and they get very hungry in consequence, and in the other case the warm

---

* I once had some full-grown trout, of the peculiarly large variety found in Monadnoc Lake, confined in a small pond, and one autumn had occasion to remove them, and put in a number of small brook trout. The pond was a covered one, and the fish were not particularly examined through the winter. In the spring, when the cover was removed, it was found that more than one half of the brook trout had disappeared. A thorough search of the pond revealed a large and very fat Monadnoc trout hidden in a dark hole, where he had been overlooked in the removal of the others. He had eaten at least one hundred two or three ounce trout during the winter.

winter days sharpen their appetites. In either case, if you do not anticipate the cravings of their instincts with your food, the smaller trout will pay the penalty of their lives. It makes no difference with the large ones whether they can wholly swallow those they kill or not. They seize them by the middle, whirl them round as herons do, and swallow them head down. If they cannot swallow the whole fish at first, they will begin digesting the end that is down, and swallow the rest as it comes along.

I will also suggest the following precaution here, though it is a little out of place. If you have two ponds on the same brook, one below the other, with large fish in one and small fish in the other, make it doubly sure that none of the large ones can by any possibility escape into the pond of smaller ones. Do not be satisfied with leaving things so that you *think* this cannot happen, but make it impossible by any mishap short of an earthquake, for the possible consequences cannot be exaggerated ; and what makes it all the worse is that, should a large trout get among the small ones, and adopt cannibal habits, he would keep himself completely hidden, — such is the habit of cannibal fish, — and you might not discover him till his ravages had been very disastrous. Fix your ponds, therefore, so that no freshet, or clogging up of the screens, or other contingency, can make it possible for the large ones to jump over, creep under, or in any other way get into the pond of small ones.

6. *Never let the water get foul.* The source of foulness in the water, whenever it occurs, is, of course, the

feed which falls to the bottom of the pond and the effete matter coming from the fish. If these accumulate in any great quantity, danger is imminent. The fish are, so to speak, on the edge of a precipice, and the first warm day may bring great loss.

There is but one remedy for a foul pond, except removing the fish and digging it out anew, and that is the use of earth. This remedy, though the only one, is a sure one. Earth, as is now well known, is a wonderful absorbent of foul gases. Therefore, when the bed of your pond gets foul, and it is not convenient to clean it out, throw in a layer of three inches, or, if very foul, of six inches of common earth. This will make the pond as sweet and clean as it ever was, and the fish, too, will be better for it. Do not be afraid of muddying the water. Muddy water never killed a trout yet, though thousands have died for the want of it.

Beginners are here cautioned against drawing down the pond, when it gets foul, in order to remove the fish, for this is the very surest thing to make matters worse. The water becomes thick with the offending matter, when the pond is drawn off, and it will certainly sicken the fish and check their growth, if it does not kill them outright. It is not so dangerous with large trout as with young fry, thousands of which have been killed by this practice ; but it is bad enough with fish of any size, and never ought to be resorted to.

It is a good plan to keep a few moderate-sized suckers or mullets (*Catostomi*) — mullets are the handsomer fish — in your ponds for scavengers. They do good service at this work, they are perfectly harmless, and will clean the bottom of the pond of whatever food escapes the mouths of the trout. Every trout pond, I think, should contain one or more of them.

7. *Protect from natural enemies.* The natural enemies of large trout in New England are herons, fish hawks, and minks. Kingfishers are also very destructive to yearlings, and will *kill* two-year-olds, if they do not *eat* them. Snakes also prey on yearlings, and will sometimes swallow a two-year-old; but these two latter enemies are chiefly formidable to yearlings. The best protection against the birds is to cover the pond. A plain rack, made of inch-strips of pine, laid about two inches apart, answers very well for this purpose. The birds will not go through the slats for the fish. The rafts which are put on the pond to shade it are some protection against birds, especially kingfishers; but herons will stand on the rafts themselves, and with their long necks reach the incautious trout in their hiding-places underneath. Herons have very capacious throats, a passion for fish, and a rapid digestion. They are consequently very much to be dreaded. They do their mischief evenings and mornings, but mostly in the early morning; and as they are not very wary birds, you can usually shoot them, if you get up early enough. They are waders, also, and, having very long feet, they are easily caught alive, by setting traps in the mud where their foot-tracks have been discovered. I once caught a large blue heron so, with five two-year-old trout in his throat. If you get one alive, and are at all incredulous about their trout-

destroying capacity, keep him till he is hungry, and then give him a panful of live minnows to eat. He will soon show what herons can do in stowing away fish, and will remove, I think, all scepticism from your mind henceforth about the destructiveness of herons among trout. The kingfishers are easily shot. They generally come early in the morning, or about three hours before sundown ; but, if not molested, they will stay around all day, and increase in numbers very fast. Approach them with a gun, if you can. If you are not able to get within gunshot, lie in wait for them near one of their favorite perches about the ponds, and they will usually soon come within gunshot of their own accord. You can also trap them, by erecting a tall pole over the pond, and, setting a steel trap or bird-trap on the top of it ; it will not be long before the kingfisher will alight on the pole to watch for his prey, and will be caught. The same trick answers for hawks. Minks are not so easy to manage. The best chance is to trap them on their way to the ponds in the fall, as that is the time when they make their way up the brooks. Green's method of trapping minks, which is the best I know of, is as follows : " Make a box eighteen inches long by six inches broad and deep, leaving one end open. Set a common game-trap (such as is used for catching muskrats) in the open end of the box, in such a position that when the jaws are closed they will be in a line with the length of the trap. If it is set crossways it will be apt to throw the mink out, instead of catching it. Put the bait in the further end of the box (a piece of meat or a dead fish will answer for bait), set the trap, and cover it over with a large leaf. Now there is only one way for the mink to get at the bait, which is by walking over the trap." You will be very likely to catch the mink in this way, though you will probably get a few house cats first. When minks begin to infest your waters, you will see the advantage of plank ponds over earth ponds ; for in plank ponds the minks cannot hide permanently, but must come and go every time they make a meal off the fish. On the contrary, in the earth ponds they will find some old muskrat-hole or other place where they will probably take up winter quarters ; and when the ground is frozen solid for a foot or two below the surface it will be found very hard to dislodge them. It is almost impossible to trap them then, for two reasons. In the first place, as they have a subterranean passage to their daily food they seldom appear above ground, where they can be caught or shot ; and, secondly, having plenty of the food which they like best, namely, live trout, you have nothing better to tempt them into a trap with. Your only chance is this. Place a dry plank on the north side of the pond, so that one end rests in the water and the other slants some ways up the bank. Put a steel trap on the plank, near the lower end, and fasten it so that the mink, if caught, will throw it into the water. Minks like to sun themselves in the winter, and though your intrenched enemy will not be baited into a trap, he will sometimes step into one in trying to get to a dry spot in the sun. If minks are so troublesome as to warrant the outlay.

enclose the pond on all sides and on the top so tightly that a mink cannot get in ; then you are safe.

There is no way to manage the snakes but to kill them ; but they are not so very destructive to large trout ; and, if you keep off all other enemies, I do not think you will suffer much from snakes.

POACHERS.

I know the prevailing opinion is now that there is not much danger from poachers. I wish to lift up my voice against this delusion. Your trout in an exposed pond are just about as safe as your money would be in it ; indeed, in some respects, not so safe, for there are people who *will steal trout* who would not steal money. Yet persons will lock up their money in vaults in banks, and then not feel safe, and will leave a hundred or a thousand dollars' worth of trout in an unprotected pond and think there is not much risk. It is a great mistake. I would throw every barrier I possibly could between my trout and trout-thieves, and would make my ponds just as secure from poacher raids as the value of their contents will warrant.

Poachers are of three classes. First, the regular thief. He steals the trout the same as he steals his firewood and poultry, because he prefers to get his living that way. He comes regularly, but, with a thief's caution, by the least suspected path, and usually takes just enough each time not to have them missed. A year's steady work at it, however, will leave its marks on your trout stock, you may depend. Possibly the *rôle* will be changed some time, and all your trout be taken off in one night and shipped to market and sold. It is of no use to say that the law will keep this kind off. The law has no effect on them. They make a business of breaking the law, and if it does not keep them from other property it will not keep them from trout.

The second class of poachers are those who steal the fish partly for the lark of it, and partly because they want the fish, and have not enough principle to care whether it is right or wrong. The law restrains these somewhat, and makes their visits scarcer, but does not keep them off entirely.

The third class are those who have principle enough not to steal other things, but seem to have such a passion for trout fishing that a stocked trout pond is a temptation they cannot resist. I will only say of these, that the sight of their names in print would be a startling revelation of what otherwise respectable persons can be sometimes tempted into doing.

With these three classes of poachers about, your trout are never secure. So I would say, make the safety of your ponds just as near a certainty as you can. Do not trust to people's being too honest, or too indolent, or too unenterprising to take your trout, for there are dishonesty, cunning, and enterprise enough in the world to steal them twenty times over, and it is more than likely that these qualities exist in the very neighborhood of your ponds. The true plan is to put temptation out of the way of all by interposing impassable barriers between the trout and the thieves; and as a guide to what may be done, we will give a brief description of the safeguards employed at the Cold Spring Trout Ponds. There is, first, an admission-fee to the grounds, and visitors are required to register their names. This has a good effect in various ways. It keeps the crowd unfamiliar with the temptation, which is a good deal; for persons who have never seen the trout in the daytime are much less likely to come for them at night than those who have seen them often. Poachers might say of trout what Pope said of vice, —

> When "seen *too oft*, familiar with its face,
> We first endure, then pity, then embrace."

An admittance fee also makes the number of visitors so small that any suspicious persons taking observations for a midnight raid are likely to be noticed. At all events, it makes you feel safer than if there were people around your ponds all day that you did not know anything about. Finally, if a fee is objectionable to your taste, you need not *take* it any oftener than you like. Giving notice that one is charged will answer the purpose.

Secondly, a copy of the statute in regard to poaching is placed where all can read it. This has a good effect, for a quiet contemplation of six months' imprisonment, as the penalty is in New Hampshire, or $ 100 fine, as it is in some other places, is a serious damper on the ardor of at least some minds possessed of poaching proclivities.

Thirdly, a tight board fence eight feet high (and it should be higher), closely spiked at the top, surrounds the ponds of large trout. This, it is true, will not prevent a resolute thief from climbing over and getting the fish, if he has made up his mind that he will have them, but it nevertheless reduces the number very much of the dangerous ones, and limits them to the very enterprising only. There are a hundred poachers who will steal up and throw their lines into an open pond, where there is one who will bring a ladder and scale a spiked fence and descend on the other side, where he does not know how many spring guns, or bull-dogs, or what not, there may be inside to receive him. A spiked enclosure lessens the chances of loss by poaching very much.

Fourthly, there is at the Cold Spring Trout Ponds a dog whose ferocity I have never seen surpassed except in a chained tiger (one of Van Amburgh's) at a menagerie we once visited, and who is as stanch and as incorruptible as he is ferocious. This dog "Jack" is the last thing in the world a poacher would like to encounter in a spiked enclosure, and adds very much, I think, to the safety of the fish. He is certainly a terror to all who know him. It is true a watch-dog can be shot or poisoned, and so be got out of the way; but he is at least another barrier to danger, and as long as he lives, at all events, he is a protection.

There are other safeguards inside of the fence which are disclosed only to the poachers themselves, but which make the way of the transgressor exceedingly perilous. We would add here that the racks which are put over the ponds to keep off the birds are also a protection against a line being thrown over the fence among the trout. But for all the protection of these safeguards there is one better than all, and that is to have your dwelling-house or your keeper's house either over or close to the ponds. Then with a dog that will give the alarm at the approach of danger you may consider your trout as near safe as the nature of the case permits.

SECTION IV. — ADULT TROUT. — HOW TO GROW TROUT TO A VERY LARGE SIZE, AND RAPIDLY.

Trout show their keeping as well as any other creature, and more than most. I have seen a trout that was reasonably believed to be but two years old that weighed a pound, and I have seen one of the same age that barely turned the scales at half an ounce. The larger one had been in a warm stream which swarmed with blood-suckers, than which there is no more growing food in the world for trout. The other happened to be confined in a small enclosure of very cold water, almost destitute of food. These instances show what a difference unlike conditions will make in the growth of a trout. You can grow them at an almost incredible rate, or you can dwarf them to an almost incredible degree.

If you want to dwarf trout, keep them in cold sunless water, in close confinement, and with little food, and you will do it.

If you want to grow them fast and large, observe the following directions : —

1. *Give them plenty of water.* Of two similar lots of trout confined in the same amount of space and kept on the same amount of food, those which have the largest supply of water will grow the best.

2. *Give them plenty of food.* Trout will not grow in exact proportion to the food which is given them, because their growth is modified by so many other conditions; but you may be sure of this, that the more you feed them, and the more often, under any conditions, the better they will grow.

3. *Keep them where the water warms up in the summer, say to* 65° *or nearly* 70°. You cannot grow trout fast or large in very cold water. Feed them and care for them the best you can, they must, nevertheless, have comparatively warm water; and in such water, with plenty of food, range, and space, their rate of growth is simply wonderful.

4. *Give them range.* If you want to grow your trout very large, you must give them range. I say if you want to grow them *very large*. Range is not necessary, by any means, to the *average* growth of trout, for they will grow to a very good size in small places, and it is also generally incompatible with trout growing as a business to give them great range; but, if you want to raise the very largest trout, you must give them the very largest range. Trout will not grow beyond a certain size in confinement. They will stop or nearly stop growing when they have reached a certain limit. Range also influences the *rate* of growth. Large ponds grow trout faster, as a rule, than small ponds. Put ten trout into a pool three feet square, and ten others in a pond three rods square, and those in the pond will grow very much faster than those in the pool, on the same food. In a pond of three acres they would grow faster yet.

5. *Give them plenty of space.* I mean by space the amount of cubic feet of room to each fish in a pond. This, of course, is not synonymous with range. As, for instance, a thousand head of cattle in a pasture would have as much range as ten head, but ten head confined in it alone would have a hundred times the space. Space is something which cannot be afforded by trout growers generally, but it is necessary to the very large and rapid growth of trout. Put one thousand trout in a pond twenty feet square, and ten trout in another pond of the same size, and keep both lots on the same food, and you will be astonished to see how much the growth of the smaller lot exceeds that of the larger lot. Much space is not necessary to keep trout alive in and doing well, but it is nevertheless indispensable to very large growth.

The suggestions of this chapter are intended more for amateurs and those who wish to experiment on raising very large trout than for those who make a business of trout raising; for though the raising of very large trout is a desirable thing always, it is not often consistent with the best economy, — smaller trout and more of them, with perfect security, being a more profitable end to seek.

Section V. — Daily Care of the Large Trout.

The mere daily care of the large trout is almost nothing, if the arrangements for keeping them are right to begin with. I know of no domesticated creature which requires so little daily care. With the exception of feeding them once a day, and keeping the inlets and outlets clear, you need not bestow a thought on them for weeks. They do not require daily grooming like a horse, or daily milking like a cow, or careful housing in winter like sheep, or watching like poultry. If you have made the ponds safe from the changes of weather and the attacks of enemies, the trout will be, summer and winter, their own keepers, with your assistance once a day in giving them their food, and twice a year in sorting them. They can even be kept without eating for several days without the injurious results which would follow similar neglect with other domesticated creatures. There is also seldom or never any sickness among large trout kept in suitable waters. This is a very striking feature of trout growing, and a very favorable one. It is astonishing how many you can keep in a pond of good water the year round without danger of sickness or loss by death. Fowls confined in numbers get sick and die. Disease breaks out and spreads among large flocks of sheep and herds of cattle when confined, but you can keep thousands of trout in a very small enclosure of good water in perfect health all the year round. Indeed, there is no other creature above the grade of insects, except other fish, that you can keep in such large numbers and in so small a space with so little risk of disease and death. This is one of the most remarkable points about growing the large trout, and reduces the labor of taking care of them to a minimum. To be sure, the general work *connected* with keeping the large trout is very considerable, such as taking the eggs, preparing the spawning-beds, and the like; but the mere daily care of the fish themselves is very trifling.

SECTION VI. — MARKETING THE LARGE TROUT.

Marketing the trout is a simple process. You take a pail, some small pieces of ice, a little food, and a hard-wood stick about a foot long, or a piece of iron, to kill the trout with, and go to the pond. Place a large tub near where you are going to take out the fish, fill it half full of water, throw a little food into the pond, and, when the fish come for it, take out a netful, and empty them into the tub. Sort out what fish you want to kill, and throw back the rest, then, lifting the fish up one by one with the left hand, strike a sharp blow on the top of the skull with the instrument in the right. This will kill them at once, which is an important point gained. Put the dead ones immediately with the ice in the pail, and take them to the scales to weigh them. Having noted down their weight, pack them in a box of pounded ice and sawdust, nail up the box, label it, and send it to the express-office. In filling a twenty-pound order, this can be done so quickly that the trout can be on their way within half an hour after you go to the ponds for them, and they need not have been exposed to the air (without ice) three minutes in all. Killed and packed in this way, they will open twenty-four hours afterwards as fresh and hard as when they were taken out of the ponds, and will be a great deal harder than trout caught by fishermen in the wild brooks the same morning. The proprietor of the Parker House at Boston, to whom I have furnished trout for several years, said that the Cold Spring Trout, which were killed and packed in this way, came the best of any they had ever had in the house. Yet his house is one hundred and twenty miles from the ponds.

The best time to kill fish for the table is, as a rule, that season of the year which is the antipodes of the spawning season. The best time, therefore, to begin to market trout is in the spring, just after their spring appetite comes on. They are then hard and plump, and in first-rate condition. From then till July they do very well to market. After that they steadily deteriorate. As the spawning season approaches, their flesh weighs less compared with their size. They gain very much in weight between April 1st and July 1st, sometimes fifty per cent and over, which makes it desirable on that account to hold them till July. On the other hand, the prices are best at the beginning of the season, and fall very considerably by July. My trout, sent to Fulton Market, New York, and sold on commission, April 1, 1871, brought $ 1.25 per pound. Before the month was out the price had fallen to 90 cents.

The question as to the age at which it is most profitable to market trout is an important one. I think that it is the spring of the fourth or fifth year. It cannot be earlier than this, for the trout get some of their best, if not their very best, growth the third year, and to kill them before they are three years old would cut off nearly all the increase from them.

There are also reasons why they are most profitably killed before they are older than four years. The ratio of their growth to the cost of keeping has then reached its maximum, at least in small artificial ponds, and is on the wane. Every year after that they are kept also increases the general risk. They are at this age of the best marketable size, — very large trout not being as salable as pound-trout or less.

This question, however, of the most profitable age to market the fish varies with circumstances, and it is one which every trout breeder will doubtless best settle for himself, though the above suggestions may perhaps, in some measure, serve as a guide.

The New York market is the best market in the country for first-class trout, as it is for game of every description. The Boston market falls very much below it, and most of the smaller cities are very poor places indeed to which to send trout for sale in the public markets.

CHAPTER VI.

CONCLUDING CHAPTER.

Section I.—The Work in General at a Trout-Breeding Establishment.

THE work at a trout-breeding establishment varies with the season of the year. In the summer, when the work is the lightest, it is a routine nearly as follows. You go to the ponds in the morning, examine the streams,* and clean the screens. You then take the meat as the butcher has left it, sort it for the different sizes of fish, grate the liver for the young fry, chop the heart in the cutter for the yearlings, run the rest through the sausage-grinder for the large trout, and give the refuse to the dog. You next take the feeder and feed the fry, and examine them thoroughly; then the yearlings, then the large fish. You then feed the

---

* I would like here to caution beginners, when going the rounds for the purpose of seeing if everything is right, never to take anything for granted, but, on the contrary, to look over the works with the *expectation* of finding something wrong. Though you may have left everything perfectly safe, as you supposed, the day before, a dozen things may have occurred during the night to make trouble. I could mention numberless instances where losses have occurred from the keeper taking for granted that everything was right, and consequently overlooking something that was wrong.

11

P

young fry again, and if in spring water, give them earth twice a week. Set things in order, observe the progress of your experiments if you have any, see that everything is left right, and then, if no accident has happened, your work is done for the morning.

In the afternoon you feed the young fry again twice and the yearlings once, leave things right for the night, and the work is done for the day, if it is a fair day. If it is a rainy day, the streams and screens will need more watching and care, and there will perhaps be gates and flash-boards to alter.

You will also during the summer probably have some improvements to make, and some changing and sorting of the young fry, if you have many.

As the spawning season approaches, there will be, among other things, in addition to the routine work, the spawning races to clear out and bed with clean gravel, the hatching troughs to clean out and prepare for use, new flannel filters to make, moss to get in for packing the eggs, traps to set, and special precautions to take against the fall freshets.

After the spawning season begins, there will be the feeding, the spawning the fish, the laying down of the eggs, orders to fill, and the daily examination of the eggs. If you secure a good impregnation this latter job will not be much, but if you have poor luck impregnating, it will be a great burden all through the winter, increasing every day till long after the fish begin to hatch. After the hatching commences, and the empty eggs are all picked out, there is a lull in the work till the new fry begin to feed. It is then very cold. The old trout will need to be fed but three or four times a week, the yearlings not much oftener, the young fry only once or twice a day, and there will now be no more bad eggs to pick out. Thus the work is very much lessened ; but it is the lull before the storm, if this expression may be used, for soon the young fry begin to feed, and their thousands or hundreds of thousands of mouths must be fed five or six times a day. The shells of the hatched eggs, now being constantly shed by the young fish, clog up the screens, and make incessant watching of them necessary.

Very likely the frost and muskrats are making trouble with the ponds or aqueducts outside, and altogether this is usually made a very busy time, the burden of which is not at all lessened by the shortness of the days and the excessive cold. As the spring advances the young fry are thinned out by sales, they require to be fed less often, the fry of last year have become yearlings, the days lengthen, the weather grows warmer, and the work becomes easier and pleasanter, until the sales of the young fry are over. The balance of them are soon turned into their nurseries, rearing-boxes, or ponds, and the labor is reduced again to the mere routine of the summer.

The cares of a trout-breeding establishment in full operation are very considerable most of the time, and few beginners will be wholly able to free themselves from consequent anxiety ; but this is more than balanced a hundred times over by the constant interest and ever-increasing enthusiasm which the beautiful creatures inspire at every stage of their growth. There is no time when they are not beautiful and intensely interesting, and it is not exaggerating to say that at some particular periods, as, for instance, the spawning season, the first appearance of the embryo in the egg, and the hatching of the egg, afford to a lover of nature a most pleasurable excitement, which would seem to be satisfying even to those who think that it takes a good deal of excitement to satisfy them.

On the whole, I should say that the work of a trout farm is attended with considerable care, and at first with some anxiety, but also with a corresponding interest and enjoyment, and not without a very considerable degree of pleasurable excitement at times.

The Pecuniary Aspect of Trout Culture.

One of the chief inquiries at the present time in regard to trout culture is whether it can be made a profitable business. In reply to this inquiry I have no hesitation in saying that I think trout breeding can be made profitable anywhere in the settled portions of this country where there is plenty of suitable water; but to be very profitable it must be on a large scale. It will not pay great profits to raise a thousand trout a year, but a handsome income will be made from raising ten thousand a year.

I find that the cost of growing trout is very small indeed, and that the returns are very large indeed.

It costs no more to keep a thousand trout each, of the three different sizes, springlings, yearlings, and two-year-olds, than it does in the country to keep a horse, and what would keep a pair of horses at a stable in the city would enable a man to turn out five thousand pound of trout a year.

The current expenses of a trout-breeding establishment consist of three classes, viz. : 1. The rent of the place or the interest on the original outlay, plus the wear and tear, which together should be reckoned at 12%. 2. The care of the fish, which is not much for a small stock of trout, and grows (comparatively) less the more fish you have. 3. The cost of feed, which is very small, amounting, perhaps, to 3 cents a pound. All which items of expense do not make the full-grown trout cost over 15 or 20 cents a pound, if successfully raised.

On the other hand, trout bring from 50 cents a pound to $1.25, 75 cents being, I should say, a fair average, at the present time, in the neighborhood of Boston and New York.

Here we see a large margin for profit, and I think it is a fair one, when a man raises his trout successfully. It all depends on this, of course. If he cannot keep his trout alive and secure, he cannot expect to make anything at the business.

I should say the following estimate approximated the truth : —

If you have first-rate water facilities, and should hatch 20,000 young fry and raise them all to be four years old on food at 3 cents a pound, they would cost you, after you began to market the fish, not over 18 cents a pound. If you raise half, all your expenses being the same, with the exception of food, they will cost about 24 cents a pound. If you raise one fourth, they will cost somewhere near 36 cents a pound. If you raise one eighth, about 54 cents a pound. If you raise less than this, they will cease to pay a profit.

To assist the beginner in estimating his expected expenses and returns, I will give the following maxims: —

a. Under favorable circumstances, five pounds of meat food may be considered an equivalent for one pound of trout growth with two-year-olds and three-year-olds.

b. For any given quantity of two or three year olds one per cent of their weight may be regarded as an adequate average daily ration the year round.

c. Two and three year olds will double their weight annually, and can be *made* to do so in the six months from May to September, by extra care and feeding.

d. Good food for grown-up trout, namely, lungs and plucks of slaughtered animals, can be purchased anywhere for two or three cents a pound. The cost of the actual food of the young fry the first six months is inappreciable. For further information see chapter on food.

e. First-class trout bring $ 1.00 a pound in Fulton Market in April, and can be forced, almost any time, when in season, at 50 cents.

f. Freshly killed trout, well packed in ice and sawdust, will stand a direct journey in the summer, by rail, of five hundred miles, without injury.

Mr. Stephen H. Ainsworth's estimate of profits, published five years ago (1866), is as follows: —

```
Cost of buildings and fixtures .    .    .    .    . $ 6,000
5,000 parents for spawn, at 50 cents    .    .    .      2,500
Three men's labor for four years, at $300 per year    3,600
Cost of food for 1,000,000 trout for 4 years   .    . 20,000
   "       "       "       "      3 years .    .   10,000
   "       "       "       "      2 years   .    . 4,000
   "       "       "       "      1 year .    .    1,000
                                               ___________
                                    Total  $ 47,100
```

Now for their value. The million of four-year-olds will average a pound each, and are worth at least twenty-five cents per pound in the pond, which makes the

```
1,000,000 4-year-olds worth       .    .    .    . $ 250,000
    "     3-year-olds, ½ pound each    .    .      175,000
    "     2-year-olds, ¼ pound each .    .    .      87,000
    "     1-year-olds, 7 oz. each    .    .    .      30,000
                                               ___________
The worth of all trouble at the end of four years  $ 542,000
Deduct the price of growing    .    .    .    .      47,000
                                               ___________
Profit .    .    .    .    .    .    .    .    . $ 495.000
```

As these figures stand, they cannot serve as a guide to fish-breeders at present, for no one begins to carry on the business on this immense scale. But suppose we divide the figures by 50, which brings the scale within reach, we then have a profit of $ 10,000 on an establishment turning out 20,000 four-year-old trout annually. This, I believe, would be not far from the truth but *for one item*, which Mr. Ainsworth did not take in, but which closely follows every business like an evil genius, namely, *risk*. What this fluctuating item ought to be in the above calculation, I will not attempt to say, but I am afraid that at the time the estimate was made it was more than enough to swallow up the profits. It has been growing less and less

every year, as trout growing has become better understood, and I believe the time is near at hand when
Mr. Ainsworth's figures may be realized on a reduced
scale, with not more than 50% deducted from the
profits to cover the items of risk.

It may occur to some to inquire what makes the
item of risk so large. I will reply that it is because
the business is new, and but little understood, the
subject-matter is of a peculiarly hazardous sort, and,
perhaps more than all, fish-breeders will not take pains
to insure the security which is absolutely necessary to
success, and which has been dwelt upon so emphati-
cally in earlier portions of this treatise. These things
have made the risk very great, and account for the
very significant fact, that, in the five years since Mr.
Ainsworth's table was published, no one has made
a fortune by raising trout for the table, or even to my
knowledge derived any very extraordinary income from
this source alone.

I think, however, the next five years will tell a different story, and I am very much mistaken if some of
the trout ponds now under way do not yield within
that time some very handsome returns from their mar-
keted trout.

Thus far we have considered the business of trout
growing in only one of its branches of profit, namely,
raising marketable trout. There are, as is well known,
two other sources of revenue :—

1. The sale of spawn.

2. The sale of young stock.

The first branch can hardly be considered a legitimate branch on which to base permanent returns, because the sale of spawn is limited to establishments that are just commencing operations. This trade is a large one now, because so many establishments are starting ; but these will soon furnish their own spawn and become sellers instead of buyers, and when the prospective fish-breeding operations of the country are all under way there will be a great supply of eggs with a very disproportionate demand. Indeed, the prospect is that the spawn trade will not be a permanent one of any great value, and therefore cannot be regarded, in its present state at least, as a legitimate ground for basing permanent expectations.

It is not so, however, with the trade in young fry and yearlings for stocking other waters. It is a universal custom now with owners of small gardens to buy their young cabbages and tomatoes, and other vegetables, of the large producers, because it is cheaper than to start them themselves. Farmers also buy their pigs, instead of breeding them, from the same cause. Now it is only reasonable to expect the same rule to prevail in fish raising, as it certainly does at present. Many persons who have ponds and streams, and want to keep them stocked, will prefer, and will find it cheaper, to buy their young stock every year than to work all winter at hatching the eggs. The trade in young stock, therefore, looks as if it would be permanent, and appears to be a *legitimate* source from which to expect an income in trout-raising.

This forms at present a very considerable item in the business. Young fry are in great demand in New

England* at $25 a thousand, and yearlings at $100 a thousand. Many thousands of them could be sold at this day for these, and even at an advance on these prices, if the fish could be had. The supply this year (1871) has not nearly kept up with the demand.

We here find in the sale of young stock quite an addition to the sources of the trout grower's income, and I am informed by those who are operating near the large cities that a very considerable revenue could be obtained at their places by charging an admission-fee to visitors.

There is also money to be made by buying and fattening trout for the market, when you can buy them cheap enough. 'Good thriving trout less than four years old will double their weight in a year, and sometimes much more. Therefore, if you put a thousand pounds of them in a pond, securely protected, they will

---

* The price-list of Cold Spring Trout Ponds for 1871 is as follows : —

Trout Spawn, warranted live and healthy, per thousand	$10.00
Young Trout, one inch long, first thousand . . .	30.00
Each additional thousand	25.00
Yearling Trout, four or five inches long, per thousand	100 00
Trout for the Table, dead weight, per pound . . .	1.00
Salmon Spawn, warranted live and healthy, per thousand	50.00
Each additional thousand	25.00
Young Salmon, first thousand	100.00
Each additional thousand	50.00
Young Black Bass, first thousand	50.00
Each additional thousand	25.00

This is a fair statement of prices current. Some dealers charge more, some charge less.

in a year become two thousand pounds, and the feed in the mean time will not cost over one hundred and fifty dollars. That is to say, the increase will cost you not over fifteen cents a pound.

When these various sources of income are taken into account, in connection with the wide margins for profit, it is obvious that successful operations cannot but pay well. I would say, however, in conclusion, that I do not wish to hold out false inducements to persons to go into the business with the hope of making great fortunes. The item of risk is a very serious one yet, and small operators cannot expect to make more than a fair living. With many it will not pay at all, while it is reserved only for the very successful, and for those who have the few great water facilities of the country, to make the great fortunes.

Section II. — Recapitulation.

WATER.

Cautions to be observed in selecting Water for Trout Breeding.

Beware of,

1. Insufficient water.
2. Freshets.
3. Water that heats in the summer.
4. Water intrinsically unsuitable.

PONDS.

Points to be secured in building Ponds.

1. Excavate, rather than dam up.
2. Build compactly.

3. Build small ponds for business.
4. Be able to draw off the water.
5. Avoid hiding-places.
6. Protect ponds thoroughly.

BUILDINGS.

A full set of buildings or rooms consists of,
1. Hatching apartment.
2. Meat apartment.
3. Store-room and carpenter's shop.
4. Office.
5. Ice-house.

THE HATCHING APPARATUS.

The hatching apparatus consists of,
1. Supply reservoir.
2. Aqueduct.
3. System of filters.
4. Hatching apparatus proper.

THE NURSERY.

The points to be secured about the nursery are,
1. A fall of water.
2. A current.
3. Protection from suction against the screens.
4. Security from overflow.
5. Absence of fixed hiding-places.
6. Compactness.
7. Protection against natural enemies.
8. Perfectly tight compartments.

TAKING THE EGGS.

The directions for taking the eggs are,

1. Use eggs that flow easily, and no others.
2. Use ripe milt, and no other.
3. Make quick work.
4. Stir well while stripping.
5. Allow time for eggs to separate.
6. Rinse thoroughly.

HATCHING THE EGGS.

Dangers.	*Remedies.*
Fungus.	Carbonized wood.
Sediment.	Flannel filters.
Living enemies.	Covers.
Byssus.	Daily examination.

ALEVINS.

Dangerous Instincts.

1. To hide.
2. To pursue a current of water.

THE YOUNG FRY.

Directions.

1. Have healthy well-fed breeders.
2. Develop strong and healthy embryos in the egg.
3. Provide suitable place for young fry.
4. Take good care of them.

LARGE TROUT.

Precautions.

Guard against,
1. Freshets.
2. Overstocking.
3. Heated water.
4. Careless handling.
5. Cannibalism.
6. Fouled water.
7. Natural enemies.
8. Poachers.

HOW TO GROW VERY LARGE TROUT.

Give them,
1. Plenty of water.
2. Plenty of food.
3. (Relatively) warm water.
4. Wide range.
5. Ample space.

APPENDIX.

APPENDIX I.

A NEW DISCOVERY.—CURE FOR FUNGUS.

Salt a Cure for Microscopic Parasites on Trout.

IN the spring of 1872 I began some microscopic examinations of the parasites on large and small trout, which
led to the discovery of a cure for what has hitherto been
thought to be incurable disorder.

It is well known that when trout become injured or un-
healthy a fungoid growth appears in blotches over the surface of their backs, usually terminating in fatal results in a
few days.

It has hitherto been supposed, I believe, that the fungus
eats into the tissues of the fish, and destroys it. The microscope revealed, however, that it was not the fungus that
penetrated into the fish, but a multitude of microscopic
worms of the shape and appearance given on page 258.
The worms are never found in the upper parts of the fungus, but just below at the roots, or where the fungus joins
on to the surface of the skin. Here between the roots of
the fungus and the body of the fish are found hundreds of
these creatures incessantly in motion and apparently eating vigorously. They are about $\frac{1}{80}$ of an inch in length
and $\frac{1}{200}$ of an inch in diameter, and are provided with a
mouth at one extremity and at the other with about twenty
claw-like appendages for fastening on to the fish on which
they feed. They are continually eating into the tissues of
the fish, and the twenty tentacles enable them to fasten on
so tightly that the fish cannot shake them off. These parasites appear to live on the flesh of the fish, and the fungus

to live on the digested matter into which they transform it.

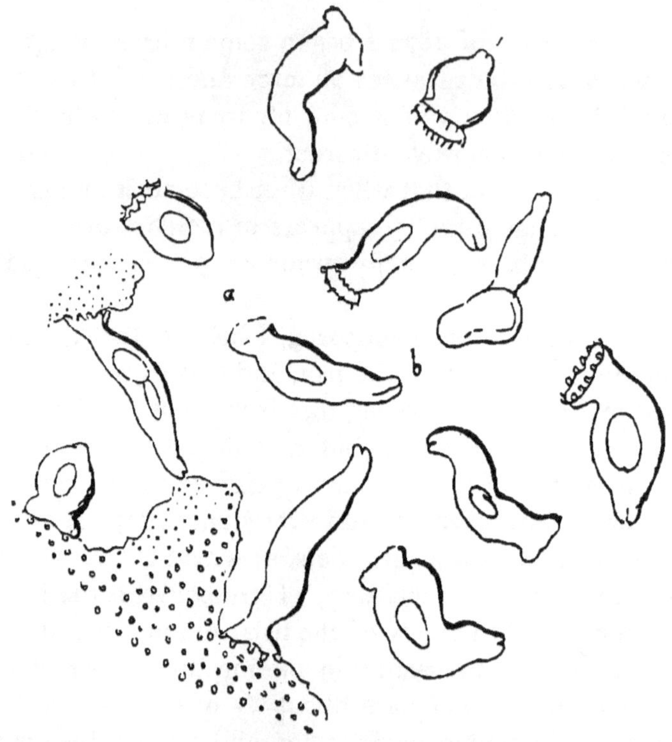

Parasites which attack Large Trout. *a* Tentacles for fastening to the fish; *b* Mouth.

This discovery led to some experiments in search of a remedy, and it was found that a strong solution of salt destroyed the parasites. Experiments were then made of immersing trout in salt water, and it was found to be perfectly harmless, if not too long continued. A method was thus found of killing the parasites without killing the fish, which fact was confirmed by actually taking a trout covered with fungus and immersing him in a salt bath for a moment or two, and afterwards keeping him by himself for several days. The fungus peeled off, the parasites were killed, the bare spots healed over, and the trout got well.   Others were tried; some died and some lived.

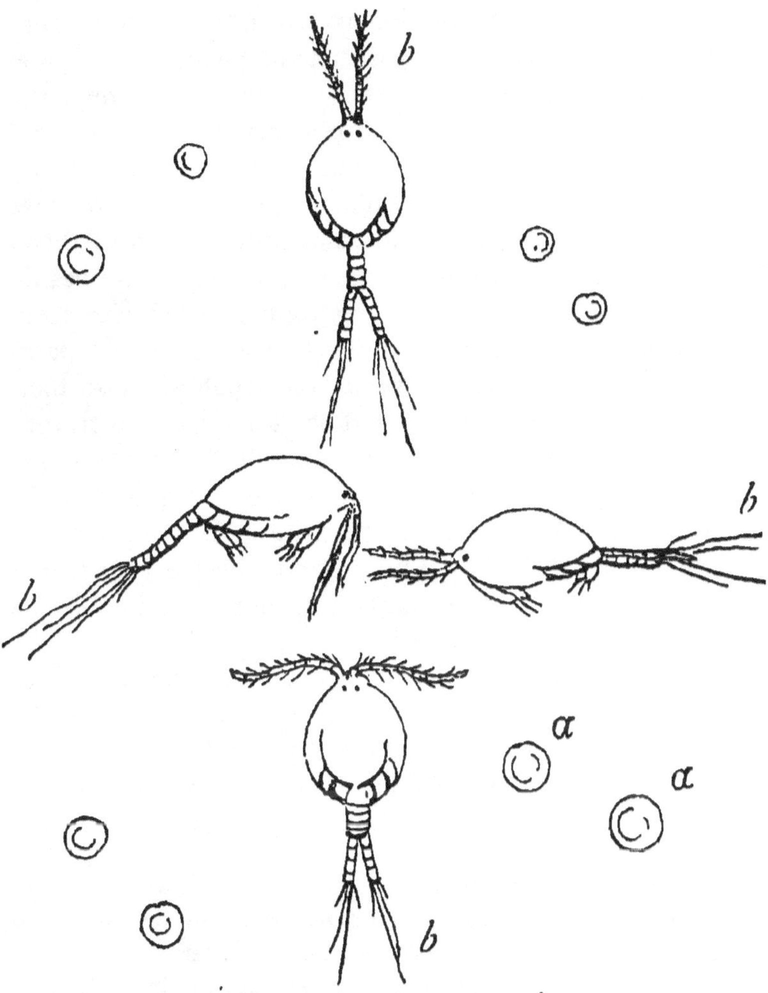

a Microscopic parasites which attack trout fry : *b* Water insects supposed to be destructive to trout eggs.

From all which circumstances we may, I think, draw the following conclusions : That it is the worm, and not the fungus, which eats into and kills the fish ; and that the fish can be cured, when not too much weakened, by immersion in a strong solution of salt.*

A similar series of experiments led to the discovery that salt is also a cure for the parasites on young fish. These parasites are smaller than those which infest the large fish.† They have a circular form with a diameter of about $\frac{1}{50}$ of an inch. They are extremely thin, and progress by a rotatory movement. They sometimes swarm in immense numbers upon the young fish that are attacked by them. They do not cause a fungoid growth, as the larger ones do in the larger fish, but the young trout affected with them appear outwardly as clean and well as ever. If the parasites are not removed, however, the trout will lose their strength and drift down toward the screen, on which they will probably be finally caught and die.‡ Salt destroys the parasites, and does not injure the young fry. It is, therefore, a remedy for the parasites. Hundreds of experiments which I tried of putting the affected young trout in salt water had the same result, which was to kill the parasites and restore the fish.

I will also add in this connection that the salt bath seems to improve the young fish in other ways than by killing the parasites, and one lot of young fry in particular, confined in a small box, which I cured in this way, and to which I gave a pint of salt every day, appeared better than

* I used a table-spoonful of salt to a pint of water, and kept the fish in it till he went over on his back, and then took him out and put him instantly into cold running water.

† I have sometimes found the larger parasites in small numbers on the small trout, but have never found the circular parasite on large trout.

‡ This furnishes one explanation of what so many trout breeders have remarked, that their young fry seemed to die when they appeared perfectly healthy.

any other young fish that I had. I have accordingly come to the conclusion that salt is beneficial to the young fish, and that large quantities can be used to advantage in the nurseries of the young fry, not only for the purpose of immersion, but to furnish an essential element in which the water has become deficient. All spring water, it is said, contains a modicum of salt. Perhaps this slight trace of salt is essential to the health of the fish. If so, then salt ought to be supplied artificially when trout are kept in a spring stream where the supply of salt is insufficient.

APPENDIX II.

JOURNEYS OF LIVE FISH AND EGGS.

BELOW will be found a brief account of some journeys with live fish, which may serve as a guide to beginners.

1. In May, 1868, I sent 15,000 trout fry to New York City and various intermediate points, in care of Mr. Frank H. Osgood. They left the ponds about 6 A. M., and were carried in ten twelve-gallon tin cans about two thirds full of water. The temperature was kept low and even with ice. The last of the lot did not reach their destination till eleven o'clock the next morning. The water was not changed, but was kept well aerated during the journey. Very few died. *Mem.:* New tin answers very well to transport fish in, but after it has been standing a long time it should be carefully scoured, as it gathers an oxide which seems to be partly soluble in water, and, at all events, is poisonous to the fish. The young salmon for the Delaware River were lost this spring from a similar cause.

2. The same season I sent by express two lots, of 500 trout fry each, to Providence, R. I., about 120 miles, without an attendant. They all died on the way. A lot of 500 bass fry sent by express to Framingham, Mass., about 100 miles, with two changes of cars, met the same fate. *Mem.:* It is not safe usually to send live fish without an attendant, at least a part of the way.

3. In the fall of 1868 Mr. Osgood took several yearling trout to the New England Agricultural Fair at New Haven, 157 miles, and exhibited them for several days

in a tank, occasionally changing the water. They bore the journey and exhibition admirably and without loss, receiving a well-deserved diploma.

4. In the fall of the same year we caught live salmon in a stake net on the Mirimichi River, confined them for a while in a pen made in the river, conveyed them from the pen eleven miles, closely packed in a creel, and put them into a pond. At first many of them became covered with fungus and died, but as the water grew colder the transportation injured them less and less, and late in the fall they suffered very little from handling.

5. In December, 1868, in very cold weather, nearly 200,000 salmon spawn, the eye-spots then becoming visible, were packed, at the salmon establishment on the Mirimichi, in moss in baskets, and the baskets in large boxes, and taken 100 miles on a sled, 100 miles by rail, 250 miles by steamer, and 220 miles more by rail. They arrived at the Cold Spring Trout Ponds in good condition.

6. The same winter salmon spawn and trout spawn packed in moss were sent to Hon. Frank T. Buckland, H. B. M. Commissioner of Fisheries. The trout spawn arrived in England in first-rate condition, and also that portion of the salmon eggs which did not hatch on the way, but it was so late in the season that some of the embryos hatched and perished.

7. In the spring of 1869, 3,000 salmon fry were sent in two twelve-gallon cans to the South Side Sportsmen's Club, Long Island, in care of an attendant. The water was kept cold with ice, and the salmon did well till about 10 P. M., when they were on the New York steamer, and had been sixteen hours on their journey. At this time the water was partly changed, and water from the boat was used. Nearly 2,000 died immediately, the rest reaching their destination safely.

8. Another lot of 2,000, to make up this loss, was sent

soon afterwards, in a similar way, but the *water was not changed during the journey*, though ice was used freely. They all reached their destination safely, after a journey of about thirty. hours. *Mem. :* It is much safer to keep the fish in water that you are acquainted with than to use that with which you are not acquainted.

9. In the spring of 1869 I had three lots of Lake Champlain and Missisquoi River fish transported to Charlestown, N. H., consisting of Black Bass (*Grystes fasciatus*); Glass-eyed Pike (*Lucioperca*); Red-fin Mullets (*Catostomus*); White-tailed Mullets (*Catostomus*); Lake Champlain Shad, Whitefish (*Coregonus*); Suckers (*Catostomus*) : Mascalonge (*Esox*, gill-covers bare); Pickerel (*Esox*, gill-covers scaled); Hornpouts, Bull-heads (*Pimelodus*); Yellow Perch (*Perca flavescens*); Sheep's Head, Drumfish (*Amblodon*). Their journey was a long and severe one. They were first taken in a seine, and confined in a pound a day or two, then transferred to a hundred-gallon wooden tank, and conveyed ten miles in a row-boat to the village of Swanton, Vt., thence to the railroad station by wagon, thence to St. Albans by rail, where they waited several hours for the connecting train. They then travelled 152 miles by rail to Charlestown, where they were received in a wagon and driven to the Ponds. Ice was used plentifully on the way, probably too much, they being warm-water fish, and the water was more or less aerated. The result was very different with different fish. There were about forty fish in the tank each time, all full grown, and averaging two pounds apiece. All the shad (whitefish) died almost immediately, most of the sheep's-heads died early also, and almost all the glass-eyed pike. The mullets, perch, suckers, hornpouts, and pickerel lived. Most of the black bass lived. The survivors are still at the Cold Spring Trout Ponds, and are doing well. *Mem. :* Ice should be used cautiously with warm-water fish. The

Lake Champlain shad (whitefish) cannot be transported in the spring.

10. In September, 1869, ten large trout, hatched at Charlestown, and measuring nearly a foot in length, were taken for exhibition at the Mechanics' Fair in Boston. They survived the journey very well, although they were kept two days and one night in a tank of forty gallons of water. They were ultimately placed in a glass tank in the rotunda of Quincy Hall, where an arrangement had been made to run a constant stream of water over them. The temperature of the water varied from 65° to 73°, but was kept down somewhat with ice. The trout lived about ten days when they all died. A second lot was sent for, which survived the remaining two weeks of the exhibition. They received a silver medal and the diploma of the Association.

11. In May, of 1870, I transported 1,000 yearling trout to North Brookfield, 109 miles, three changes of cars, twelve hours' journey. They were taken in a tank and two barrels, with about eighty gallons of water, which was kept very cold, and well aerated. Forty-one died on the journey.

12. On the 20th of May, the same year, one very hot day, I carried 10,000 trout fry to Bristol, Conn., 138 miles, twelve hours, with three changes of cars. They were carried in six twelve-gallon cans, with about fifty gallons of water. Only *seven* died on the way.

13. In the fall of 1870 I carried 20,000 trout spawn, just taken, in a pail of water, seven miles in a wagon, without loss.

14. In the spring of 1871 I sent 10,000 trout fry to Norway, Me., 120 miles by rail, 100 by boat, and 40 miles more by rail. The journey took twenty-eight and a half hours. They were carried in a tank, in forty to fifty gallons of water, and plenty of ice. There was a loss of about 500, many of which had been bruised by the ice.

12

15. In the same spring I took 500 yearlings and 12 large trout, very fat, in the same tank, in forty gallons of water, to Webster, Mass., 110 miles, in thirteen hours, with three changes of cars. All seemed in first-rate condition, with the exception of half a dozen yearlings, which appeared to have been bruised. *Mem.:* In travelling by rail with fish, it is better to have one large tank than several smaller ones, provided you do not carry over about fifty gallons of water. More than this makes it too heavy to be handled safely in the hurry of railway travel.

16. On the 20th of November, 1871, 10,000 trout eggs were packed in sphagnum moss in a common wooden box about a foot square, at Charlestown, N. H. They went from Charlestown to Boston, 120 miles by rail, on the same day. They remained in Boston over night, and the next morning were put on board the ocean steamer which sailed that day. They had a long passage of eighteen days to Liverpool, and a considerable journey by rail afterwards from Liverpool to Keswick. At the end of the journey two thirds were found in good condition, although some hatched on the way and died, and the byssus generated by these, and by some of the eggs that were killed during the first part of the trip, made great havoc in places.

APPENDIX III.

ODDS AND ENDS.

CONTAINING tables of spawn in various fishes; the seasons when fish spawn; the months when fish are in good condition; of water plants suitable for fish ponds; the months when it is illegal to catch trout in the various States; also trout breeding outfit, tricks for managing domesticated fish, tricks for managing the enemies of fish, etc.

NUMBER OF SPAWN IN DIFFERENT FISH.

*Buckland's Table.**

Species.	Weight of fish.	Total number of eggs.
Trout	1 lb.	1,008
Jack	$4\frac{1}{2}$ lbs.	42,840
Perch	$\frac{1}{2}$ lb.	20,592
Roach	$\frac{3}{4}$ lb.	480,480
Smelt	2 oz.	36,652
Lumpfish	2 lbs.	116,640
Brill	4 lbs.	239,775
Sole	1 lb.	134,466
Herring	$\frac{1}{2}$ lb.	19,840
Mackerel	1 lb.	86,120
Turbot	8 lbs.	385,200
Cod	20 lbs.	4,872,000

* Buckland's Fish Hatching, p. 13.

Atkins's Table.[*]

Species.	Weight of fish.	Number of eggs.
Yellow Perch	$3\frac{1}{2}$ oz.	9,943
River Smelt	2 oz.	25,141
Fresh-water Smelt	10 oz.	80,000
Whitefish (*Coregonus*)	2 lbs.	25,076
Schoodic Salmon (average)	$\frac{1}{2}$ lb.	about 600
Sebago Salmon (full count)	2 lbs. 10 oz.	2,368

Number of Spawn in other Fish not mentioned in the above Tables.

Species.	Weight of fish.	Number of eggs.
Herring	$5\frac{3}{4}$ oz.	265,650
Flounder	—	1,000,000
Mullet	—	13,000,000
Tench	—	383,250
Bream	—	137,800
Carp	66 lbs.	342,140
Sturgeon	200 lbs.	7,000,000
Pike	—	272,160

The following table gives the number of salmon eggs taken at the writer's establishment at Mirimichi in 1868. The fish averaged in weight about nine pounds, and were found to yield, like salmon everywhere else, a very uniform average of 1,000 eggs to the pound, when all the eggs were saved.

October 15, 1868,	80,000 eggs from 8 salmon.
" 16, "	55,000 " " 5 "
" 17, "	81,500 " " 12 "
" 20, "	8,000 " " 2 " partly spawned.
" 21, "	53,000 " " 8 "
" 23, "	5,000 " " 1 "
" 24, "	18,000 " " 3 "

[*] Maine Fisheries, Report, 1869, p. 24.

October 26, 1868,   21,000 eggs from 4 salmon.*
   "   29,   "   10,600 "   " 2   "

The following table is a portion of Seth Green's report to the New York Commissioner of Fisheries of the shad spawning on the Hudson in 1870, showing the number of spawn in shad.

Extracts from Report of Shad Fisheries in the Hudson in the State of New York, 1870.†

May 26, caught 20 shad at night, 2 ripe fish, 70,000 spawn.
  " 27, caught 12 shad, 1 ripe fish, took 40,000 spawn.
  " 30, fished at night, got 23 shad, 9 ripe fish, 260,000 spawn.
  " 31, caught 74 shad, 8 ripe fish, took 210,000 spawn.
June 1, caught 35 shad, 4 ripe fish, took 100,000 spawn.
  " 2, caught 108 shad, 6 ripe fish, took 150,000 spawn.
  " 3, caught 90 shad, 12 ripe fish, took 250,000 spawn.
  " 4, caught 133 shad, 7 ripe fish, took 165,000 spawn.
  " 11, caught 86 shad, 7 ripe fish, took 165,000 spawn.
  " 12, caught 70 shad, 11 ripe fish, took 240,000 spawn.
  " 13, caught 39 shad, 6 ripe fish, took 120,000 spawn.
  " 14, caught 32 shad, 2 ripe fish, took 55,000 spawn.

The following is the record of the trout spawning during the month of October, 1870, of one pond at the Cold Spring Trout Ponds. The trout averaged about half a pound in weight.

	Number of eggs.	Number of fish.
October 12	1,000	2
" 15	600	1
" 18	2,400	3
" 19	2,400	4

* It should be observed that the salmon in the river finished spawning by the 24th of October, and that the eggs taken after that time were from the fish captured in the artificial ponds.

† New York Citizen, October 15, 1870.

	Number of eggs.	Number of fish.
October 20	2,500	3
" 21	2,500	4
" 22	1,800	3
" 23	1,800	3
" 24	1,200	3
" 25	2,300	4
" 26	4,150	8
" 27	4,600	10
" 28	5,400	11
" 29	2,200	4
" 30	4,200	10
" 31	7,400	13

The following table shows the time of spawning in the latitude of Northern New England of some of our more common American migratory and fresh-water fishes.

Migratory Fishes.

Smelt (*Osmerus viridescens*)	April.
Shad (*Alosa prestabilis*)	May and June.
Alewife (*Alosa tyrannus*)	May and June.
Menhaden (*Alosa Menhaden*)	May and June.
Striped Bass (*Roccus lineatus*, Gill, *Labrax lineatus*, Cuv.)	July.
Salmon (*Salmo salar*)	October.

Fresh-water Fishes.

Perch Pike (*Lucioperca*)	Last of April.
Pickerel (*Esox reticulatus*)	Last of April and first of May.
Yellow Perch (*Perca flaviscens*)	April and May.
White Perch (*Merone americana*)	June.
Roach (*Pomotis appendix*)	May.
Sunfish (*Pomotis vulgaris*, Cuv.)	May.
Sucker (*Catostomus*)	May.
Rock Bass (*Centrarchus æneus*)	May.
Bottom Pike (variety of *Lucioperca*)	May.

Mullet (*Catostomus*)	June.
Black Bass (*Grystes fasciatus*)	June.
Hornpout, Catfish (*Pimelodus*)	September.
Trout in ordinary brooks (*Salmo fontinalis*)	October and November.
Blue-back Trout (*Salmo oquossa*)	October.
Schoodic Trout (*Salmo sp.*)	November.
Sebago Salmon (*Salmo sp.*)	Last of Oct. and first of Nov.
Lake Trout, Togue (*Salmo toma*)	Last of Oct. and first of Nov.
Whitefish (*Coregonus albus*)	November.
Trout in spring water (*Salmo fontinalis*)	Nov., Dec., Jan., Feb.

Table of M. Coste.

PERIODS OF SPAWNING OF CERTAIN KINDS OF (EUROPEAN) FISH WHICH
REPRODUCE IN FRESH WATER.

Name of the species.	Time of spawning.
Salmon (*Salmo salar*)	From November to February.
Salmon Huch (*S. hucho*)	April and May.
Trout (*S. fario*)	From October to February.
Common Ombre (*S. thymallus*)	April and May.
Ombre Chevalier (*S. umbla*)	February, March, and April.
Lavaret (*S. Wartmanni*)	August, September, and Oct.
Fera (*Coregonus fera*)	January and February.
Shad (*Clupea alosa*)	March, April, and May.
Pike (*Esox lucius*)	February, March, and April.
Carp (*Cyprinus carpio*)	From May to September.
Bream (*C. brema*)	End of April and May.
Gibele (*C. gibelio*)	May, June, and July.
Tench (*C. tinca*)	June and July.
Perch (*Perca fluviatilis*)	March, April, and May.

Note.—The periods indicated in this table, varying according
to places and climates, must not be considered as fixed, but as
terms considering which it is possible to guess pretty nearly the
times at which the eggs of the different species will be likely to
hatch by artificial means.

TIMES WHEN IT IS ILLEGAL TO TAKE TROUT IN SOME OF THE STATES.

Maine : October, November, December, January.

New Hampshire : September, October, November.

Vermont : September 15th to 30th, October, November.

Massachusetts : September 20th to 30th, October, November, December, January, February, March 1st to 20th.

Rhode Island : July, August, September, October, November.

Connecticut : September, October, November, December, January, February, March.

New York : October, November, December, January, February.

New Jersey : September, October, November, December, January, February.

Pennsylvania : August, September, October, November, December, January, February, March.

California : January, February, March, April, May.

THE MIRIMICHI AND MISSISQUOI RIVERS.

There are two rivers in the vicinity of New England so prolific in fish that they should be known to every one who is interested in fishes as they swim, and who enjoys studying them and their habits.

These two rivers are the Missisquoi and the Mirimichi. The first produces chiefly warm-water fishes ; the second, migratory fishes of the best sort, and each is a marvel of its kind.   The fish, at the right season, fairly swarm in both of these rivers.

To illustrate the vast quantities of fish in the Mirimichi, it is only necessary to say that within five years one haul of the net drew out 10,600 striped bass * at North Esk. Smelts were so plenty, previous to 1868, that they were literally scooped up out of the water by barrels full, and used to manure the ground.   Salmon sold for 60 cents apiece,

---

* At Fulton Market prices, this one haul would bring ten thousand dollars.

and trout were so plenty that they had no sale at all.* Very fine eels were killed by the barrel full by rapping them on the head with a stick as they came up the small brooks by night.

The writer, in connection with Mr. Joseph Goodfellow of Mirimichi, shipped to Boston and New York, during the three months, January, February, and March, 1869, 30,490 pounds of striped bass, frozen; 46,946 pounds of smelts, frozen; 8,908 pounds of sea trout, frozen.

Previous to our starting this work, these enormous supplies of fish were of no value to the inhabitants. Since then a lucrative trade in these fish has been continued.

We paid at first, in 1868, 3½ cents per pound for striped bass, 2½ cents per pound for smelts, 3½ cents per pound for trout. The prices have risen very much since the trade was opened, and make these fisheries a considerable source of revenue to the Mirimichi people.

The Mirimichi River rises near the head-waters of the St. John, and flows northeasterly into the Gulf of St. Lawrence. To go to the Mirimichi River from Boston, you take a steamer to St. John, 300 miles, the cars from St. John to Shediac, 100 miles, and steamer from Shediac to New Castle, Mirimichi, 100 miles more.

The most valuable fish caught in the Mirimichi are Salmon (*Salmo salar*); Striped Bass (*Labrax lineatus*); Sea Trout (*Salmo trutta*); Brook Trout (*Salmo fontinalis*); Smelt (*Osmerus viridescens*); Sturgeon (*Acipenser*); Eel (*Anguilla*).

The Missisquoi River, though not so rich in fish as the

---

* The writer saw repeatedly a school of about two hundred large trout under a bridge where the most travelled highway crossed a small brook emptying into the Mirimichi. These trout summered here. No one thought them worth molesting, and they consequently lost their shyness, so as not to be at all afraid of the teams and persons passing.

Mirimichi, is yet deserving of acquaintance from the general variety and abundance of its inhabitants. This river, which is in the northern part of Vermont, empties into Lake Champlain at Missisquoi Bay, very near the Canada line. You can go directly from Boston *via* Fitchburg, Cheshire, and Vermont Central Railroads, leaving the cars at the Swanton Station, distance 288 miles. The chief fisheries are between Swanton Village and the Lake. The fishing is done in the spring of the year, with sweep seines, as soon as the ice goes out.

The fish caught in the Missisquoi River and Bay are, Red-fin Mullet (*Catostomus*) ; White-tail Mullet (*Catostomus*) ; Glass-eyed Pike, Perch Pike (*Lucioperca*) ; Lake Champlain Shad, Whitefish (*Coregonus albus*) ; Sheephead, Drumfish (*Amblodon*) ; Mascalonge, gill-cover bare (*Esox*) ; Pickerel, gill-cover scaled (*Esox*) ; Bottom Pike (*Lucioperca*) ; Black Bass (*Grystes fasciatus*) ; Oswego Bass (*Coregonus otsego*) ; Mud Fish, Fresh Water Lusk (*Lota*) ; Ling* (*Lota*) ; Sturgeon (*Acipenser*) ; Shiner (*Leuciscus americanus*) ; Bullhead, Catfish (*Pimelodus*) ; Rock Bass (*Centrarchus æneus*) ; Sunfish (*Pomotis vulgaris*) ; Sucker (*Catostomus*) ; Yellow Perch (*Perca flavescens*) ; Eel† (*Anguilla*) ; Salmon, fifty years ago (*Salmo salar*).

With the exception of the Trout, Salmon, and Whitefish, all these fish spawn in the spring and summer.

The following list contains the names of some water plants suitable for trout ponds and nurseries : —

Arrowhead (*Sagittaria sagittifolia*) ; Arrowhead (*Sagittaria acutifolia*) ; Water-cress (*Nasturtium officinale*) ; Water-cress (*Nasturtium hispidum*) ; Winter-cress (*Barbarea vulgaris*) ; Yellow-eyed Water Grass (*Schollera*

---

* This fish is thought by the fishermen to be the parent of the eel.

† Is the eel a hybrid ? No eggs or young are ever found in eels.

graminea); Water-lobelia (*Lobelia dortmanna*); Water-milfoil (*Myriophyllum verticillatum*); Water-milfoil (*Myriophyllum ambiguum*); Water-weed (*Anacharis canadensis*); Water-lily, white (*Nymphea odorata*); Water-lily, yellow (*Nuphar advena*); Water-lily, small yellow (*Nuphar pumila*); Northern Calla (*Calla palustris*); Floating Bur-reed (*Sparganium natans*); Pond-weed (*Potamogeton natans*); Pond-weed (*Potamogeton setaceum*); Sweet-flag (*Acorus calamus*); Starwort, broad-leaved (*Calletriche verna*); Starwort, narrow-leaved (*Calletriche autumnalis*); Hornwort (*Ceratophyllum demersum*); Tapegrass (*Vallisneria americana*); Common Rush (*Juncus*); Club Rush (*Scirpus*); River-weed or Thread-foot (*Podostemon ceratophyllum*), Duck Meat (*Lemna minor*); Duck meat (*Lemna gibba*); Sphagnum Moss (*Sphagnum*).

List of the most necessary and convenient articles that are used about a trout-breeding establishment : —

Meat-cutter and stand. Grater for preparing meat for young fry. Tin boxes for sending spawn. Water pails. Cans for carrying young fry. Small fine nets for catching young fish. Landing-net for large fish. Small sweep-seine. Flannel for filters. Fine copper-wire netting. Coarse galvanized iron-wire netting. Shears for cutting wire netting. Brush for cleaning screens. Sponge. Broom. Small shovel for moving gravel in troughs. A good meat-knife. Spouts for temporary use. Portable trap-boxes for temporary use. Large boxes for holding gravel. Traps for muskrats, minks, and kingfishers. Homœopathic bottles for specimens of embryos, etc. Alcohol for preserving specimens. Feathers and nippers for picking over eggs. Gun. Common agricultural tools, as shovel, etc. Common carpenters' tools, as hammer, saw, etc. Thermometer. Microscope.

To be used at the spawning beds : —

Large tubs. Three large pails. Landing net. Impregnating pans. Timepiece. Thermometer. Note-book.

Tricks with Trout.

If you want to make the colors of trout deep and dark, grow them over a black, muddy bottom, well shaded. If you want to cultivate light and delicate tints, grow the trout on a light, open, gravelly bed.

If you want to have trout short and deep, and, to use an expressive Americanism, "chunky,"* grow them in a deep, still pond. If you want to have them long and slim, grow them in a shallow, swift current.

If you want to have the trout in your ponds come to spawn any particular day, turn on a large, swiftly running stream, and they will come up. If you wish to retard their spawning for a day, let a small slow stream over them, and they will wait.

If there is a fall of water where trout run wild, set a common bushel basket behind the fall in a perpendicular line with the top of the dam. The trout will spring up the fall in the line of the current in attempting its passage ; but, if not successful, will fall back in the line of gravitation and be caught in the basket. If you wish to trap trout from below into an enclosure above, on a brook, screen it at the desired place, and arrange a pendent gate or door of wire netting in the screen, as in a mouse-trap, so that they can go through, but cannot come back. This will work quite successfully in the spawning season, when the trout's instinct to go up stream is very strong.

If you wish to take trout out singly from a pond without hurting them, bait a line (without a hook) with an inch-square piece of red flannel. The trout will swallow it just far enough to allow himself to be pulled out on the bank, but not far enough to hurt him.

If you want trout to frequent a particular place in your pond, feed them there regularly. If you want them to re-

---

* Also provincial in England, I believe.

treat to any particular place in your pond, feed them regularly, excavate a hole there, and darken the bottom, placing light gravel throughout the rest of the pond. They will always go there when disturbed, unless too tame or expecting feed.

If you are carrying trout in a barrel or tank, and want to make them rise from the bottom, give the barrel a knock or a blow near the bottom. The trout will instantly rise. If you want to make them sink to the bottom of the tank, shake a white handkerchief over them.

After a trout appears perfectly dead from suffocation (want of air), you can, if he has not been left too long in this condition, bring him back to life by vigorously aerating the water

Commence tickling a trout underneath with your hand, and in a little while, if you are gentle and patient, you will so mesmerize him that you can raise him out of the water, on the open palm of your hand, without his struggling.

If you want to attract trout to your bait, use the oil of rhodum, or anise, or cumin. The smell of salmon roe also attracts them   It is said that the scent of petroleum and tar is enticing to them. Walton recommended the use of petroleum.

If you want to net out trout in the night, arrange a lantern so that you can sink it in the water. Once in the water the fish will gather around it, and will become so bewildered that you can net them out without difficulty, whether wild or tame.

If you want to prevent a lot of trout from being hooked out in the night by poachers, feed them well towards evening, and then catch out two or three with a small hook, and, after a moment or two, throw them back. They will create a panic amongst the rest. so that there will be no more fishing that night with a hook.

If you want to see whether trout notice sounds, creep up cautiously, with a bell and revolver, to where you can see them without their seeing you, then scream with all your might, ring the bell, and fire the pistol. If they do not see any of your motions, they will not move a fin.

TRICKS WITH TROUT EGGS, OTHER FISH, MUSKRATS, ETC., ETC.

If you want to have trout eggs hatch in the summer, keep them on ice for six months. If you want to hatch them in a month, keep a stream of warmish water running over them. This you can do by bedding the supply-pipe in a bank of fresh horse-manure. Make the pipe small, and give it several turns in the bank.

If you want to see a trout-egg hatch, take one that is just ready to break the shell and put it in warm water, say at 70°, the warmth will often stimulate the embryo into breaking the shell.

If you want to drive alevins from a particular corner where they have collected, pour a few cups of water over the spot, which will drive them away, then fill in with whitish gravel, which will keep them away to some extent.

If a trout, not over two and a half inches long, strikes at a black spider in the water, the spider will strike back at him, and if he takes a good aim will kill the trout instantaneously. The little fellow will not go twelve inches before he turns over on his back and drops down dead.

If you throw small balls, made of the fisher's berry (*Cocculus indicus*), into the water, the fish will eat it, become poisoned, and rise to the surface dead.

If you have occasion to carry live bullheads * any dis-

* The bullhead (*Pimelodus*) is very tenacious of life. Fishermen often, by a half-dissecting and half-flaying process, take the meat out of a bullhead's body for their chowder, leaving only the head, skin, and fins. This more than eviscerated shell of a

tance, you can do so by packing them in wet moss (*Sphag-num*). They will live forty-eight hours in it. Or, if it is in the winter, you can freeze them up and carry them, if you do not freeze them so stiff but that you can bend them easily. This you can also do with pickerel and other fish.

When muskrats begin to come up your brook in the fall, set your traps in the middle of the stream and place obstructions (stakes or anything) on each side of the trap, as far as the bank. The rats will go into the trap, rather than go around or over the obstruction. If the muskrats have succeeded in getting up into your ponds, sink a barrel into the pond, fill it a little less than half full of water, and put a sweet apple in it. The rats will get into it after the apple, and cannot get out.

If minks have got into your ponds, push one end of a plank into the water, on the north bank of the pond, and let it rest so, obliquely, on the bank, facing the south. Put your trap on the plank, so that the mink must step into it if he comes up on the plank. He will presently climb up the plank to sun himself, and will be caught.

If kingfishers or fish hawks molest your trout, erect a pole on the bank, and fasten a common steel trap on the top of it. The birds will surely light on the pole to watch their prey, and will almost always be caught. If large herons visit the ponds, place a number of steel traps in any shallow part of the pond where their tracks are seen. The heron's feet are so large that he will not be long stepping into one of the traps. The traps should be firmly fastened, of course.

If you wish to know whether poachers visit the ponds

creature will immediately gain his equilibrium in the water, and endeavor to move off with as natural a motion of the fins as if nothing had happened. This sickening sight I have often seen at the Missisquoi River.

at night, tie cords across the paths, or, if the ground is suitable, strew a layer of fine sand around the ponds. The breaking of the cords or footprints on the sand will reveal the presence of the nocturnal visitors.

FREEZING FISH.*

From the Scientific American, January, 1854.

I have witnessed repeatedly, the two winters I have been here, the resuscitation of frozen trout, pickerel, and perch, on thawing them out in fresh running water, even after they had been carried for miles.

It is only under certain circumstances, however, that they will revive. If caught on a day when it is cloudy and freezing hard, and if not hurt with the hook, and they freeze immediately on being thrown on the ice, they will revive on being thawed out. But if allowed to toss about in the sun, on a clear day, and probably not freeze for an hour or two after they are caught, then they will never revive.

It is so common a thing that I have only to go back to the last day I was fishing, for an example of it. I went down to Lake Sandford with one of our men, on the 29th ultimo, and at night we carried home in our packs eleven pickerel, all frozen hard, and bent and curved just as they happened to twist themselves before freezing. We put them into a trough of running spring water, and when thawed out found six of them alive. The others had probably been caught in the warmest part of the day, and died before they froze. The same day fifteen fine brook trout were brought from Lake Andrew, five miles distant, in a pack, and on being thawed out several of them revived, though I did not notice how many. They are, however, a much more delicate fish than the pickerel or perch, and more easily hurt and killed than either of them.

* Compare *Embryologie des Salmones*, C. Vogt, p. 17.

On the afternoon of the 24th ultimo I had fished faithfully for pickerel till sundown, without even getting an encouraging nibble; tired at last of that fun, I took out a small hook and line, and soon had twenty-five perch; they froze almost instantly; I strung them on a crotched twig, carried them so for two miles, and, when thawed out, found fourteen of them alive, the rest having been hurt either by the hook or the twig.

The pond behind the village, formed by the damming of the river, is full of young pickerel; they are all from three fish put in there last winter, one male and two females. All of them were brought from Lake Sandford frozen, and were put into the pond after they had been thawed out in a trough. The male I caught; it lay on the ice, frozen, for three hours, and then, not finding a mate for him, I ran a stick through his gills, and dragged him home on the snow, two miles, threw him into the trough, and thought no more of him till next morning, when I found him alive, and seemingly enjoying himself as well as his narrow limits would permit. I took pity on the poor fellow, carried him down to the pond, and he went off like a dart.

These are but a few instances of what occurs almost every day the winter through. The fact of their resuscitation after being frozen, as I have described, is known to every one here who is in the habit of fishing in winter, and cannot escape being noticed, as the weather is cold enough almost all the time to freeze them, and they have to be thawed out before they can be cleaned.

I have heard fishermen say that they have taken trout when frozen, and whittled the fins and tail off, and, on being thawed, found them alive; but I have never tried this or any other experiment with them, and would not vouch for the truth of it.

First Authentic Account of Fly-Fishing.

Extract from Ælian's History of Animals, XI. 1, A. D. 230.

I have heard this account of a mode of fishing in Macedonia. In a river called Astræus, which flows between Beræa and Thessalonica, are found fishes marked with various colors (spotted trout). These feed upon flies that play upon the water, which are unlike any other flies, — differing from bees, wasps, or hornets, but of a distinct species. They have the boldness of other flies, are about the size of hornets, of the color of wasps, and make a bumbling noise like bees. These they call Ἴκκουρον. These, as they sport on the surface, the fish see; and, moving slyly through the water till they get under the insect, leap upon it as a wolf upon a sheep in a flock, or an eagle upon one of a flock of geese, and, seizing their prey, sink again into the deep water. This the fishermen observed, but could not use them for bait, as, when caught in the hand, the flies lost their color and their wings; for which cause they hated them (the fishes glutting themselves upon the bait which the angler knew not how to use). But, in process of time, as their angling science advanced, they learned to outwit the fish by their ingenuity. They first wrapped around their hook some Phœnician (purple) wool, and then tied on two feathers, or the wattles of a cock's neck, of a wax color. This they threw with a pole or reed, an ὀργυια, four cubits long (there must be a mistake here, for, at the utmost, that would not be more than seven or eight feet), and a line of the same length. These cunning artifices they threw on the water, and the fish, attracted by the appearance of the pretty insect they feed upon, seized the bait, and were caught.

ANCIENT FISH STORY.*

The farthest stretch of profane writers into the history of fishing is the mention made by Diodorus Siculus (Lib. I. 52) of Moeris, the immediate predecessor of Sesostris (see Larcher, Chron. d'Hérodote, and Bähr on Herodotus, II. 100), which, according to Champollion Figeac, would put him about B. C. 1500 (perhaps a hundred years too soon). This Moeris, the historian says, constructed the famous artificial lake called by his name, which was eighty stadia long and τρίπλεθρον (say four hundred feet) broad, and it cost fifty talents to open and shut the flood-gates. In the middle he erected two sepulchral pyramids, one for himself and the other for his wife, with marble statues of them both on a throne. But it was also a vast fish-pond, having in it twenty-two different kinds of fish, which increased so fast that the most extensive preparations for salting them were not sufficient for the purpose. The revenue derived from the fishing he assigned to his wife, who had thus, out of that source, a talent ($ 10,000) a day for pin money. The passage is curious, as showing the importance of fish as an article of food.

A DISSERTATION ON SHAD.

From the Belfast Journal.

The shad was named for old Shad-rach, whom Nebu-chad-nezzar considered a scaly chap, till after he passed through his fiery furnace, when he was found to be a man of much backbone, and in this respect the shad resembles him in great quantities. Shad are nature's pin-cushions for bones. They are built of the refuse stuff that was left after all the rest of the fish were concocted. The interior

---

* Bibliographical preface to Wiley and Putnam's edition of **Complete Angler, p. viii.**

of a shad looks like a fine-tooth comb or a wool-card, and
the best way to get the meat out is to use a toothpick. A
little later in the season and the shad will make their appearance. When they come, they come a good deal; there
is many of him; he is multitudinous. We are not read
up as to where the shad lives before he comes this way,
but he boards where they set a poor table. When he first
puts in an appearance, he is extremely emaciated. He is
so thin that his skin don't fit him, hence the phrase "thin
as a shad." You can't get anything thinner than a spring
shad, unless you take a couple of them, when, of course,
they will be twice as thin. They look much like a porgie,
— about twice as much, but they are not so high-scented.
Shad fishing is a lucrative business. If the fisherman has
good luck, they will net him considerable, or he will net
them considerable, we are doubtful which. They are fast.
They don't stop to loaf any more than a thoroughbred pill,
but just keep right on about their business.

A person to like shad wants to eat them often, at near
intervals, once every twenty-four hours for eleven or nineteen weeks. The champion place for getting up an appetite for shad is at a Brooklyn boarding-house. The thing
there is reduced to a science. As soon as shad becomes
cheap and plenty, the landlady announces at the breakfast-
table that she will have shad for dinner. The boarder
immediately goes to his room and puts on the poorest shirt
he has, and when he comes to dinner he has provided himself with a magnifying glass, which makes the bones look
larger, a small basket to put the bones in, a toothpick, and
a pair of tweezers. When one eats shad he wants to eat
it; he don't want to talk or discuss the state of affairs in
France, as he will get so full of the bony parts that he will
sigh for a little more Bourbon. When he swallows a bone,
all he has to do is to take his tweezers and pull it out;
after one learns this art it is simple and even graceful. It

is calculated that during the shad season a good shad-eater
will get from ten to fifteen bushels of bones from what shad
he eats.   After the last shad is destroyed, he tears off his
shirt, sandpapers off the ends of the bones which are stick-
ing out through his skin, dons clean linen, and is himself
again.   If we have in our remarks said aught that looks
as though we had wandered from the truth, we are willing
to vouch for correctness by furnishing all sceptics with a
written affidavit.

APPENDIX IV.

PATENT CARBONIZED HATCHING TROUGHS.

WHEN the first efforts at trout breeding were made in this country, wooden troughs were used for hatching the eggs. It was soon found that the fungus which grew on wood when under water was exceedingly destructive to the eggs. Indeed, of all the dangers to which the eggs were exposed, fungus proved to be the worst. It destroyed them by thousands and hundreds of thousands, and those which it did not actually kill it rendered worthless by exhausting their vitality. It therefore became indispensable to abandon the use of wood for hatching trout eggs. The great want was, then, to find something which, by being inexpensive, accessible, and at the same time safe from fungus, would supply the place of the old wooden troughs. The emergency brought out various materials, — soapstone, slate, pottery, glass, metallic screens and pans, wood lined with glass, and other things, all of which were tried and found to be either inadequate or expensive, and the want of a cheap and safe material was still unsupplied.

It was at this time, after many useless experiments, and the loss of many thousands of eggs, that the writer hit upon charred or carbonized wood. This was tried, and found to answer the purpose beyond all expectations. Nothing could be conceived more perfect in its adaptability. The problem was solved. In carbonized wood was found an inexpensive, accessible, and perfectly effective material for hatching fish eggs, without danger from fungus. It is also one of the most durable and easily handled things in the world. And this is not all. It has invariably been my experience that in any instance where the carbonized hatching troughs have been used, not only have the eggs been free from fungus, and have therefore hatched better, but the young fry have *lived better;* and the contrast between the effect of the charred wood and the raw material in this respect has been very marked indeed. While the young fish, hatched in the old wooden troughs, seemed to drop down dead from no assignable cause, the fry hatched in the charred troughs showed a wonderful tenacity of life, that became more and more surprising every day. I have hatched over a million eggs in these troughs, and speak from experience, and my experience has been, without an exception, to confirm the belief that the fry hatched in this material *do not die* as they did under the old method. It is a fact that can be confirmed by my assistants, that in some of the charcoal troughs last year less than one-tenth per cent were lost by death in the first three months, with the exception of deformed ones. This year it has been the same; and if any one will take the pains to visit my hatching house, I will show him charred troughs, which the water has run through for six months or more, that are as clean from fungus as when the water was turned on in the fall, and also troughs of young fry, where death is a rare occurrence.

The exclusive right to use charcoal and charred wood for hatching fish eggs has been secured to the writer in the United States by letters patent; but even with the royalty paid for the right to use charred wood it is still the *cheapest* thing that can be found, as well as the *best.* The reader can see the saving in expense in the use of charcoal troughs over glass grilles by looking at the following figures : —

Glass grilles for hatching 100,000 eggs cost, say 80 at
$3.50 apiece $280
Carbonized troughs for hatching 100,000 eggs cost for
  Lumber and labor $15
  Right to use   25

                      Total cost   40

Balance in favor of charcoal troughs $240

This is an important saving of money; but there is a still greater saving in the lives of the young fish after they are hatched.

These considerations lead me to think that for business the carbonized troughs stand the test better than anything in use. I will only add that the work of preparing the carbonized lining to the trough is very trifling, and can be done in a few moments and at an insignificant expense.

APPENDIX V.

BRIEF SKETCH OF OPERATIONS AT THE COLD SPRING TROUT PONDS.

THIS establishment was the first of its kind undertaken in New England for making a business of fish breeding. It is located in Charlestown, N. H., a town on the Connecticut River, about fifty miles by rail above the Massachusetts line. The water supply consists of two streams, both fed by springs, and running about 10,000 gallons an hour in dry weather. The hatching house is built at the source of one of these streams, and has a supply of 2,000 gallons an hour, at 47° Fahrenheit. The breeding ponds are built at the junction of the two streams, and receive, when required, all the water from both.

1866.

The Cold Spring Trout Ponds commenced operations in the summer of 1866, when two or three small ponds were built, and a hatching building, 8 feet by 16, was erected. This building hatched 15,000 trout the following winter.

1867.

My whole attention was given the next year (1867) *to growing the young fry*, it being my conviction that everything now depended upon successful operations in this particular department. I felt certain that here was the weak point in trout raising. Trout had been hatched by the hundred thousand. Trout enough had come into being by artificial means to fill the market to overflowing, if they had grown up. But where were they? Domestic trout ought to have been as plenty as codfish; instead of that, there were none to be had.

I therefore made the growing of the young fish a severe and unremitting study the first year, and was rewarded with success; not that I did not lose many young fry, for I lost a great many, but I raised some, and in most instances where they died I thought I saw a removable cause. I now believed that time and study would prevent the difficulties of the first year's growth, and proceeded to extend my operations. The original hatching house was enlarged into a building 16 feet by 24, and a large new hatching house, 60 feet by 27, was put up, with 500 feet of hatching troughs. That fall over 100,000 trout eggs were laid down, beside 40,000 salmon eggs, which were sent by the Massachusetts and New Hampshire Commissioners to be hatched here for the Connecticut River.

1868.

The next spring (1868) the plan of the rearing box was completed, the object of which is to protect the young fish from accident, and from their natural enemies. It will not, of course, feed them, or keep them from dying of diseases, but it will save them from the two very prolific causes of loss just mentioned, namely, accidents and natural enemies. This spring, and during the winter, some of the salmon eggs and young fry were, with the consent of the Commissioners, sent to Professor Agassiz. They were the first live specimens of the American *Salmo salar* that the great naturalist had seen, and drawings were taken of them for his projected work on the Salmonidæ of this continent.

During the same spring another pond was built, and a few black bass introduced from Lake Champlain. There were also 100,000 young bass hatched in some small artificial ponds in New York State, which formed a branch of the Cold Spring Farm. It is a good evidence of the increased public interest in fish culture that now there is an incessant demand for black bass, while in 1868 I had but *one* order for bass fry during the whole summer. In the fall of this year I built a large salmon-breeding establishment, with extraordinary natural facilities, on the Mirimichi River, New Brunswick. Nearly half a million salmon eggs were taken here this year, one half of which went by agreement to the Canadian Department of Fisheries, and the other half were taken to the hatching house at Charlestown. Various causes had reduced the numbers, however, and each half was estimated at only 183,000; 100,000 of these were sold to the Massachusetts and New Hampshire Commissioners for $ 1,600, and sent to Messrs. Robinson & Hoyt, at Meredith Village, N. H., to be hatched by them for the Merrimack River. Other lots were sent to various parties, among others, the South Side Club, New York; W. Clift, Poheganut Ponds, Conn.; Colonel Theodore Lyman, for Massachusetts State Hatching House, and E. A. Brackett, Winchester, Mass. One lot was sent to England to Mr. Frank Buckland, British Commissioner of Fisheries, and was favorably noticed in the London Times.

One salmon of this fall's take of eggs, now three years old, was kept till last winter (1872) at Charlestown, in the fresh water it was hatched in. It is a smolt, but very much dwarfed, and is the oldest tame salmon in America.

One lot of yearling trout, hatched here in the year 1867, took a diploma at the Connecticut River Agricultural Fair. Another lot took a diploma at the New England Fair at New Haven.

1869.

In the spring of 1869 about 100 spring spawning fish were brought from the Missisquoi River to the Cold Spring Trout Ponds, consisting chiefly of black bass, glass-eyed

pike, mullet, yellow perch, and one large *Esox*, well known
to visitors as the "big pickerel." These fish are quite
large, and though of not much profit are a fine sight, and
afford observers an opportunity of studying their ways.
In the fall of this year, the trout, now two years old, which
took diplomas at the last year's agricultural fairs, received
a diploma and silver medal at Boston at the exhibition of
the Massachusetts Charitable Mechanics' Association. In
the same fall, carbonized or charred wood, for hatching
trout eggs, was tried at the hatching house in Charlestown,
and was found to answer its purpose perfectly. This was
the year of the great freshet, which wrecked so many trout
ponds. It fortunately did no harm at the Cold Spring
Farm.

1870.

The next year, 1870, the demand for trout eggs and
young trout had very much increased. Preparations to
meet this demand were made at the Cold Spring Trout
Ponds. The carbonized hatching troughs were introduced
throughout in the hatching buildings, and 250,000 trout
eggs were laid down in them. In the mean time a fine lot
of yearlings had been brought through the last year. Several consignments of large trout had been sent to Fulton
Market, New York, and one of the largest hotels in Boston had been supplied through the summer.

1871.

The next spring, 1871, the demand for eggs and young
fish was a quarter of a million more than the establishment
could furnish. The large trout brought, in Fulton Market,
in April, $ 1.25 per pound. The right to use charcoal and
carbonized wood for hatching fish was patented June 20,
1871.

Four new ponds were built this year, 1871, and lined
with carbonized two-inch plank. A large number of year-

lings were sold this year, the demand for this size being larger than ever before. In the fall of 1871 nearly 300,000 trout eggs were laid down in the hatching troughs.

Ten thousand of them were sent to Europe. Most of them arrived safely, and have since hatched. Some of them are in Mr. Frank Buckland's Museum at South Kensington, England, and were noticed by him as follows, in Land and Water, published in London.

"*Salmon and Trout Breeding at South Kensington.* — The breeding troughs at my Museum of Economic Fish Culture are now almost as full as they can be. The following is a catalogue of the eggs and fry : *Salmo fontinalis*, or American Brook Trout, brought over by Mr. Parnaby of Troutdale Fishery, Keswick.* These are beautiful little fish, of about three quarters of an inch long. They have almost absorbed their umbilical bag, and will shortly begin to feed. I propose to feed them on the roe of soles. These American fish are much more active, and, I was going to write, — it may be even so, — intelligent fish than our salmon or trout (*Salmo fario*). Possibly they have imbibed some of the national American sharpness. I think I shall consult them on the Alabama question."

The Cold Spring Trout Ponds received this fall the sole agency in the United States for the sale of the British fish hatched at the celebrated Keswick establishment, the largest in England. The experiment of taking trout eggs by the Russian or dry method of impregnation was tried this season at the Cold Spring Farm with astonishing success, the yield of fish being 95 per cent of the eggs taken. This method will be hereafter adopted here altogether.

---

* The original article in Land and Water, above quoted, states that the fish came from Mr. Wilmot's establishment in Canada. This is an error, as every *Salmo fontinalis* which Mr. Parnaby took to England came from my hatching house at the Cold Spring Trout Ponds.

1872.

In February, 1872, the trout and salmon from these ponds took a silver medal and a bronze medal at the exhibition of the New York State Poultry Society at Albany.

The trout hatched out this year have done wonderfully well; up to the present time (August), very few losses indeed have occurred.

Some of the young fry which hatched in England from the eggs sent over last fall are now in possession of Her Majesty Queen Victoria. The salmon hatched last year (yearlings) are looking finely, although much dwarfed. In June of this year, Mr. Parnaby, of Keswick, England, visited the Cold Spring Trout Ponds for the purpose of obtaining some black bass to carry across the Atlantic. A large quantity of these fish were furnished him, and were doing well, at last accounts, when the steamer conveying them sailed from New York.

The demand for trout and trout eggs has been good this year at the Cold Spring Farm, and two new plank ponds have been built. Other plans of improvement were contemplated, but the proprietor having been appointed Deputy Commissioner of the United States to conduct the salmon breeding on the Pacific Coast, has left them to be carried out by his agent in charge.

A peculiar feature about this farm is that it hatches eggs at the halves for all the neighboring trout-raisers, they preferring to have their eggs hatched so, to incurring the risk and labor of doing it themselves.

APPENDIX VI.

SALMON-BREEDING ESTABLISHMENT ON THE MIRIMICHI.

PREVIOUS to 1868 the few salmon eggs that had come into the United States to stock its depleted streams were obtained at random, and in quantities totally inadequate to the requirements of the great American salmon rivers. It was evident that something must be done on a more extended scale to carry out the now rapidly forming purpose of restoring the salmon in those rivers; and in the spring of 1868 the writer conceived the idea of organizing a large salmon-breeding establishment on one of the New Brunswick rivers, all of which are famous for the vast quantities of salmon which they contain.

The Mirimichi was chosen, on account of its accessibility and its capacity for supplying parent fish in abundance. On the farm of Mr. Joseph Goodfellow, eight miles above Newcastle, on the river, was found a very large even-flowing spring and a spring brook running within a few feet of it, and both within sixty rods of the river itself. A large hatching house, one hundred feet by twenty-seven, was built of three-inch deals, just below the spring. The house was provided with nearly an eighth of a mile of hatching troughs laid in rows parallel with its length. A pond, having an area of about an acre, was built below the house. This was connected with the river by a flume. The spring water and brook water were turned through the house, thence into the pond, and thence into the river.

Nothing could be more admirably suited to its purpose. One of the best rivers in the world to furnish the parent salmon, an inexhaustible supply of water, both brook and spring, to hatch the eggs in, a hatching house capable of turning out millions of young fry annually, and immediate communication with the river for letting the parent salmon in and out. The place was as near perfect in its adaptations as could be wished. As soon as the site was selected, and before any work was done, a plan of the whole undertaking was laid before the Hon. Peter Mitchell, the Canadian Minister of Marine and Fisheries. After some consultation, the plan was favorably received, and we were instructed by the minister to prepare a full statement in writing of our plan of operations, with a request for permission to take from the Mirimichi River the parent salmon required for our work.

This statement and petition having been prepared and submitted to the minister, he replied, upon reading it, "Go on with your work, gentlemen; your wishes will be granted." The work of building the house and pond was prosecuted without delay, and in September, the writer being then in Boston, Mr. Goodfellow, acting on the oral authorization of the minister, began fishing in the river with a stake-net for the parent salmon. The fishery wardens, acting in accordance with their general instructions, though hastily, we think, immediately took up and confiscated the large forty-fathom net which had been used, and released the captured salmon. As it was then the close season, and as the fishing wardens had received no instructions from headquarters to make an exception in favor of our nets, they were certainly only doing their duty. On the other hand, as they knew, though not through an official source, that the undertaking had the sanction of the head of the Fisheries Department, and as the salmon were not to be killed, but only confined alive in a pond close to the river, where they could be returned to it at any time, if it was found that they were wrongly captured, and especially as one half of all the young fry hatched were, according to agreement,* to go back to

* OTTAWA, September 2, 1868.

GENTLEMEN : I am directed by the minister to state, that he has considered the proposal made by your letter of 20th ultimo, in continuance of a verbal proposition made to him when at Mirimichi, having in view the establishment of breeding-beds and ponds for the artificial production of salmon at North Esk, on the northwest branch of the river Mirimichi.

The department cannot allow any bounty, such as you mention, nor attach any exclusive right to the enterprise in question, neither afford any guaranty whatever for the expense you may incur, but will extend to it such facilities as are warranted by the interest which the public may have in your success, and shall appear to be justified from time to time by the earnestness and good faith of your endeavors or the actual fruits of your operations.

At present it is deemed proper to specify in what terms the requisite authority can be conveyed to you.

1. That at private cost you shall make and keep in efficient repair suitable rearing and feeding ponds, and spawning beds, and a proper hatching house with troughs, and the other necessary appliances at a brook emptying into the northwest branch of the river Mirimichi, on the south bank thereof, on the property of Mr. Joseph Goodfellow, in the parish of North Esk, as named by you.

2. That this establishment shall be built and maintained for the *bona fide* purpose of hatching and rearing salmon.

3. That from the time of impregnation, and during the period of incubation, the salmon ova obtained for or deposited in this establishment shall be and be deemed the property of the crown, and one half of the young salmon so hatched and reared therein, or in connection therewith, shall be, and continue, the property of the crown, and shall be allowed to pass alive and healthy and well fed into, and remain in, the waters of the

13*

enrich the river, and all the salmon, when manipulated, were to be restored to it, this summary confiscation of the nets and release of the fish seemed to be hasty action, to say the least, on the part of the fishery wardens, who

Mirimichi or its branches, when and after they shall obtain the sufficient and ordinary growth of salmon fry.   And the other half shall, when hatched out, be your property.

4. That you shall be entitled to obtain from this department permission to procure fish-spawn for the sole purpose of furnishing impregnated eggs for hatching in the said establishment, such permission to be accorded for the *times*, *places*, and *means* of so taking salmon fixed in writing by the inspector of fisheries for Nova Scotia and New Brunswick, and subject to uses only under the immediate surveillance of a fishery officer or fishing warden, who shall be empowered to stop all proceedings under the said written permit the moment he finds the liberty it allows subject to abuse or injurious to the salmon fisheries, or any of these conditions evaded or violated.

5. The numbers and condition of salmon caught and manipulated, which are to be returned alive and uninjured to the stream with the dates of capture, manipulation, and release, together with the numbers of eggs obtained therefrom, and actually deposited, and also the numbers vivified, and afterwards hatched, and the numbers of young fish let into the river, to be attested on oath, by one or more of the persons engaged in the establishment.

6. That any fishery officer or warden shall at any and all times have free access to the premises.

7. That no eggs or fry shall be removed from the ponds, boxes, hatching-beds, or elsewhere, without the knowledge and consent of the local fishery officer, and the partition or releasing of young fish to fulfil the crown share shall be made in the presence of and certified by a fishery officer authorized thereto.

8. That until you have prepared the establishment to the satisfaction of the inspector of fisheries, no permit shall be delivered to you.

9. Any violation or evasion of these conditions shall forthwith

might, without injury, have left things *in statu quo* for a while, until the course of events decided whether the fishing was authorized or not. If the wardens were acting under the direction of the Inspector of the Province, it makes the matter all the worse, for he at least ought to have had intelligence enough to abstain from such intemperate haste.

As soon as the first net was forcibly taken by the wardens, Mr. Goodfellow, still relying on the authority conveyed by the last conversation with the minister, staked down another net, and continued fishing. This was immediately taken up and confiscated like the last. When another net was put down and taken, then another and another. As fast as a net was put down it was taken up, and as fast as it was taken up another was put down,* and so it continued, each net going the way of its prede-

forfeit the permit, and put an end to the privilege, besides exposing the parties to penalties provided by the laws.

The foregoing laws it has been found advisable to stipulate for the security of the public and the satisfaction of the department; but the minister expresses his confidence in the ability and energy of the parties who undertake this project, and he will view with lively expectation and assist to the utmost their *bona fide* exertions towards rendering it a practical success, at once remunerative to themselves and beneficial to the fisheries.

I have the honor to be, gentlemen,
Your obedient servant,
W. F. WHITCHER,
For the Hon. Minister of Marine and Fisheries.

* To discontinue fishing would have been fatal to the undertaking. The spawning season was near, and the best runs of fish were over, and it was evident that unless the parent salmon were caught at once it would be too late. Subsequent facts confirmed this view of the matter; for after the date (October 6) of our written permit from the inspector, we caught only twenty-eight salmon in all.

cessor, until seven or eight nets had found their way to the contraband stores of the wardens.

At length the written instructions of the Fisheries Department were received by Mr. Goodfellow, and not long after I arrived at Mirimichi. The department instructions made the fishing conditional upon a written permit from the inspector of the Provinces. On my arrival, the inspector was immediately telegraphed for. The community was by this time worked up into a state of great excitement, and the inspector had heard only the warden's side of the story. But upon seeing the works which had been constructed, and hearing a full account of the affair, and of what was contemplated, he fell in with the undertaking, and gave it his hearty support. He also gave a written permit, drawn up in the most liberal terms, for the taking of three hundred salmon from the river for the purposes of the establishment.

After receiving this permit, no pains were spared to catch as many salmon as possible ; but the good runs were over, and we captured but twenty-eight fish between this time and the spawning season, which began in one pond the 15th of October. We took on this and the two following days 226,500 eggs from twenty-eight fish. On the 20th of October we found, to our surprise, that the fish we caught that day in the river had already spawned. The writer immediately took a gang of men and a forty-fathom sweep-seine, and swept the river thoroughly for nine miles above our nets, though the floating ice had begun to run. Many salmon were caught, but all had spawned except two, one of which had been injured by a spear. The salmon in the pond continued to hold their spawn till late in November, though most of them had been found ripe, and had been stripped by the third day of that month. We took in all 443.900 eggs from forty-eight salmon. This number, reduced by removal of dead eggs and accidents to

356,000, was equally divided, by special permit from the minister, when the eye-spots appeared, and one half were brought to the Cold Spring Trout Ponds at Charlestown, N. H., and the other half left to hatch for the benefit of the Mirimichi River.

On the writer's return to New England, a very pleasant day was passed with the inspector of the Provinces at St. John, during which he renewed his assurances of his cordial support, and was even kind enough to offer capital for investment in our enterprise. This, however, was declined on the ground that the assistance was not needed, as everything was paid for; but the writer has regretted ever since that the offer was not accepted. The next time the inspector was heard from was on the occasion of his publishing a letter in a St. John paper, speaking in very detracting terms of Mr. Goodfellow and the writer. The ostensible cause was some very inoffensive remarks made by the writer at a meeting of the Fisheries Commissioners at New York. The real cause may perhaps be found to be the rejection of the inspector's offers of investment, and the opposition of Mr. Goodfellow to the government party at a recent important election. But whatever the cause, from that time the salmon-breeding establishment on the Mirimichi and its owners met only persecution from the inspector, who, in language more becoming a rowdy than a government officer, wrote most abusive letters to and about the owners of the establishment. He made a threat, in words more forcible than elegant, that the salmon works at Mirimichi should "rot where they stood," and he has since resolutely and persistently acted up to it.

The consequence is that a large * and well-appointed salmon-breeding establishment in perfect running order, located in one of the most favorable situations on the globe, is left to stand idle and useless, when it might be

* Probably the largest in the world.

adding to the world's wealth at the rate of millions of salmon a year. The short-sighted inspector, sacrificing the vast public good that could come from it to his private animosity, like the dog in the manger, will neither do anything himself, nor let any one else do anything with it. The good it might do and the credit it might reflect on his administration are sacrificed to carry out his childish threat; and there the establishment still remains, closed and useless, a monument of the inspector's malevolence and imbecility.

I am happy to say that the United States Congress has this year (1872) made an appropriation for salmon-breeding on the Pacific coast, and that in future salmon eggs will probably be obtained within the limits of the United States on even a larger scale than they could be procured on the Mirimichi.

APPENDIX VII.

EXPERIMENTS WITH TROUT EGGS AND TROUT.

I WOULD by all means have a set of hatching boxes devoted to experiments. By careful and systematic experiment more knowledge and experience are gathered than in any other way, and it is upon this that sound progress in fish culture or any other art depends.

The experiment boxes need not be large. Boxes varying in capacity from 100 to 1,000 eggs each are about the right thing. They can be separate boxes or subdivisions of the regular hatching troughs separated by screens; but whatever they are they should be perfectly isolated from each other, for where this precaution has been neglected it is a very common and provoking source of disappointment to have the eggs of different experiments wash in together and become indistinguishable. This is just as fatal, of course, to all useful results, as if the eggs had been destroyed.

The separate subdivisions should be distinctly designated, and full notes of the experiment carefully taken down in a note-book. In brief, the experiment, to be valuable, should be exact, systematic, and full in recorded detail, and the experiment boxes should be prepared to this end.

Below will be found some of the experiments in trout culture which most readily suggest themselves.

IMPREGNATING EGGS.

*Dry Method.**

1. Take ripe eggs with little milt and note the percentage of impregnation.

2. Take ripe eggs with abundant milt and note as before.

3. Try immature eggs with good and sufficient milt.

4. Try ripe eggs with poor milt.

5. After mixing milt and eggs, add water at 36°, at 45°, at 60°, and compare results.

6. Use milt that has been taken in a dry phial and corked up 24 hours, 48 hours, 96 hours, and compare results.

7. Use milt that has been bottled up and sent by mail 100 miles, 500 miles, 1,000 miles.

8. Use milt that has been forced † by putting male in warm water, and note the degree of impregnation.

9. Use milt that has been frozen.

10–12. Repeat experiments 6, 7, 9, using eggs instead of milt.

13. Put ripe eggs with milt that has been exposed to the air 5 minutes, 20 minutes, 30 minutes.

14. Put good milt with eggs that have been exposed to the air 5 minutes, 20 minutes, 30 minutes.

15. Use ripe eggs with milt that has been diluted with water 2 minutes, 5 minutes, 20 minutes.

16. Use good milt with eggs that have been kept in water 2 minutes, 5 minutes, 20 minutes, 30 minutes.

17. Compare the percentage of impregnation of eggs taken in Ainsworth's races and Collins's roller box with those taken by manual pressure.

Experiments in general with Eggs.

18. Pack eggs in wet moss (*Sphagnum*) as soon as taken, and examine when nearly ready to hatch, and note the mortality.

---

* See p. 92.   † See p. 103, note.

19. Pack eggs in moss at the first appearance of the eye-spots, examine and note as before.

20. Place eggs, as soon as taken, on ice, keep on ice, and see how long they will be hatching.

21. Freeze eggs solid, in water, at different stages of development, and note the result.

22. Freeze as before in the air.

23. Place a few eggs on a copper-wire screen, and note the discoloration and absorption of copper.

24. Allow a few eggs, after the eye-spots appear, to remain considerably covered with sediment, and note the deformity of the embryo when hatched.

25. Subject eggs of different ages to high temperatures of water, and note what degree of heat they will live through.

Experiments with Alevins and Young Fry.

26. See how long five alevins will live in a gill of water at 36°, at 42°, at 50°, at 60°, at 70°.

27. Freeze alevins solid, thaw out, and return to the water in hatching box, and watch for a month. *Mem.:* Take care, during the freezing, not to disturb the fish, as it will tear itself against the forming ice, and die from the effect of the laceration. The best way to freeze eggs or young fish is to take a dry glass tumbler which has been exposed to a great degree of cold, and pour into it the specimens to be experimented with, together with about a spoonful of water. The water, with the specimens, will immediately freeze solid.

28. Expose alevins to a rising temperature, and note what degree of heat they will survive.

Experiments with Young Fry.

29–31. Repeat with trout fry the experiments with alevins marked 26, 27, and 28.

T

32. Keep very young trout fry in pure filtered spring water, and note how long they remain healthy without the addition of earth.

33. After the fish in the last experiment begin to sicken, apply earth plentifully, and note the improvement.

34. Keep 100 young fry in a small box, and 100 in a pond, for six months ; compare the mortality and growth.

35. Feed two similar lots of young fry, one wholly on curd, the other wholly on liver, and compare results.

36. Feed young trout fry plentifully on the young of other fish, as suckers, perch, and shiners, and note the result.

37. Take young trout fry that are attacked by animal parasites, and give them a salt bath, as described on page 258, and note the result.

38. Observe the effect of the parasites on young fry not subjected to the salt bath.

Experiments with Large Trout.

39. Count the number of respirations of large trout at a temperature of 36°, 45°, 70°, and 80°, and compare the results.

40. Freeze large trout carefully, but stop the freezing before the body becomes stiff. Thaw out gradually, and note the result.

41. Let a large trout become motionless from suffocation in still water, then try the effect of vigorous aeration of the water in restoring him.

42. Ring a bell and make loud noises near trout where you can see them and they cannot see you, and note whether they appear to hear the sounds.

43. Feed one lot of trout wholly on minnows for three months, and a similar lot on worms, a third lot on meat, a fourth lot on all three, and compare results.

44. Subject a fish attacked by fungus to the salt bath described on page 258, and note the result.

45. Cross the various species of the *Salmo* family with each other, and note and publish the results.

46. Whoever has the opportunity, and sufficient patience, will render a great service to the fish-cultivating world by fully testing the experiment of breeding in and in with peculiar varieties of trout, as the Chinese do with gold fish, and publishing the results.

APPENDIX VIII.

THE PROGRESS OF DEVELOPMENT OF A SALMO
(*COREGONUS PALÆA*, Cuv.) EGG.*

WE shall try to give here a short summary of the state of the embryo at all periods of its life, indicating at which period the organs begin to form, and under what form they first appear.

At the time of spawning, the egg is composed of the yolk, of little drops of oil spread over the surface of the yolk, and forming a kind of disk; of the germinal vesicle and spots, situated in the middle of this disk; and, lastly, of the yolk and shell membranes which envelop the egg, without any intermediate space between them. Four hours after the spawning the shell membrane is detached from the yolk membrane, in consequence of the endosmotic penetration of the water through the pores of the first; it becomes inflated, and the yolk floats freely in its cavity. Twelve hours after the spawning the germ begins to rise from the middle of the oily disk under the form of a little circular swelling. Sixteen hours after spawning the germ is seen in the form of a clear, transparent vessel above the oleaginous disk. The cells of which it is composed are little delicate transparent vessels, without any traces of a nucleus. Twenty hours after spawning the germ occupies all the extent of the disk, and the furrowing begins. A large shallow furrow is first perceived, which extends in a circular direction, and affects nothing but the germ. Dur-

* Translated from the French of Vogt's *Embryologie des Salmones*, Chap. XIV., by F. W. WEBBER.

ing the second and third days the furrows develop. There
exists ordinarily, as soon as the beginning of the second
day, two furrows in the form of a cross. At the end of
the second day the mulberry form has reached its development. On the third day it is insensibly effaced, and the
germ becomes smooth ; but it is, however, opaque, owing to the cells accumulated in its interior. On the fourth
day the embryonic germ represents a hemisphere of granulated appearance, but smooth on the exterior, reposing on
the oily disk. All the cells are perfectly developed, and
all have nuclei. Those of the outer stratum are even provided with nucleated cells. From the sixth to the ninth
day the epidermoidal stratum detaches itself insensibly
from the other embryonic cells, overruns the yolk, and the
embryo separates more and more from the yolk vessel.
At the beginning of this period the germ represents a
large sunken mass, which hardly passes the borders of
the oily disk. Finally, there is only a little space in the
yolk free, the yolk cavity ; all the rest is filled up with
the epidermoidal layer. The embryo is diametrically opposite to the yolk vesicle, and it is in correspondence with
its length that the cells are the most heaped up in the
place where the primitive bands form. On the tenth day
the dorsal furrow appears and takes the form of a large
and tolerably deep fissure, but ending indistinctly in front.
The cephalic extremity of the embryo is large, square,
and truncated. The caudal extremity is lost in a vague
way in the keel surrounding the yolk cavity, which grows
continually narrower. The dorsal part of the embryo is
more narrow than the two extremities. It is, besides,
curled in a uniform manner around the yolk, and the dorsal furrow is wide open ; the germ and the yolk vesicle are
diametrically opposite. On the eleventh and twelfth day
the dorsal furrow ends in front, and shows the first traces
of the enlargements which correspond to the three cere-

bral divisions. The space corresponding to the mesencephalon is the largest, and in profile it is easily discerned by its enlargement, which begins near the ocular lobes. The dorsal furrow is closed in tube form on the back. The vertebral divisions begin to show, but almost exclusively upon the front turned against the yolk. The part of the dorsal furrow which is still open is very narrow. The cells of the epidermoidal stratum have lost their nucleoli and represent a tessellated epethelium. At the place where the dorsal cord shows, cells are to be seen, filled with an opaque and granulated alimentary substance. From the thirteenth to the sixteenth day the three cerebral divisions are characterized in the most distinct manner. The ocular lobes of the mesencephalon become more and more distinct and completely enclosed on the side of the mesencephalon as in a vault. The dorsal cord appears under the form of a simple string, solid and transparent, in the middle of the embryo. The vertebral divisions are perfectly distinct. The caudal extremity of the embryo is circumscribed on the side of the yolk. ·The yolk is surrounded on all sides by the epidermoidal stratum. The yolk cavity has disappeared. Towards the end of the sixteenth day the beginning of the crystalline coating can be remarked in the eye. The rudiment of the ear appears at the same time under the form of an elliptical vesicle, with a clearer space in the centre; it is situated a little in front of the nuchal bow. This, as well as the cephalic bow and the curvature of the trunk, is well marked out. The yolk vesicle, on the contrary, is very much reduced. The epencephalon shows a few swellings analogous to the "*ganglions persistans des Trigles.*"

From the seventeenth to the twentieth day the tail begins to show itself, and the embryo uses it to give vigorous shakes by striking with it laterally. The cephalic bow becomes level. The crystalline coating develops and hardens. The choroid cleft is just formed. The prosencephalon, with its prolongation towards the extremity of the snout; the mesencephalon, which is hollowed completely into the form of a cavity; and the epencephalon, with the cerebellum, which are beginning to form, — are now very easily distinguished. In front of the extremity of the cord, which is still homogeneous, is accumulated at the base of the brain the thick blastema of the basis of the cranium. Then under the dorsal cord, between it and the yolk, forms a thick layer of cells larger than the properly called embryonic cells, and provided with opaque nuclei, the layer of intestinal cells representing the mucous leaflet. This layer is divided into two rows, the lower one designed to form the intestine, the upper designed for the *corpus Wolfianum*. The intestine begins to be transformed into a tube behind and in front, in proportion as the embryo disengages itself more and more from the yolk. An enlargement (a *posterior allantois*) shows itself at the extremity of the secretory canal of the *corpus Wolfianum*. The heart forms in a swelling of the embryonic mass on the side of the yolk, in the middle of the space between the ear and the eye. At first solid, and composed of simple embryonic cells, it is soon transformed into a cavity, in which globules of blood can be seen to rise and fall in cadence, conforming to the repeated contractions of this organ. The heart is at a right angle with the axis of the body, and reposes vertically upon the yolk, the middle of which it occupies. Behind the heart can be remarked a little angular protuberance, the first vestige of the pectoral fin. The blood-producing layer is seen to appear upon the yolk in the neighborhood of the heart, giving to the yolk a spotted appearance. The first traces of the black pigment show in the choroid; the cells of brown pigment are created at the same time in the vicinity of the eye. The vertebral divisions are very distinct.

The tail grows larger. The first traces of the odd fin are formed by the epidermoidal layer upon the circumference of the embryo ; the yolk vesicle disappears.

From the twenty-third to the twenty-seventh day the first rudiments of the nasal cavities are seen to appear on the lower front of the head. The prolongation of the prosencephalon, forming the olfactory nerve, stretches so as to reach the nasal cavities. The head rises, disengages itself from the yolk in consequence of the strengthening of the nuchal bow. The yolk begins to separate from the head, and the separation of the belly follows at the same time that an uneven ventral fin shows, formed from the epidermoidal layer. The choroid surrounds nearly all the bulb of the eye ; the coloboma of the iris appears under the form of a light cleft. The thick blastema of the base of the cranium is very distinct. In the dorsal cord the little cells develop in the form of little isolated vesicles, which increase and occupy all the cord in front and behind. The blood-producing layer extends over the yolk. The choroid can be recognized by the naked eye in consequence of the accumulation of pigment, and the eyes can be distinguished through the shell membrane under the form of two black points. The intestine and the urethra are transformed into complete tubes, not showing any trace of cellular structure. The anus is still closed.

From the twenty-seventh to the thirtieth day the pineal gland appears in the form of a little globulous accumulation of cells in the semicircular cavity situated behind the prosencephalon. The interior formations of the mesencephalon begin to show. The thick blastema of the base of the cranium contracts very distinctly in the neighborhood of the hypophysis. The ear is much nearer to the eye than formerly. The first traces of circulation appear in the beginning, under the form of two similar currents, one of which is destined for the head and the other for the body. These currents come out from the heart by the aorta and the carotid arteries, and return to the heart by the anterior and posterior yolk veins. The two anterior yolk veins disappear first, and after them the left posterior vein. The hematogenous layer has completely overrun the yolk, and there exist no capillary ramifications except upon the latter. The pectoral fin, which at first was pendent, rises, and keeps up a continual motion. The formation of cells is complete in the dorsal cord, and the intercellular substance has almost entirely disappeared. The liver begins to form, its communication with the intestine is very distinct, and capillary networks form in its interior towards the end of this period. The posterior yolk vein stretches along the lower front of the intestine, and bends back in the neighborhood of the liver. The odd fin which surrounds the body grows larger. The first traces of the otoliths appear in the ears. The different divisions of the heart are visible externally, and the rudiments of the opercle become more and more distinct.

From the thirty-first to the fortieth day the nose begins to show very distinct outlines. The buccal cavity forms, and on both sides can be seen the first rudiments of the upper jaw, under the form of two prolongations. The choroidal fissure closes, and the development of black pigment in the eyes prevents any further study of them. The branchial fissures appear one after the other, and each of the branchial arches receives a vascular arch. At the end of this period there are five arches, the first of which is the hyoidal arch. The semicircular grooves begin to form in the ears. The cells of the muscles are arranged in threads. The cells of black pigment in the epidermoidal layer of the back are seen to appear. The whole circulation undergoes important modifications while penetrating into the tail, where it gives birth to a cardinal vein. The circulation of the head becomes symmetrical, the right carotid being more active than the left, and the left jugular more active than the right. The aortic arch at the right is also more powerful. Intestinal arteries form. The liver develops more and more to the detriment of the yolk circulation. The little drops of oil unite in one great drop. The buccal intestine enters into communication with the branchial cavity.

From the forty-first to the sixtieth day the embryo becomes ready to hatch. The nose draws insensibly near the extremity of the head. The cartilaginous bases of the head form from the thick blastema of the base of the cranium. In the eye the cornea and the sclerotic separate from the tissues of the choroid. The ear approaches the eye. The interior parts of the eye completely develop. The heart takes a horizontal position in consequence of the proximity of the yolk and the body,—a proximity which itself depends upon the disappearance of the pericardial sac and the abdominal sac of the epidermoidal membrane. The yolk disappears from sight. Peristaltic motions and very decided movements of mastication can be perceived in the intestine. The mouth, situated between the eyes, is transversal. The embryonic odd fin shows cavities in the places where it is designed to be absorbed. The yolk circulation disappears, that of the liver or the circulation of the portal system is entirely established. The sixth branchial arch, or the pharyngian arch, receives a vascular arch. The hyoidian arch has disappeared. The head contracts as the formation of the cartilages progresses. The vertebræ become cartilaginous. The muscular fibres take transverse striæ.

Immediately after the spawning the essential modifications are as follows : The yolk is little by little completely absorbed. The oil drop lasts the longest, but it also finally disappears. The yolk circulation passes entirely to the liver, and there completes the circulation of the portal

system.   The opercular parts develop backwards, the
lower jaw forwards, without, however, reaching the extremity of the snout.   The lower extremity of the dorsal
cord rises.   The odd fins take their shape definitely and
receive their rays.   The pectoral fins are very large in
proportion.   The fringes of the capillary arteries begin to
develop upon the branchial arches.   The metallic pigment
of the choroid appears.   The swimming bladder unfolds.
The cartilaginous skeleton begins to turn to bone, and the
rudiments of the teeth appear in the mouth.

APPENDIX IX.

PERCH HATCHING.

I THINK that the most wholesome food for very young trout fry will be found to be the still smaller and younger fry of spring-spawning fish, and I venture to predict that the time will come when this natural food will be generally used when practicable. The Yellow Perch (*Perca flavescens*), which spawns in April, is an admirable fish for the purpose, as it is very abundant, and its eggs are numerous, easily obtained, and very easy to impregnate and hatch. With this end in view, the following notes are given in regard to hatching perch eggs.

It is the easiest and simplest thing in the world to manipulate perch and take their eggs artificially, and hatch them. I have taken millions in that way, and have hatched hundreds of thousands of them. Indeed, after my first experience, during the year 1868, I found it vastly easier, and had better luck, than with the salmon family.

It is not only very easy to take perch eggs by hand, but you can generally impregnate the whole of them, or very nearly the whole of them. If any one would like to see how easy it is, let him take a good-sized milk-pan, nearly full of water, and having found a ripe pair of golden perch, — this is easy enough, I have found hundreds just ripe, — let him impregnate the water well with the milt of the male, and proceed as follows with the female : —

Hold the fish just over the edge of the pan, so as to let the exterior end of the roe rest, as it comes out, on the further edge of the pan. It will stick in a moment. Then draw the fish slowly over the pan to the opposite edge, letting the roe fall in the water, and fasten the other end of it, as before, to that edge of the pan. You will then have the roe suspended in the water in such a way that it cannot get together and stick, and suffocate itself, as it surely would if it had a chance. Shake the pan a little. In an hour rinse the eggs, change the water twice a day, and in twenty days, if the water is not too cold, your eggs will hatch. 60 degrees Fahrenheit is a very good temperature to hatch them in, but they will stand a temperature as high as 85 degrees, at which point their development is very rapid. At 95 degrees they die. If you put a couple of large stones in the pan, to rest the ends of the roe on, it is better than to stick them to the edge of the pan.

The development of the perch embryo is exceedingly interesting. A very singular feature of it is the movement of the embryo in the egg, which begins almost as soon as the form of the fish is visible. The little creature jumps from one wall of the egg to the other, with a quick spasmodic movement, like that observed in the animalculæ in a drop of water under a very high magnifying power. This motion is as regular, when the eggs are not disturbed, as the ticking of a watch, and never ceases, day or night, except when the eggs are shaken, when, by an instinctive consent, every fish stops as if by magic. In a second or two the movement begins again.

The viscous matter which envelops the eggs and holds them together is finally wholly absorbed, and the eggs fall apart. They now consist of merely a frail shell, containing the embryo. This shell easily breaks, and the young perch is set free. He is very small, not more than half as large as a black bass just hatched, or one fourth as large as a whitefish an hour old.

The roe of the yellow perch comes in folds from the

fish, in the form of a long, narrow, adhesive ribbon, with the appearance of having been packed very compactly. In a few moments it swells to such a size that you could not get more than one third of it into the fish again.

After the expansion is completed, an average roe of a six-ounce Missisquoi River perch will measure about 36 inches in length by about 3 inches in width, or 108 superficial inches. I estimate that there are about 64 eggs to the square inch, which would give 6,912 eggs to the roe. I do not claim any exactness in this estimate, but I think it approximates the truth.

There is one more feature about the spawn in question which should be noted. After a little while it loses its tendency to stick to foreign substances, although it still adheres together, and it can be taken up in the hand and carried about, and even handled quite roughly, without damaging the eggs.

APPENDIX X.

ORGANIZATION OF AMERICAN FISH CULTURISTS' ASSOCIATION.

New York City, December 20, 1870.

A MEETING of practical fish culturists was held in this city to-day, in compliance with a call, issued November 1, by W. Clift, A. S. Collins, J. H. Slack, F. Mather, and L. Stone.

The place of meeting was subsequently changed to the rooms of the New York Poultry Society, to which society the delegates are much indebted, both for the use of the rooms and for various other courtesies extended to them during the day.

The delegates having assembled, a temporary organization was formed, with Rev. W. Clift as chairman and Mr. L. Stone as secretary. It was then unanimously resolved to form a permanent organization of fish culturists, and Dr. Edmonds and Mr. Stone were appointed a committee to draft a constitution for such an organization, to report when ready. On the presentation of their report, the following constitution was adopted, namely : —

CONSTITUTION.

Article I.

Name and Objects. — The name of this Society shall be "The American Fish Culturists' Association." Its objects shall be to promote the cause of fish culture; to gather and diffuse information bearing upon its practical success; the interchange of friendly feeling and intercourse among the members of the association; the uniting and encouraging of the individual interests of fish culturists.

ARTICLE II.

Members. — All fish culturists shall, upon a two-thirds vote of the society and a payment of three dollars, be considered members of the association, after signing the constitution. The commissioners of the various States shall be honorary members of the association, *ex officio.*

ARTICLE III.

Officers. — The officers of the association shall be a president, a secretary, and a treasurer, and shall be elected annually by a majority vote. Vacancies occuring during the year may be filled by the president.

ARTICLE IV.

Meetings. — The regular meetings of the association shall be held once a year, the time and place being decided upon at the previous meeting.

ARTICLE V.

Changing the Constitution. — The constitution of the society may be amended, altered, or repealed by a two-thirds vote of the members present at any regular meeting.

The constitution having been adopted, the following officers were chosen for the ensuing year : W. Clift, Mystic Bridge, Conn., President; L. Stone, Charlestown, N. H., Secretary; B. F. Bowles, Springfield, Mass., Treasurer.

It was then resolved that an effort be made to secure an exhibition of live fish at the next meeting, and that the following gentlemen be requested to prepare papers, to be read at the next meeting, on the subjects annexed to their names : —

A. S. Collins, on "Spawning Races and the Impregnation of Eggs."

J. H. Slack,

W. Clift, on "The Culture of Shad."

Dr. Edmonds, on "The Introduction of Salmon into American Rivers."

B. F. Bowles, on "Land-locked Salmon."

Dr. Huntington, on "Fish in the North Woods of New York.

L. Stone, on "The Culture of Trout."

It was decided to hold the next meeting and exhibition in connection with the New York Poultry Show next year. It was voted to send a report of the meeting for publication to the New York Citizen and Round Table, the New York Tribune, the Springfield Republican, the New York Poultry Bulletin, and other papers at discretion; and the secretary was instructed to mail the published reports of the meeting to fish culturists generally.

LIVINGSTON STONE,
Sec'y Fish Cult. Ass'n.

14*   U

APPENDIX XI.

SPECIMENS OF SALMONIDÆ FOR PROF. AGASSIZ.

Cold Spring Trout Ponds,
Charlestown, N. H., January 24, 1871.

To Fishermen and Sportsmen.

GENTLEMEN: Professor Agassiz is preparing an illustrated work of the American Salmonidæ, including all the trout and salmon, as well as whitefish, of this country. To enable him to make this work complete, he requires live specimens of every variety of trout, salmon, and whitefish found on this continent. The American Fish Culturists' Association are endeavoring to help him in this great undertaking, and would beg you to send to Professor Agassiz,* for his investigation, any specimens of these varieties that may come within your reach, — alive, if possible; if not, dead, — and especially to forward to him any new or rare specimens that you may discover. Samples of the winninish, land-locked salmon, and the rarer kinds of the lake trout and sea trout, are particularly requested. Further appeal for your co-operation seems unnecessary, as you cannot but feel that no American can do too much for Professor Agassiz. All specimens should be directed to Professor Agassiz, Museum

---

* If the specimens cannot be kept alive, and are small, put them just as they are into a bottle of alcohol and water, and send them. If the specimens are large, treat them thoroughly with a wash of carbolic acid, and express them at once to the Museum, or skin them, without severing the head or tail, and send the skin, head, and tail in the same way, or in alcohol.

of Comparative Zoölogy, Cambridge, Mass., and should be labelled with the name in full of the exact locality from which they are taken.

Yours very truly,
LIVINGSTON STONE,
Sec'y A. F. C. A.

The following letter is added, at Professor Agassiz's suggestion : —

CAMBRIDGE, January 20, 1871.

DEAR SIR : I am greatly obliged to you for your kind offices in helping me to secure the necessary materials for a proper investigation of our salmon, etc.

A single specimen of any fish of this family, even the common brook trout, from any locality, with label attached, mentioning the name of the place, would be very accept-able, as indicating the range of distribution. Of the rarer varieties, *several* specimens are desirable. Besides the specimens that may be thus brought forward, I would like an opportunity to critically study the specific characters of all the different species of the family found upon this continent. To this effect I should have *a large number of specimens* of each species, in every stage of growth, *collected in the same locality*, so that there could be no doubt of its being the same kind of fish, and yet a chance be afforded of studying all the variations of age, sex, sea-son, etc. For the salmon, for instance, it would be neces-sary to have very young ones, others two, three, four, five inches, etc., to full-grown ones, *from one place*, where the *true* salmon alone is found ; then the same for the land-locked salmon ; then the same again for the Sebago sal-mon. This would settle the question whether we have one, two, or three species of salmon. Next, I would wish for the same opportunity of studying, in every stage of growth, the lake trout, the brook trout, the grayling, and the different kinds of whitefish. Single specimens sent from different localities — and the more such are sent the better — will settle the question of the distribution of each species ; but you see that it will never do to attempt identifying the species from specimens gathered at random in different localities ; *that* study must be made from specimens collected in the same region, independently of the study of the distribution of species. And now that you know my plans, I leave the matter in your hands.

Very truly yours,
L. AGASSIZ.

Livingston Stone, Esq.

APPENDIX XII.

I NOW give the different ways of marking.

1. Cut off the dead or adipose fin altogether with sharp surgical scissors. This test, however, is liable to mislead. Everybody cuts off this fin, so that future diagnosis is difficult. I do not know what use the salmon makes of the adipose fin. It seems to have been put on his back by nature for the convenience of us pisciculturists, on purpose to be cut off, or otherwise experimented on.

2. Slit the adipose fin right down the middle again with sharp scissors. Rub the cut edges well with stick nitrate of silver; these edges will never again unite as long as the fish lives, unless the salmon has a submarine hospital, and a piscine doctor to bring the edges together, and keep them there in a scientific manner.

3. Cut a V-shaped bit out of the front of the adipose fin on its anterior margin.

4. Cut a V-shaped bit out of the posterior margin.

5. Cut a V from the top of the adipose fin, from above downwards.

6. Get some little metal clips, such as are used to keep loose papers together, make a hole with a pen-knife between the rays of the edge of one of the fins, not the tail or pectoral fins, run in the letter clip, expand the two arms, and Mr. Fish is marked. Do not put the clip too tight, or it might slough out. A bull never sheds the iron ring in his nose, but recollect the ring is loose, not tight.

There might be a danger that these clips would not stand sea water; they might easily be galvanized over, or covered with a waterproof varnish.

7. Wipe the fish's face quite dry. Light a Vesuvian match (not a flamer), and burn the skin of his cheek; burn marks never come out in men and animals, why should they not also be permanent in fish? The Vesuvian marks can be varied, — one on the right cheek for 1870, two on the left cheek for 1871, and so on.

8. Get a saddler's punch, such as is used for making holes in stirrup leathers. Punch a hole in his gill-cover; the hole will only let a little more water into his gills, on the principle that they slit the nostrils of the mules that carry copper ore up the Andes, — it lets more air into their lungs.

9. Get a sharp clip, such as is used by the " tickets, please," man at the railway station. Clip bits out of the edges of the fish's gills, or out of his anal fin. This fin is the least serviceable fin to the fish, therefore utilize it; but interfere with his tail fin, that is, his screw propeller, as little as possible.

10. Get a set of doctor's cupping instruments, cup the fish on his side; six beautiful slits are made in a moment. Rub in gunpowder, and the fish is tattooed.

11. Fasten silver wire loose around the first ray of the back fin, or round the hindermost ray of the anal fin. The wire must not be too loose, or it might catch in weeds, etc. I am afraid tickets, unless very small, with numbers, might interfere with the fish's movements.

Whatever you do, take care not to touch or injure the fish's gills. If the fish is obstreperous, do not fight with him; let him dance about a bit on the grass. A silk pocket-handkerchief is the best thing to hold a slippery fish; a flannel blanket is also a useful thing.

Do not return the fish rudely into the water; if he is

faint, go in with him, and support his head against the stream till he swims away of himself. If there are many fish, keep them till wanted in the water in a large hoop, or, as I call it, a "crinoline" net. This net can easily be made with two common hoops, as used by boys, and a bit of spare netting.

I am afraid Mr. Colam and the Cruelty to Animals Society may be down on me for my suggestions on marking fish; but I really do not think the cold-blooded, scale-wearing fish can possibly have an acute sensation of pain. Besides which, even suppose it was cruel to mark fish, the operations are done in the cause of science, and for the advancement of general 'knowledge of the habits of the salmon.

October 20, 1870.

APPENDIX XIII.

ARE THE FISH IN THE SEA DIMINISHING?

Extract from Bertram's Harvest of the Sea, Chap. XI.

THE idea of a slowly but surely diminishing supply of fish is no doubt alarming, for the public have hitherto believed so devoutly in the frequently quoted proverb of " more fish in the sea than ever came out of it," that it has never, except by a discerning few, been thought possible to overfish ; and, consequently, while endeavoring to supply the constantly increasing demand, it has never sufficiently been brought home to the public mind that it is possible to reduce the breeding stock of our best kinds of sea fish to such an extent as may render it difficult to re-populate those exhausted ocean colonies which in years gone by yielded, as we have been often told, such miraculous draughts. It is worthy of being noticed that most of our public writers who venture to treat the subject of the fisheries proceed at once to argue that the supply of fish is unlimited, and that the sea is a gigantic fish-preserve into which man requires but to dip his net to obtain at all times an enormous amount of wholesome and nutritious food.

I would be glad to believe in these general statements regarding our food fisheries, were I not convinced, from personal inquiry, that they are a mere coinage of the brain.

There are doubtless plenty of fish still in the sea, but the trouble of capturing them increases daily, and the instruments of capture have to be yearly augmented, indicating but too clearly to all who have studied the subject that we are beginning to overfish. We already know, in the case of the salmon, that the greed of man, when thoroughly excited, can extirpate, for mere immediate gain, any animal, however prolific it may be. Some of the British game birds have so narrowly escaped destruction that their existence, in anything like quantity, when set against the armies of sportsmen who seek their annihilation, is wonderful.

The salmon has just had a very narrow escape from extermination. It was at one time a comparatively plentiful fish, that could be obtained for food purposes at an almost nominal expense, and a period dating eighty years back is thought to have been a golden age so far as the salmon fisheries were concerned. But, in my opinion, it is more than questionable if salmon, or indeed any of our sea or river animals, ever were so magically abundant as has been represented. At the time — a rather indefinite time, however, ranging from the beginning to the end of the last century, and frequently referred to by writers on the salmon question — when farm servants were compelled to eat of that fish more frequently than seemed good for their stomachs, or when the country laird, visiting London, ordered a steak for himself with "a bit o' saumon for the laddie," and was thunderstruck at the price of the fish, we must bear in mind, as a strong element of the question, that there were few distant markets available ; it was only on the Tweed, Tay, Severn, and other salmon streams, that the salmon was really plentiful.

No such regular commerce as that now prevailing was carried on in fresh salmon at the period indicated. In fact, properly speaking, there was no commerce beyond an occasional despatch to London per smack, or the sale of a few fish in country market-towns, and salmon has been known to be sold in these places at so low a rate as a penny or twopence a pound weight. Most of these fish, at the time I have indicated, were boiled in pickle, or split up and cured as kippers. In those days there were neither steamboats nor railways to hurry away the produce of the sea or river to London or Liverpool. It is not surprising, therefore, that in those good old times salmon could almost be had for the capturing. Poaching — that is, poaching as a trade — was unknown. As I have already stated, when the people resident on a river were allowed to capture as many fish as they pleased, or when they could purchase all they required at a nominal price, there was no necessity for them to capture the salmon while it was on the beds in order to breed. Farm-servants on the Tay or Tweed had usually a few poached fish, in the shape of a barrel of pickled salmon, for winter use. At that time, as I have already said in treating of the salmon, men went out on a winter night to "burn the water," but then it was simply by way of having a frolic. In those halcyon days country gentlemen killed their salmon in the same sense as they killed their own mutton, namely, for household eating; there was no other demand for the fish than that of their own servants or retainers. Farmers kept their smoked or pickled salmon for winter use, in the same way as they did pickled pork or smoked bacon. The fish, comparatively speaking, were allowed to fulfil the instincts of their nature and breed in peace ; those owners, too, of either upper or lower waters, who delighted in angling, had abundance of attractive sport ; and, so far as can be gleaned from personal inquiry or reading. there was during the golden age of the salmon a rude plenty of home-prepared food of the fish kind, which, even with the best-regulated fisheries, we can never again, in these times of increasing population, steam power, and augmented demand, hope to see.

At present the very opposite of all this prevails. Farmers or cottars cannot now make salmon a portion of their winter's store. Permission to angle for that fish is a favor not very easily procured, because even the worst upper waters can be let each season at a good figure; and more than all that, the fish has become individually so valuable as to tempt persons, by way of business, to engage extensively in its capture at times when it is unlawful to take it, and the animal is totally unfit for food. A prime salmon is, on the average, quite as valuable as a Southdown sheep or an obese pig, both of which cost money to rear and fatten; and at certain periods of the year salmon has been known to bring as much as ten shillings per pound-weight in a London fish-shop. There have been many causes at work to bring about this falling off in our supplies; but ignorance of the natural history of the fish, the want of accord between the upper and lower proprietors of salmon rivers, the use of stake and bag nets, poaching during close times, and the consequent capture of thousands of gravid fish, as well as the immense amount of overfishing by the lessees of fishing stations, are doubtless among the chief reasons.

If these misfortunes occur with an important and individually valuable fish like the salmon, which is so well hedged round by protective laws, and which is so accessible that we can watch it day by day in our rivers, — and that such misfortunes have occurred is quite patent to the world; indeed, some of the best streams of England, at one time noted for their salmon, are at this moment nearly destitute of fish, — how much more is it likely, then, that similar misfortunes may occur to the unwatched and unprotected fishes of the sea, which spawn in a greater world of water, with thousands of chances against their seed being even so much as fructified, let alone any hope of its ever being developed into fish fit for table purposes. In the sea the larger fish are constantly preying on the smaller, and the waste of life, as I have elsewhere explained, is enormous. The young fish, so soon as they emerge from their fragile shell, are devoured in countless millions, not one in a thousand, perhaps, escaping the dangers of its youth. Shoals of haddocks, for instance, find their way to the deposits of herring-spawn just as the eggs are bursting into life, or immediately after they have vivified, so that hundreds of thousands of these infantile fry and quickening ova are annually devoured. The hungry codfish are eternally devouring the young of other kinds, and their own young as well ; and all throughout the depths of ocean the strong fishes are found to be preying on the weak, and a perpetual war is being waged for daily food. Reliable information, it is true, cannot easily be obtained on these points, it being so difficult to observe the habits of animals in the depths of the ocean ; and none of our naturalists can inform us how long it is before our whitefish arrive at maturity, and at what age a codfish or a turbot becomes reproductive ; nor can our economists do more than guess the percentage of eggs that ripen into fish, or the number of these that are likely to reach our tables as food.

As has been mentioned in a previous chapter of this volume, the supply of haddocks and other *Gadidæ* was once so plentiful around the British coasts that a short line, with perhaps a score of hooks frequently replenished with bait, would be quite sufficient to capture a few thousand fish. The number of hooks was gradually extended, till now they are counted by the thousands, the fishermen having to multiply the means of capture as the fish become less plentiful. About forty years ago the percentage of fish to each line was very considerable : eight hundred hooks would take about seven hundred and fifty fish ; but now, with a line studded with four thousand hooks, the fishermen sometimes do not take one hundred fish. It was recently stated by a correspondent of the *John o' Great*

Journal, a newspaper published in the fishing town of Wick, that a fish-curer there contracted some years ago with the boats for haddock at 3 s 6 d. per hundred, and that at that low price the fishing ýielded the men from £ 20 to £ 40 each season ; but that now, although he has offered the fishermen 12 s. a hundred, he cannot procure anything like an adequate supply.

As the British sea fisheries afford remunerative employment to a large body of the population, and offer a favorable investment for capital, it is surely time that we should know authoritatively whether or not there be truth in the falling off in our supplies of herring and other whitefish. At one of the Glasgow fish merchants' annual soirées, held a year or two ago, it was distinctly stated that all kinds of fish were less abundant now than in former years, and that in proportion to the means of capture the result was less. Mr. Methuen reiterated such opinions again and again. " I reckon our fisheries," said this enterprising fish merchant, on one occasion, " if fostered and properly fished, a national source of wealth of more importance and value than the gold mines of Australia, because the gold mines are exhaustible, but the living, propagating, self-cultivating gift of God is inexhaustible, if rightly fished by man, to whom they are given for food. It is evident anything God gives is ripe and fit for food. ' Have dominion,' not destruction, was the command. Any farmer cutting his ripe clover grass would not only be reckoned mad, but would in fact be so, were he to tear up the roots along with the clover, under the idea that he was thus obtaining more food for his cattle, and then wondering why he had no second crop to cut. His cattle would starve, himself and family be beggared, and turned out of their farm as improvident and destructive, who not only beggared themselves, but to the extent of their power impoverished the people by destroying the resources of their country. The farmer who thus destroys the hopes of a rising crop by injudicious farming is not only his own enemy, but the enemy of his country as well." Such evidence could be multiplied to any extent, if it were necessary; but I feel that quite enough has been said to prove the point. It is a point I have no doubt upon whatever, and persons who have studied the question are alarmed, and say it is no use blinking the matter any longer, that the demand for fish as an article of food is not only beginning to exceed the supply, but that the supply obtained, combined with waste of spawn and other causes, is beginning to exceed the breeding power of the fish. In the olden time, when people only caught to supply individual wants, fish were plentiful, in the sense that no scarcity was ever experienced, and the shoals of sea fish, it was thought at one time, would never diminish; but since the traffic became a commercial speculation the question has assumed a totally different aspect, and a sufficient quantity cannot now be obtained. Who ever hears now of monster turbot being taken by the trawlers? Where are the miraculous hauls of mackerel that used to gladden the eyes of the fishermen? Where are now the wagon-loads of herring to use as manure, as in the golden age of the fisheries? I do not require to pause for the reply; echo would only mock my question by repeating it. Exhausted shoals and inferior fish tell us but too plainly that there is reason for alarm, and that we have in all probability broken at last upon our capital stock.

It seems perfectly clear that we have hitherto seriously exaggerated the stock; it could never have been of the extent indicated, because then no draughts could have had any great effect, no matter how enormous they might have been. From various natural causes, some of which I have indicated in a former chapter, the stock has been kept in balance, and it seems now perfectly clear that by a course of fishing so extensive as that carried on at present, coupled with the destruction incidental to unprotected breeding, we must at all events speedily narrow, if not exhaust, the capital stock. We have done so in the case of the salmon; and the best remedy for that evil which has yet been discovered is cultivation,—*pisciculture*, in fact, —which science, or rather art, I have already treated of on its own merits. In ancient days the land yielded sufficient roots and fruits for the wants of its then population without cultivation; but as population increased, and larger supplies became necessary, cultivation was tried, and now in all countries the culture of the land is one of the main employments of the people. The sea, too, must be cultivated, and the river also, if we desire to multiply or replenish our stock of fish.

APPENDIX·XIV.

BOOKS ON FISH CULTURE.

List of Published Works relating in whole or in part to Fish Culture.

ΌΠΠΙΑΝΟΥ 'ΑΛΙΕΥΤΙΚΩΝ, βιβλια πεντε. 12mo. Florentiæ. CDXV.

Booke of Fishing with Hook and Line, and all other Instruments thereunto belonging; with Remarks on the Preservation of Fish in Ponds. Leonard Mascall. 4to. London. 1590.

Certaine Experiments concerning Fish and Fruite. John Taverner. 4to. 1600. Very rare.

The Perfect Husbandman. C. H. B. C. and C. M. 4to. London. 1658. Pages 346–355 of Fish Ponds and Fish.

The Angler's Vade Mecum, together with a Brief Discourse on Fish Ponds. Thomas Barrett. 8vo. London. 1681.

Country Gentleman's Vade Mecum. Giles Jacob. London. 1717. Pages 25–31 on Fish, Angling, and Fish Ponds.

Discourse of Fish and Fishing. Roger North. 8vo. London. 1718. Large 4to. London. 1770.

An Account of the Fishpool. Sir Richard Steele. 8vo. London. 1718.

History of the Chinese Empire. Vol. I. John Baptiste Duhalde. 1735.

Memoirs of the Swedish Royal Academy of Sciences. Vol. XXIII. German Ed. 1761.

Philosophical Trans. Royal Society of London. Vol. LVII. 1768.

Icthyologie, ou histoire naturelle générale et particulière des poissons, traduit de l'allemande par Laveaux. Marc. Eliez. Bloch. 12 vols. Berlin. 1785–97.

Berisch Anweisung zur Zahmen und Wilden Fischerei. Leipzig. 1794.

A Plain and Easy Introduction to the Knowledge and Practice of Gardening, with Hints on Fish and Fish Ponds. Charles Marshall. 12mo. London. 1796.

Natural History of British Fishes. O. Donovan. 5 vols. London. 1802–08.

History of Fishes. Vol. I. Noel de la Morimière. 1815.

Histoire naturelle des poissons. Cuvier et Valenciennes. 8vo. Paris. 1828.

Salmonia; or, Days of Fly Fishing. Sir Humphry Davy. 8vo. London. 1828.

History of British Fishes. William Yarrell. 2 vols. London. 1835–36.

Histoire naturelle des poissons d'eau douce de l'Europe centrale. Agassiz. 2 vols. 1839.

Experimental Observations on the Development and Growth of Salmon Fry, etc. John Shaw. Edinburgh. 1840.

Political Economy of the Romans. Vol. II. Dureau de la Malle. 1840.

Journal of the Agricultural Union of the Grand Duchy of Hesse. No. 37. 1840.

Memoirs of the Central Society of Agriculture. Vol. XLVIII. 1840.

Transactions of the Royal Society of Edinburgh. Vol. XIV. 1840.

Embryology of the Salmon, Natural History of Fresh Water Fish. L. Agassiz. 1842.

Zoölogy; or, New York Fauna. Part IV. Fishes. James E. De Kay. 4to. 1842.

A Treatise on the Management of Fresh Water Fish. Gottlieb Boecius. London. 1841.

The Complete Angler, with a Bibliographic Preface, giving an Account of Fishing and Fishing-Books from the earliest Antiquity to the Time of Walton. Walton and Cotton. 12mo. New York and London. 1847. Wiley and Putnam's edition.

Natural History of the Salmon. Wick. 1848.

Comptes Rendus of the Academy of Sciences. Vols. XXVII., XXVIII., XXXIII., XXXVI., XXXVIII. 1848.

Revue des Deux Mondes. January 1, 1849.

Annals of the Natural Sciences. Third Series. Vol. XIV. 1850. Vol. XIX. 1853.

The Norman Annual. 1850 – 54.

Artificial Fecundation of Fish. Society of Emulation of the Doubs. 1851.

The Book of the Salmon, by Ephemera, assisted by Arthur Young. 1851.

The Agronomic Annals. Vol. I. 1851.

Bulletin of the Agricultural Society of Paris. Vols. VI., VII., VIII. 1851 – 53.

Report upon the Facts proved at Huningue, from May 6, 1851, to May 7, 1852. Messrs. Detzern and Berthol.

Bulletin of the Society of Agriculture of L'Herault. July, 1852.

Journal of Practical Agriculture. June 5, 1852.

Practical Instructions upon Pisciculture. M. Coste. 1853.

Haxo d'Espinal on the Artificial Fecundating and Hatching of the Eggs of Fish. Second Edition. 1853.

Memoirs of the Society of Agriculture of Lyons. May, 1853.

Report to the Director-General of Waters and Forests, upon the Repopulating of the navigable and floating Watercourses. M. de Saint Ouen, Administrator of the Forests. March, 1853.

Annals of the Forests. July and August, 1853.

Handliedung tol de Kumtmatige Veremenigouldigen var Vischen. 1853.

Analytic Sketch of the Labors of the Academy of Rouen. 1853.

Researches into the Natural History of the Salmon. 1853.

Propagation of Salmon and other Fish. Edward and Thomas Ashworth. Stockport. 1853.

Researches on the Composition of Eggs in the Series of Animals. Valenciennes and Frémy. 1854.

Guide du Pisciculture. J. Rémy. Paris. 1854.

Natural History and Habits of the Salmon, etc. Andrew Young. 1854.

Pisciculture pratique et sur l'éleve et la multiplication des sangsues. Quenard. Paris. 1855.

Pisciculture, Pisciculteurs, et Poissons. Eugene Voel. Paris. 1856.

Pisciculture et la production des sangsues. Auguste Jourdier. Paris. 1856.

Sea-Side and Aquarium. John Harper. Edinburgh. 1858.

Fish Culture: a Treatise on the Artificial Propagation of Fish. Theodatus Garlick, M. D. New York. 1858.

The Family Aquarium. H. D. Butler. New York. 1858.

Notice historique sur l'établissement de pisciculture de Huningue. Berger Levrault. Strasbourg. 1862.

Natural History of the Salmon, as ascertained at Stormontfield. William Brown. Glasgow. 1862.

Fish Hatching. Frank T. Buckland. 1863.

Guide pratique du pisciculture. Pierre Carbonnier. Paris. 1864.

Propagation of Oysters. M. Coste and Dr. Kemmerer. Brighton. 1864.

Fish Culture : a Practical Guide to the Modern System of breeding and rearing Fish. Francis Francis. London. 1865.

Artificial Fish Breeding. W. A. Fry. New York. 1866.

Harvest of the Sea. James G. Bertram. New York. 1866. A most excellent and valuable book.

The Stormontfield Piscicultural Experiments. Robert Buist. Edinburgh. 1866.

Harper's Magazine. November, 1868.

Practical Water Farming. William Beard, M. D. Edinburgh. 1868.

American Fish Culture. Thaddeus Norris. Philadelphia. 1868.

Directions for Raising Trout. Livingston Stone. Boston. 1868.

Fishing in American Waters. Genio C. Scott. New York. 1869.

Trout Culture. Seth Green. Caledonia, New York. 1870.

Pisciculture dans l'Amérique du nord. J. Leon Souberain. Bulletin de la Société d'Acclimatation. January and February, 1871.

Selection of Species in relation to Sex. Charles Darwin. 2 vols. London and New York. 1871.

Domesticated Trout: How to Breed and Grow them. Livingston Stone, A. M. Boston. 1872.

LIST OF BOOKS WITH DATES NOT GIVEN.

Artificial Spawning, Breeding, and Rearing of Fish. Gottlieb Boccius. Van Voorst. Paternoster Row.

De Piscibus et aquatilibus omnibus. Conrad Gesner.

De Re Rustica. Book VIII. Columella.

Easy Method of Catching Fish. William Arderon.

Fur, Fin, and Feather. A Compilation of Game Laws. New York. M. B. Bowen & Co.

Husbandman's Jewell, with the Art of Angling, including Fish and Fish Ponds.

Importanza economica dei pisci e del coro allevamento artificiale. Signor F. Defillippi.

Instructions pratiques sur la Pisciculture, suivies de mémoires et de rapports sur la même sujet. M. Coste. Paris.

Multiplication artificelle des poissons. J. P. J. Koltz. Paris.

Pisciculture et culture des eaux. P. Trigneaux. Paris.

Pisciculture pratique, considerations générales et pratiques sur le repeuplement des eaux de la France. M. G. Millet. Bordeaux.

Pisciculture pratique, rapport sur les mesures à prendre pour assurer le repeuplement des cours d'eau de la France. M. G. Millet. Paris.

Pisciculture, rapport sur le repeuplement des cours d'eau et sur les travaux de pisciculture de M. Millet. Paris. Auguste Goin, Editeur.

Pisciculture : considerations générales et pratiques sur la pisciculture marine. M. G. Millet. Paris.

Pisciculture : observations sur la communication verbale de M. Coste. M. Millet. Paris.

Report on the Species of Fish in Prussia which might be imported and acclimated in the fresh waters of France. M. Valenciennes.

Reports of Fisheries Commissioners of Maine, New Hampshire, Vermont, Massachusetts, Rhode Island, Connecticut, New York, New Jersey, Pennsylvania, and other States. Annuals.

Supplementary Report on the Rivers of Spain and Portugal. Manchester.

The Oyster : where, when, and how to find, breed, cook, and eat it.

The Salmon and its Artificial Propagation.   Robert Ramsbottom, Clitheroe.   London.

Translation of the Proceedings of the French Pisciculturists.   William H. Fry.   Appleton : New York.

Voyage d'exploration sur le littoral de la France et de l'Italie.   M. Coste.   Paris.

THE END.

www.ingramcontent.com/pod-product-compliance
Lightning Source LLC
Chambersburg PA
CBHW051123120726
47905CB00005B/1396